THE MESSERSCHMITT BF 110 STORY

JAN FORSGREN

FONTHILL

Fonthill Media Language Policy

Fonthill Media publishes in the international English language market. One language edition is published worldwide. As there are minor differences in spelling and presentation, especially with regard to American English and British English, a policy is necessary to define which form of English to use. The Fonthill Policy is to use the form of English native to the author. Jan Forsgren was born and educated in Sweden; therefore British English has been adopted in this publication.

Fonthill Media Limited
Fonthill Media LLC
www.fonthill.media
office@fonthillmedia.com

First published in the United Kingdom and the United States of America 2024

British Library Cataloguing in Publication Data:
A catalogue record for this book is available from the British Library

ISBN 978-1-78155-916-1

Typeset in 10pt on 13pt Sabon
Printed and bound in England

CONTENTS

Acknowledgements 5
Glossary 6
Introduction 11

1 The *Zerstörer* Heavy Fighter Concept 13
2 The Other *Kampfzerstörer* Contenders 15
3 Development of the Long-Range Strategic Fighter Outside of Germany 18
4 The Messerschmitt Bf 110 23
5 Developing the Messerschmitt Bf 110 26
6 French Interest in the *Zerstörer* 29
7 Into Service 31
8 *Blitzkrieg* Operations 32
9 Battle of Heligoland Bight 34
10 Operation *Weserübung* 36
11 Invasion of France and the Low Countries 42
12 Swiss Interlude 44
13 The Battle of Britain 46
14 Rudolf Hess Flies to Scotland 53
15 The Balkans and Greece 57
16 Invasion of Crete 60
17 Iraqi Venture 62
18 North Africa 65
19 The Eastern Front 72
20 Defending the Reich by Night and Day 76
21 Swiss Bargain 87
22 Italian Interlude 90
23 The End 92
24 Other Uses 95
25 Messerschmitt Bf 110 *Experten* 97

26	Messerschmitt Bf 110 Units	102
27	Technical Description	117
28	Messerschmitt Bf 110 Variants	123
29	Messerschmitt Bf 110 Armament	127
30	Airborne Intercept Radars	131
31	Foreign Operators	133
32	Preservation	145

Appendix: Messerschmitt Bf 110 Production 152
Endnotes 155
Bibliography 157
Index 159

Acknowledgements

As usual, many people have kindly aided in creating this book, whether by suppling photographs or information. Gregory Alegi provided details of the Bf 110 in *Regia Aeronautica* service; Niclas Amrén, Lennart Berns, John Chapman, Boris Ciglic, Philippe Couderchon, and Jean-Pierre Dubois gave information on the sole *Armée de l'Air* Bf 110; Egil Endrese (Flyhistorisk Museum, Sola) and Carl-Fredrik Geust provided pictures and information on the Bf 110s used in the USSR; José Luis Gonzales Serrano, Tomislav Grzetic, and Bengt Hermansson supplied photographs of the Bf 110s that came down in Sweden; Jack Herris, Dave McDonald, Kaj Mecklin, and Wolfgang Mühlbauer provided numerous photographs from the DEHLA Archives; Bob Ogden, Miro Patocka, and Neil Page (FalkeEins blog) provided many pictures and valuable information; Johan P. Petersen (Flyhistorisk Museum, Sola), Jean-Louis Roba, Janne Salonen, Bruno Schmäling, and Hans-Heiri Stapfer gave assistance in sharing numerous photographs and information; Csaba B. Stenge provided the background of the Bf 110s' use in Hungary; and Greg VanWyngarden supplied details on Rudolf Hess's early flying career.

I would also like to thank my commissioning editor at Fonthill, Jay Slater, for his continued faith in my writing capabilities.

Apologies to the ones I have forgotten!

Glossary

AGO:	*Aktien Gesellschaft Otto Flugzeugwerke GmbH*
AHB:	Air Historical Branch
AM:	Air Ministry
ARR:	*Aeronautica Regâlã Româna* (Royal Romanian Aeronautics)
Aufklärer:	Reconnaissance aircraft
BFW:	*Bayerische Flugzeugwerke* (Bavarian Aircraft Works)
Bordfunker:	radio operator/gunner
Dipl. Ing.:	*Diplom Ingeneur* (Master of Science)
DVS:	*Deutsche Versuchsanstalt für Luftfahrt* (German Aviation Experimental Establishment)
E-Stelle:	*Erprobungsstelle* (German test establishment for aircraft and equipment, similar to the RAE at Farnborough)
Experten:	Luftwaffe terminology for ace (i.e., a pilot with more than five victories)
FA:	*Fernsteueranlage* (remote control system)
FDL 131:	*Fernbetätige Drehlafette 131* (remote control moving mount)
Fernaufklärungsgruppe:	long-range reconnaissance group
Flak Fliegerabwehrkanon:	anti-aircraft gun
Frei Jagd:	free hunt
FuG:	*Funk Gerät* (radio, also applicable to radar)
GAFEC:	German Air Force Equipment Centre
Geschwader:	wing
Gruppe:	group
Gruppenkommendeur:	wing commander
HE:	high explosive
HZIS:	*Hrvatska Zrakoplovna Izobrazbena Skupina* (Croatian Air Force Training Group)

Kampfzerstörer:	combat destroyer
LT:	local time
MG:	*Maschinengewehr* (machine gun)
MiA:	missing in action
MK:	*Maschinenkanone* (automatic cannon)
MKHL:	*Magyar Királyi Honvéd Legierö* (Royal Hungarian Air Force)
Nachtjagd:	night fighter
NII VVS:	*Nauchno-ispytatel'skij institute Voyenno-vozdushnykh Sily* (Research Institute of the Air Force)
RA:	*Regia Aeronautica* (Royal Italian Air Force)
RAE:	Royal Aircraft Establishment
RAF:	Royal Air Force
RAAF:	Royal Australian Air Force
RIAF:	Royal Iraqi Air Force
RLM:	*Reichsluftfahrtministerium* (German Air Ministry)
Rottenflieger:	wingman
SAAF:	South African Air Force
SC:	*Sprengbombe Cylindrisch* (cylindrical HE bomb. For example, SC 50 indicates a 50-kg bomb)
Schnellbomber:	fast bomber
s/d:	shot down
SKG 210:	*Schnellkampfgeschwader* 210 (Fast Bomb Wing 210)
Staffel:	squadron
Staffelkapitän:	squadron leader
Stkz:	*Stammkennzeichen* (factory-applied individual aircraft code)
USAAF:	United States Army Air Force
VVKJ:	*Vazduhoplovstvo Vojske Kraljeve Jugoslavije* (Royal Yugoslav Air Force)
W Nr:	*Werk Nummer* (construction number)
w/o:	written off
Zerstörer:	Destroyer

Luftwaffe Aircraft Damage Table

During the war, any Luftwaffe aircraft damaged or destroyed in combat was surveyed, following which the extent of damage by a rising percentage scale was established. This system also applied to aircraft damaged (or destroyed) in accidents. During the latter stages of the war, many aircraft suffering damage of up to 59 per cent (i.e., repairable) may have been declared a write-off anyway, instead being used for spares or as a decoy. Repairing a damaged aircraft occasionally lasted longer than the time required to build a new one. At this juncture, the

Luftwaffe did not lack aircraft, but rather trained and experienced pilots and aircrew. Additionally, by late 1944, the rapidly worsening fuel supply chain resulted in many Luftwaffe units being grounded.

Damage by per cent	Remarks
0–9	Minor damage, which can be partly repaired by the unit's head mechanic
10–24	Minor damage, repairable at unit level
25–39	Major damage, requiring rebuild or repair at unit level
40–44	Damage to engine or aircraft systems (e.g., electrical) requiring replacement at unit level
45–59	Heavily damaged, but repairable by exchanging major components
60–80	Written-off, with minor components reusable
81–99	Total loss, over own territory
100	Total loss, either over sea or enemy territory

Comparative Luftwaffe, RAF, and USAAF Ranks

Luftwaffe	Abbreviation	RAF	Abbreviation	USAAF	Abbreviation
Generalfeldmarschall	*Gen. FM*	Marshal of the RAF	MRAF	General (Five Star)	Gen. (Five Star)
Generaloberst	*Gen. Ob*	Air Chief Marshal	ACM	General (Four Star)	Gen. (Four Star)
General der Flieger	*GdF*	Air Marshal	AM	Lieutenant-General	Lt-Gen.
Generalleutnant	*Gen. Lt*	Air Vice-Marshal	AVM	Major-General	Maj.-Gen.
Generalmajor	*Gen. Maj.*	Air Commodore	Air Cdre	Brigadier-General	Brig.-Gen.
Oberst	*Ob.*	Group Captain	Grp Capt.	Colonel	Col.
Major	*Maj.*	Squadron Leader	Sqn Ldr	Major	Maj.
Hauptmann	*Hptm.*	Flight Lieutenant	Flt Lt	Captain	Capt.
Oberleutnant	*Oblt*	Flying Officer	Fg Off.	First Lieutenant	1Lt
Leutnant	*Lt*	Pilot Officer	Plt Off.	Second Lieutenant	2Lt
Unteroffizier	*Uffz.*	Non-Commissioned Officer	NCO	Corporal	Cpl
Fahnenjunker	*Fhj.*	-	-	-	-

Oberfeldwebel	*Obfw.*	Flight Sergeant	FS	Master Sergeant	MSgt
Feldwebel	*Fw.*	Corporal	Cpl	Technical Sergeant	TSgt
Obergefreiter	*Obgfr*	Leading Aircraftsman	LAC	-	-
Gefreiter	*Gfr*	Aircraftsman 1st Class	AC1	Private First Class	P1C
Flieger	*Fl.*	Aircraftsman 2nd Class	AC2	Private Second Class	P2C

Luftwaffe Organisational Structure

Officially formed on 26 February 1935, the Luftwaffe was subdivided into *Luftflotten* (air corps), numbered 1 to 6 and 10, and from February 1944, *Luftflotte Reich*. Each *Luftflotte* operated within specific regions of Germany and occupied Europe. Normally, each frontline combat unit was organised into the regional *Luftflotte*. There were also smaller, local *Fliegerführer* (air command) units operating within specific geographical areas, such as *Fliegerführer Afrika* (Air Command North Africa) and *Fliegerführer Irak* (Air Command Iraq).

The *Geschwader* was the basic Luftwaffe flying unit. The *Geschwader* was roughly comparable to an RAF Wing and consisted of three *Gruppen* (the *Nachtjagdgeschwader* units usually consisted of four or even five *Gruppen*), which was made up of three *Staffeln* (squadrons). The *Aufklärung* (reconnaissance) units never reached *Geschwader* strength, being organised through up to six *Staffeln* within one or two *Gruppen*.

In theory, a *Geschwader* could field between ninety and 120 aircraft (the actual number could vary significantly due to a number of reasons—for example, combat and non-operational losses, maintenance issues, transfers to and from other units, etc.—with each *Gruppe* usually having between thirty and forty aircraft. Each *Staffel* could have between ten and sixteen aircraft. Each *Geschwader* also had a *Stab* (staff) flight, which on average had between two and four aircraft, with each *Gruppe* also having a *Stab* flight. The *Gruppe* designator consisted of a Roman numeral—I for the first *Gruppe*, etc.—with the *Staffel* designator consisting of an Arabic numeral—3 for the third *Staffel* of the first *Gruppe*.

During the entire war, it was common practice for the various *Gruppen* and *Staffeln* of a *Geschwader* to operate independently of each other on the Western and Eastern Fronts as well as in North Africa. As described in the chapter on unit histories, it was fairly common for the respective *Geschwader*, *Gruppe*, or *Staffel* to be disbanded, with some being reformed, while others were redesignated.

Messerschmitt Bf 110 Unit Codes Explained

Every Luftwaffe aircraft was assigned a *Stammkennzeichen* (individual aircraft factory code) prior to delivery to the Luftwaffe. This consisted of a four-letter code (e.g. AB+CD) appearing on both sides of the fuselage and on the lower surfaces of the wings.

Upon delivery to a combat unit, the *Stammkennzeichen* was usually replaced with a *Verbandkennzeichen* (unit code). For most of the Bf 110 units, this consisted of a four-letter alphanumeric code, with the first two identifying the specific *Geschwader* or *Gruppe*. For instance, M 8 indicated *Zerstörergeschwader* (ZG) 76. The third letter (A to Z) indicated the individual aircraft, being painted or outlined in the respective *Staffel* colour, with green indicating the *Stab* (staff) flight and blue being the regular *Staffel* colour. The fourth and last letter indicated the respective *Stab* and *Staffel* within the *Geschwader*: A (*Geschwader Stab*), B (*Stab* I *Gruppe*), C (*Stab* II *Gruppe*), D (*Stab* III *Gruppe*), E (*Stab* IV *Gruppe*), and G (*Stab* V *Gruppe*) (NJG 5 only). This fourth letter appeared in blue for the *Geschwader Stab* (A) and in green for the respective *Gruppe* (B to G). The respective 1 to 15 *Staffeln* (each *Gruppe* each having three *Staffeln*) were identified by the following letters: H (white), K (red), L (yellow), M (white), N (red), P (yellow), R (white), S (red), T (yellow), U (white), V (red), W (yellow), X (white), Y (red), and Z (yellow). If necessary, for the respective 16 to 20 *Staffeln*, the following letters were used: Q (white), J (red), O (yellow), E (white), and I (red). The letter 'O' was briefly used in 1943 by 6./NJG 5, as well as the *Einsatsschwärme* (operational sections) of NJG 101 and 102.

This system was slightly amended in 1943, with the colours of the following letters being changed: M (blue), N (white), P (red), R (yellow), V (yellow), W (blue), Q (blue), J (white), O (red), E (yellow), and I (blue).

Introduction

Originally conceived in 1934, the Messerschmitt Bf 110 was intended as a twin-engined *Zerstörer* (heavy fighter), as well as being intended as a long-range heavily armed bomber escort and reconnaissance aircraft. One might call the Bf 110 the first strategic fighter, capable of carrying out several different types of missions.

Simultaneously, although to some extent unrelated, specifications for what might be classified a *Zerstörer* aircraft were presented in France and in Poland. Aircraft manufacturers of other nations also developed specific types of aircraft for the twin-engined heavy fighter concept.

First flown on 12 May 1936, the Messerschmitt Bf 110 was used in a wide variety of roles by the Luftwaffe. Entering service with the Luftwaffe in 1938, the Bf 110 was one of only a handful of Luftwaffe combat aircraft that did not see service with the *Legion Condor* during the 1936–1939 Spanish Civil War. It was, however, one of only a relatively few Luftwaffe combat aircraft that saw action throughout the entire Second World War.

The Bf 110 made its combat debut over Poland in September 1939, where the *Blitzkrieg* (lightning war) tactics employed were perfectly suited for the Bf 110 units. With the Luftwaffe quickly achieving aerial superiority against the obsolete fighters of the Polish Air Force, the Bf 110 appeared to prove the usefulness of the *Zerstörer* concept. In December 1939, Bf 110s claimed several RAF Vickers Wellington bombers during daytime raids over the Heligoland Bight on the German North Sea coast.

During the invasion of Norway, Bf 110s fitted with auxiliary fuel tanks were the only long-range fighters available to the Luftwaffe that were able to cover the long distances involved. Bf 110 units also saw large-scale operational use during the invasion of France and the Low Countries. During the Battle of Britain, *Zerstörer* Bf 110s were used as long-range bomber escorts, while one unit, *Erprobungsgruppe* 210, was specifically formed for developing *Jagdbomber* (fighter bomber) and ground attack tactics. The Bf 110 also served in the aerial reconnaissance role.

However, clashes with RAF single-seat Hurricanes and Spitfires resulted in severe losses of highly trained aircrew and aircraft. Despite its heavy armament, by the latter stages of the battle, it had become obvious that the Bf 110 was not particularly suited for daytime operations in areas where the Luftwaffe had not achieved aerial superiority.

The Bf 110 was the aircraft of choice for the Deputy *Führer* Rudolf Hess during his long-distance flight to Scotland on 10 May 1941.

By the autumn of 1941, Bf 110 production was gradually being reduced in anticipation of its replacement, the Messerschmitt Me 210, entering service. In fact, Bf 110 production was almost coming to an end in February 1942.

However, with the Me 210 proving a dismal failure, this resulted in the Bf 110 being reinstated in series production in the spring of 1942. In the event, Bf 110 production had to be substantially increased in order to meet Luftwaffe demand. With RAF bombers attacking Germany on an almost nightly basis, the basic Bf 110 was developed into a highly efficient night fighter. The introduction of airborne intercept radar and the *Schräge Musik* armament in particular proved vital to the success of the Bf 110 in the night fighting role. Between late 1943 and early 1944, dedicated night fighter units were also used against USAAF daylight bomb raids, usually with disastrous results.

By 1944, the Bf 110s had begun to be replaced in the night fighting role by Heinkel He 219s and, in particular, late-model Junkers Ju 88s. However, despite its increasing obsolescence, the Bf 110 night fighter proved to be the most successful night fighter of the war.

Nevertheless, Bf 110s were still rolling off the production lines until the very end of the war, with about 6,000 being completed, making it the fifth most-produced Luftwaffe aircraft after the Messerschmitt Bf 109, Focke-Wulf Fw 190, Junkers Ju 88, and Heinkel He 111.

The vast majority of the Bf 110s built were delivered to various *Zerstörergeschwadern* (destroyer wings), *Nachjagdgeschwadern* (night fighter wings), and, to a minor extent, to *Aufklärungsgruppen* (reconnaissance groups). However, many Bf 110s also saw service with a variety of Luftwaffe units for a wide range of various second-line duties, such as advanced training, glider towing, as well as liaison and communications duties.

Although the export of Bf 110s was frowned upon by the *Luftfahrtministerium* (Air Ministry, RLM), a few were nevertheless operated by the Hungarian, Italian, and Romanian air forces, with others seeing brief use with French and Soviet forces. Interestingly, the first export customer was the USSR, which ordered five Bf 110s in 1940. Additionally, Bf 110s were also evaluated by the RAF and the USAAF. None remained airworthy beyond 1945.

Only a few Bf 110s have survived, with none being in flying condition.

1

The *Zerstörer* Heavy Fighter Concept

Although aircraft saw some use in wars prior to 1914, the First World War of 1914–1918 saw the heavier-than-air aircraft coming of age, being developed for use in specific military roles, including fighter, bomber, and reconnaissance. Aerial tactics also developed from using unarmed lumbering observation biplanes to deploying large numbers of single-seat fighters to multi-engined strategic bombers.

Following the German defeat in 1918, and until the early 1930s, aerial warfare tactics underwent few radical changes. The main strategy during the interwar years involved in securing victory in any future war was by destroying the enemy's military and industrial capacity, as well as breaking the morale of the civilian population, through strategic bombing campaigns. This aerial warfare doctrine was based on the writings of Italian General Giulio Douhet, who in his 1921 treatise *Command of the Air* had argued that destroying 'vital centres' through strategic bombing would negate the need for conventional armies.

According to Douhet, the bloody business of trench warfare, which had characterised the First World War, could be avoided through the use of strategic bombing. As a result, the bomber was seen as the most important combat aircraft.

The single-seat fighter had changed little since the First World War, with biplane designs armed with rifle-calibre machine guns still serving with the majority of the world's air arms until the early 1930s. Given the short range of such fighters, their main role was seen as local defence.

After the Nazi party rose to power in January 1933, rearmament plans of the still-secret Luftwaffe involved designing modern combat aircraft for which new aerial warfare tactics would have to be developed. Among the earliest of such new types of combat aircraft was the *Kampfzerstörer* (literally combat destroyer) concept. The primary role of the *Kampfzerstörer* was to fly ahead of the bombers and destroy any aerial opposition. Other roles envisaged for the *Kampfzerstörer* included bomber escort, light bombing, aerial reconnaissance, and attacking ground targets. Particular emphasis was placed on speed, range, rate of climb, and manoeuvrability.

The 1934 *Reichsluftfahrtministerium* specification for a *Kampfzerstörer* called for a twin-engined, three-seat aeroplane, constructed entirely out of metal, featuring heavy cannon armament. The new aircraft was to have two engines, a crew of three or four, an armament consisting of two 20-mm cannons and one 7.9-mm machine gun, a maximum speed of 400 kph at an altitude of 6,000 metres, a 10,000-metre service ceiling, a maximum range of 2,000 km, all-weather (i.e., day and night) capability, and a landing speed of less than 100 kph. The latter requirement would mean a wing loading of less than 100 kg per square metre, an impossibility without the addition of slats on the wing's leading edges.

In late 1934, the specification for a *Kampfzerstörer* was issued to no less than seven manufacturers: AGO, BFW (Bayerische Flugzeugwerke), Dornier, Focke-Wulf, Gothaer Waggonfabrik, Heinkel, and Henschel (interestingly, apart from BFW, two of these companies, Focke-Wulf and Gothaer Waggonfabrik [commonly known as Gotha] would eventually produce large numbers of Bf 110s under licence).

From the start, there was some internal opposition to the *Kampfzerstörer* concept from two different quarters. The Luftwaffe's *Generalstab* (general staff) believed that such aeroplanes would be the equivalent to the medieval battle tactic known as *Verlorenen Haufen* (lost crowds). The *Verlorenen Haufen* tactic involved troops storming heavily fortified enemy positions, taking heavy casualties in the process. The *Generalstab* thought that sending *Kampfzerstörers* to clear a path for the bombers would prove to be both ineffective and expensive, with the potential risk of a high loss rate.

The technical department (*C-Amt*) of the *Luftfahrtskommissariat* aimed its criticism against the many different roles (heavy fighter, light bomber, ground attack, and reconnaissance) that the aircraft was intended to perform. According to the *C-Amt*, this meant the aircraft's overall performance would suffer unduly due to the various things, such as heavy armament, large fuel capacity, large crew, etc., necessary to carry out all the roles envisaged. Simply put, the *Kampfzerstörer* would according to the *C-Amt* become a jack-of-all-trades and master of none, perhaps capable to perform one or two roles outlined in the specification, but definitely not all of them.

Nevertheless, an initial assessment of the various *Kampfzerstörer* contenders took place in December 1934. The leading contenders were the Focke-Wulf Fw 57 and Henschel Hs 124, with the design submitted by BFW seemingly appearing to ignore some of the specific demands of the *Kampfzerstörer* specification.

As a result, the BFW offering, the Messerschmitt Bf 110, seemed almost out of the competition. Another factor was that Willy Messerschmitt was a rather unpopular figure among RLM officials, particularly with Erhard Milch, the state secretary of the *Reichsluftfahrtministerium*; Milch was instrumental in the establishment of the reformed Luftwaffe. Nevertheless, through the intervention of Ernst Udet, *Technisches Amt* director of research and development of new aircraft, the RLM reluctantly placed an order for three Bf 110s.

In the event, even before any of the contenders had been flown, the RLM had begun to reconsider its original *Kampfzerstörer* specification. Instead of having a multi-role aircraft, specific aircraft were to fulfil the specific roles of *Schnellbomber* (fast bomber) and a dedicated *Zerstörer* (destroyer) aircraft. The aircraft eventually selected for the former role was the Junkers Ju 88.

2

The Other *Kampfzerstörer* Contenders

The aeroplanes that adhered most closely to the RLM specification were the Focke-Wulf Fw 57 and Henschel Hs 124. The *Gothaer Waggonfabrik*'s offering was the *Projekt 3*, which was a twin-boom design somewhat similar in appearance to the later Fokker G.I. However, the *Projekt 3* did not proceed beyond the drawing board.

The Focke-Wulf Fw 57

The Focke-Wulf Fw 57 was a large, twin-engined, low-wing, and single-fin aeroplane with a retractable undercarriage. The Fw 57 was by a considerable margin the largest of the three *Kampfzerstörer* contenders. For instance, the Fw 57 had a wingspan of 25 metres, some 7 metres more than the Hs 124 and Bf 110.

The Fw 57 was the first Focke-Wulf aircraft of all-metal design, with detail design work being assigned to *Dipl.-Ing.* Wilhelm Bansemir. As opposed to the Bf 110 and Hs 124, the Fw 57 only had a single fin/rudder. The first prototype, the Fw 57 V1, was completed in early 1936, with *Flugkapitän* Wolfgang Stein performing the maiden flight. As it turned out, the Fw 57 was seriously underpowered and overweight, seemingly confirming the critical view of the *Kampfzerstörer* concept held by the *Generalstab*.

One glaring example of the aircraft's weight issues was that the structural weight of the wing structure was five times that of the original calculations. The Fw 57 was seriously overweight—the empty weight, even without armament, was no less than 63 per cent higher than that of the Hs 124. As the Mauser dorsal gun turret had yet to be completed, a mock-up turret was fitted. In the event, no armament was fitted to the aircraft. The Fw 57 V1 was eventually written off in a landing accident in the summer of 1936. Nevertheless, two further prototypes, the Fw 57 V2 and V3, were completed and briefly test flown. Overweight and cumbersome, with a disappointing overall performance, the Fw 57 development programme was quietly cancelled in late 1936. The role envisaged for the Fw 57 had been overtaken by new, more specialised aircraft.

Focke-Wulf Fw 57 Technical Data and Performance Characteristics:

Engines: 2 × 920-hp Daimler-Benz DB 600 inverted liquid-cooled V-12 engines
Wingspan: 25 m
Length: 16.40 m
Height: 4.10 m
Wing area: 73.50 m^2
Empty weight: 6,805 kg
Loaded weight: 8,307 kg
Maximum speed: 404 kph at 3,000 m
Maximum cruising speed: 373 kph at 3,000 m
Range: n/a
Service ceiling: 9,100 m
Armament (proposed): Two 20-mm MG FF cannons on flexible mountings in nose section, one 20-mm cannon in electrically operated dorsal turret. Internal bombload consisting of six 100-kg bombs

The Henschel Hs 124

Designed by *Dipl.-Ing.* Friedrich Nicolaus, the Henschel Hs 124 was the company's first twin-engined aircraft, as well as the first with a retractable undercarriage. Of all-metal construction, the Hs 124 was to have a crew of three: pilot, radio operator/gunner in the rear fuselage, and a gunner in the forward gun turret. The Hs 124 appeared to be a slightly more promising design than the Fw 57.

The Hs 124 V1 prototype was flown for the first time on 10 October 1935. As had been the case with the Fw 57, it was fitted with a mock-up gun turret, as the Mauser turret had not yet been fully developed. However, as described above, the Hs 124 became surplus to requirements even before the aircraft had been flown.

Nevertheless, construction of five Hs 124 prototypes began, with the first being the Hs 124 V1(W Nr 0268). As Henschel had been unable to secure delivery of DB 600 engines (as had been specified by the RLM), these had to be replaced with two 700-hp Junkers Jumo 210 inline engines. This resulted in the aircraft being somewhat underpowered. The Hs 124 V1 was written off on 10 April 1937.

The Hs 124 V2 (W Nr 0269) featured an improved undercarriage and redesigned nose section. Powered by two 880-hp BMW 132 Dc radial engines, the Hs 124 V2 was flown for the first time in January 1938, the substantial delay being due to the redesign of the basic airframe. The aircraft did not last long, being scrapped on 25 February 1938.

The third prototype, the Hs 124 V3, was a mock-up for a proposed high-altitude reconnaissance variant. In the event, the Hs 124 V3 was not completed, with the project being abandoned in mid-1938.

The Hs 124 V4 (W Nr 0270) featured a redesigned forward fuselage, otherwise being basically similar to the first prototype. On 2 June 1939, the Hs 124 V4 arrived at *E-Stelle* Travemünde for further, undetermined, testing.

The fifth prototype, the Hs 124 V5, first flew in July 1936. Although intended for unspecified tests, the aircraft was subsequently scrapped in late 1936.

Henschel Hs 124 V1 Technical Data and Performance Characteristics:

Engines: 2 × 880-hp BMW 132Dc nine-cylinder radial engines
Wingspan: 18.20 m
Length: 14.50 m
Height: 3.75 m
Wing area: 54.60 m^2
Empty weight: 4,245 kg
Loaded weight: 7,221 kg
Maximum speed: 435 kph at 3,000 m
Maximum cruise speed: n/a
Range: 4,200 km (with auxiliary fuel tank fitted in bomb bay)
Service ceiling: N/a
Armament (proposed): Two 20-mm Mauser cannon in flexible mountings in nose section, one 7.9-mm MG 15 machine gun in flexible mounting in rear gunner's dorsal position. Internal bombload consisting of six 100-kg bombs, or twelve 50-kg bombs on external bomb racks

3

Development of the Long-Range Strategic Fighter Outside of Germany

It is interesting to note that the development of the long-range strategic fighter as a new type of combat aircraft began almost simultaneously in France, Germany, and Poland, with the resulting aircraft, the Potez 630/631, the Messerschmitt Bf 110, and PZL.38 respectively, showing a remarkable degree of similarity to each other.

It may be of some interest to describe, very briefly, the respective French and Polish aircraft.

The Potez 630/631 Series

Acutely aware of the commencement of Bf 110 design and development in Germany, the French *Service Technique de l'Aeronautique* (STAé) initiated a requirement on 31 October 1934 for a three-seat heavy fighter. This was to serve in the fighter direction (leading formations of single-seat fighters over the frontline), daytime ground attack, escort for army co-operation and reconnaissance aircraft, and as a two-seat night fighter. No less than seven different aircraft manufacturers responded to the STAé specification: Breguet, Dewoitine, Hanriot, Loire-Nieuport, Potez, Payen, and Romano. Out of the various submissions, the Dewoitine D.630/631, the Loire-Nieuport 20, and the radical Payen Pa 321 remained stillborn, while only two Hanriot H.220 prototypes were built (the basic design was eventually developed into the Centre NC 600), with the Romano R.110 remaining a single prototype. The two remaining contestants, the Breguet 690 and Potez 630, were selected for production.

The Breguet 690 series eventually saw service in the ground attack and light bomber roles, with some 350 being built. Following the invasion of France, the Breguet 690 units suffered horrendous losses, particularly from *Flak* during low-level ground attack sorties.

The Potez 63 was built in five main variants: the Potez 630 and 631 two- and three-seat day and night fighters; the Potez 633 two-seat light bomber; the Potez

637 three-seat reconnaissance aircraft; and the Potez 63.11 three-seat army co-operation aircraft.

Flown for the first time on 25 April 1936, the Potez 630 showed a marked similarity to the Bf 110, having twin fins and an elongated greenhouse canopy. Powered by two 580-hp Hispano-Suiza HS 14 radial engines, the Potez 630 showed much promise. The HS 14 engines would become standard on the Potez 630 simply due to the severe delays the delivery of the Gnôme-Rhône K 14 radial engine. The basically similar Potez 631, powered by Gnôme-Rhône K 14s, was flown in early 1937.

A projected variant, the Potez 635CN2 was to be fitted with two 20-mm cannons in the upper fuselage, firing upwards and forwards at a 20-degree angle. This was very similar to the later *Schräge Musik* armament as fitted to the late-model Bf 110s.

The nationalisation of the French aircraft industry implemented on 23 December 1936 wreaked havoc, disrupting supply lines of essential equipment and parts. It was not uncommon for otherwise completed aircraft to remain grounded for several weeks due to the non-delivery of engines, propellers, and armament. It is also interesting to note that the workers at Potez (which had become part of the *Société Nationale de Constructions Aéronautiques du Nord*) and other French manufacturers threatened to go on strike if any aeroplanes were sold abroad! Nevertheless, two Potez 630s and one Potez 631 were exported, to Switzerland and Yugoslavia respectively.

In the event, eighty-eight Potez 630s and 215 Potez 631s were completed. By late 1939, most of the Potez 630s had been modified as conversion trainers. The Potez 631 were armed with two 20-mm cannons and one 7.5-mm machine guns. Some aircraft were retrofitted with an additional two 20-mm cannons and four 7.5-mm machine guns housed in a pod beneath the fuselage.

Following the German invasion of France, Potez 631 crews claimed seventeen aerial victories. The Potez 631's great similarity to the Messerschmitt Bf 110 caused severe problems, with both *Armée de l'Air* and RAF fighters frequently misidentifying the two types of aircraft. After three *Armée de l'Air* Bloch 152 fighters had shot down a Potez 631 in error on 23 May, special markings were immediately introduced on the Potez 631s. A broad horizontal white band was painted on both sides of the fuselage national insignia, with the national insignia also being increased in size.

Following the French surrender, the remaining Potez 630s and 631s were transferred to the post-armistice Vichy Air Force. When, in November 1942, German forces occupied Vichy France, large numbers of Potez 631s were seized. The Gnôme-Rhône K 14 engines were determined to be the only useful asset, subsequently being fitted to Gotha Go 244 transports and Henschel Hs 129B ground attack aircraft.

Potez 630/631 Technical Data and Performance Characteristics

	Potez 630	Potez 631
Engines	2 × 670–720-hp Hispano-Suiza HS 14 Ab	2 × 660-hp Gnôme-Rhône GR 14 K
Wingspan	16 m	16.00 m
Length	11.07 m	11.07 m
Height	3.62 m	3.62 m
Wing area	32.70 m²	32.70 m²
Empty weight	2,450 kg	2,450 kg
Loaded weight	3,850 kg	3,760 kg
Max speed	N/a	442 kph at 4,500 m
Armament	N/a	2 × 20-mm cannons and one 7.5-mm machine gun

The PZL.38 *Wilk*

At the same time, design work of an aircraft similar in both concept and configuration to the Bf 110 and Potez 630 commenced in Poland. Although dimensionally smaller and less powerful than the French and German aircraft, the Polish PZL.38 and PZL.48 designs were intended for the same basic roles as the Potez 630 and Bf 110 respectively.

Discussions between the Polish Air Force and the Department of Aeronautics regarding a twin-engined multi-role combat aircraft—which, apart from the primary role as a bomber interceptor, was to have dive bombing and ground attack as secondary roles—resulted in the PZL.38 *Wilk* (Wolf). Essentially a development of the PZL.37 *Łos* (Elk) medium bomber, the PZL.38 *Wilk* was to be armed with two 20-mm cannons and four 7.7-mm machine guns, also being able to carry 300 kg of bombs. Two main variants were planned, the PZL.38, a high-altitude, general-purpose escort fighter and attack aircraft, and the P.39, intended for strike and interceptor duties, replacing the P.11 gull wing fighters (in the event, the proposal to replace agile single-seat fighters with a heavy, twin-engined two-seat fighter was not accepted, with PZL initiating development of the PZL.50 *Jastrzab* [Hawk] instead). The P.39 was also to serve as a dive bomber. In the event, the P.39 was dropped altogether, with development of the PZL.38 being continued. Protracted problems, particularly with the indigenous Foka engines, resulted in the PZL.38 *Wilk* prototype (actually the second prototype) not being flown until May 1938, being powered by American Ranger engines. It was not until January 1939 that the PZL.38 was flown with 420–620-hp Foka II engines.

By that time, the Polish Air Force were committed to a developed variant, the PZL.48 *Lampart* (Leopard). The PZL.48's fixed forward-firing armament was to consist of either two 20-mm cannons and four 7.7-mm machine guns, or eight 7.7-

mm machine guns. It was planned to order 200 PZL.48s for the Polish Air Force. Construction of two PZL.48 prototypes were underway when Germany invaded Poland in September 1939. A more heavily armed variant, intended to carry two 20-mm cannons and six 7.7-mm machine guns in the nose, the PZL.54 *Ryś* (Lynx), did not progress beyond the drawing board.

German forces captured both of the PZL.38 prototypes, with the aircraft's final fate being unknown.

PZL.38 Wilk and PZL.48 Lampart Technical Data and Performance Characteristics

	PZL.38 *Wilk*	PZL.48 *Lampart*
Engines	2 × 450-hp Ranger SGV-770B/2 × 420–620-hp Foka II	660–730-hp Gnôme-Rhône K 14M05 Mars
Wingspan	11.05 m	11.5 m
Length	8.35 m	8.7 m
Height	2.50 m	2.50 m
Wing area	19.00 m²	19.50 m²
Empty weight	1,715 kg	N/a
Max weight	2,770 kg	3,500 kg
Max speed	465 kph at 4,000 m	560 kph at 3,500 m
Service ceiling	10,000 m	N/a
Range	1,250 km	1,500 km

NB: all performance data for the PZL.48 are estimations.

Although other countries other than Germany, France and Poland did invest in the development and production of twin-engined heavy fighters during the mid-1930s, these were a mixed bag of aircraft, ranging from the excellent to the indifferent.

Among the former was the Fokker G.I. A private venture design intended as a *Jachtcruiser* (heavy fighter); the Fokker G.I was of twin-boom configuration, being powered by two 730-hp Bristol Mercury VIII engines. Flown for the first time on 16 March 1937, the Fokker G.I was armed with two 23-mm cannons and three 7.9-mm machine guns, also being capable of carrying up 400 kg of bombs. Much interest was evinced in the Fokker G.I, with the *Luchtvaartafdeeling* (Royal Netherlands Army Air Force) placing an order for thirty-six aircraft. Out of these, twenty-six were in service on 10 May 1940. During the German invasion of the Netherlands, Fokker G.I crews shot down fourteen Luftwaffe aircraft. Several Fokker G.Is were captured by the Germans, with another batch already under construction being completed on behalf of the Luftwaffe. Interestingly, the Luftwaffe sent their Fokker G.Is to Wiener Neustadt in Austria for use as Bf 110 conversion trainers with *Flugzeugführerschule* (B) 8.

One non-starter was the Bell YFM-1 Airacuda. A twin-pusher engine design intended as a long-range bomber destroyer, the Airacuda was supposed to intercept enemy bombers beyond the range of single-seat fighters. Carrying a crew of five and an armament consisting of two 37-mm cannon, two 12.7-mm machine guns, and two 7.62-mm machine guns with a maximum take-off weight of 9,809 kg, the Airacuda had a futuristic appearance. In reality, the Airacuda was a badly flawed design, suffering from poor flight characteristics, engine cooling issues, as well as a complicated electrical system. A total of thirteen Airacudas were built for evaluation in 1937–38, with negative results.

It can be said that the US aircraft closest in concept to the Bf 110 was the Lockheed P-38 Lightning, which proved highly adaptable as a long-range escort fighter and reconnaissance aircraft.

Perhaps the closest British equivalent of the Bf 110 was the Gloster F.9/37. A single-seat twin-engined heavy fighter, the Gloster F.9/37 first flew on 3 April 1939. The first Gloster F.9/37 prototype was powered by two 1,050-hp Bristol Taurus radial engines, giving the aircraft a maximum speed of 579 kph at an altitude of 4,600 metres. With a wingspan of 15.24 metres, a length of 11.27 metres, and a wing area of 35.85 square metres, the Gloster F.9/37 was somewhat smaller in size than the Bf 110. A second Gloster F.9/37 prototype was powered by two 885-hp Rolls-Royce Peregrine engines. The projected fixed forward-firing armament was to consist of two 20-mm cannons and four 0.303-inch machine guns. Although the Gloster F.9/37 proved itself to have excellent flight and handling characteristics, it remained a prototype.

4

The Messerschmitt Bf 110

With the failure of the Fw 57 and Hs 124, the BFW candidate now became the aircraft of choice as the Luftwaffe's new *Zerstörer*. The rearmament of Germany, which had been secretly ongoing since Hitler's rise to power, was announced publicly on 16 February 1935. On this date, Hitler declared that Germany was no longer bound to the Treaty of Versailles with regards to limitations to its armed forces. Barely two weeks later, on 26 February, the Luftwaffe was officially re-established.

Dipl.-Ing. Walter Rethel was appointed as chief designer for the Bf 110, with some preliminary design work having been carried out by Robert Lusser. Construction of the first Bf 110 prototype at Augsburg proceeded quickly, with the ground trials commencing in the first months of 1936. With its long, sleek fuselage, the Bf 110 had the appearance of a shark with wings. The first Bf 110 prototype was powered by two DB 600 A engines, with Handley Page-type slots being fitted to the wing's leading edges.

On 12 May 1936, the Bf 110 V1 (W Nr 868, registered as D-AHOA) took to the air for the first time. As a safety precaution, the undercarriage remained lowered during the entire ten-minute flight. Messerschmitt's Chief Test Pilot Hermann Wurster later recalled the flight:

> Lastly I tested the stall characteristics while the engines were idling.
>
> I did this mostly to find out what was the safe speed on finals. In those days, the approach speed had to be found out by the test pilot, today it is given by the aerodynamics bureau!
>
> The aircraft showed good control efficiency which emboldened me, even at this very early stage, to do some rather steep turns. Stability around the three axes was perfect. When stalling the aircraft did not fall off one wing but pitched down straight forward. The landing too was uneventful, although after touching down I found that the undercarriage brakes were too weak and that idling was too high. I had to switch off the ignition so that I didn't run into a hangar.

Immediately after completing the first flight, Wurster spoke to Willy Messerschmitt:

> Controls of the 110 are very good in both horizontal flight and while turning. When stalling the aircraft shows no tendency dangerously to fall off a wing or to spin. The flaps are adequate for landing. I believe that we will not have any difficulties with the 110 as concerns the landing characteristics.[1]

Wurster did, however, express his reservations about the engine rpm idling, as well as the insufficient brakes to the company chief engineer.

The second flight took place on 25 May. With the undercarriage retracted during this flight, the Bf 110 nevertheless showed itself to take a considerable amount of time to pick up speed. Even if some characteristics seemed disappointing, the Bf 110 appeared to be a promising design. This became evident on 27 August, when Ernst Udet visited Augsburg. Udet expressed a desire to stage a mock dogfight against the Bf 110. With Udet flying a Bf 109 prototype, and Wurster the Bf 110 V1, the former First World War ace attempted, and continuously failed to out-turn the bigger and heavier Bf 110. According to Wurster: 'Udet did not succeed in getting me into his sights'.[2]

As a result, Udet became very enthusiastic about the Bf 110's potential as a combat aircraft.

There were some considerable drawbacks though. Although a top speed of 505 kph had been achieved, continued testing showed the unreliability of the DB 600 A engines. During take-offs and landings, the Bf 110 showed itself to exhibit a potentially dangerous torque effect—i.e., turning sideways in a manner that could result in ground loops. Although adjusting the undercarriage camber subsequently reduced this problem, it would remain an issue for the rest of the Bf 110's career.

The protracted engine problems resulted in the second Bf 110 prototype not flying until 25 October.

Messerschmitt Bf 110 Prototypes

Prototype	W Nr	Registration	First Flight	Remarks
Bf 110 V1	868	D-AHOA	12 May 1936	
Bf 110 V2	869	D-AQYE	24 October 1936	
Bf 110 V3	870	D-ATII	24 December 1936	
Bf 110 V4	910	D-AISY	21January 1938	
Bf 110 V5	911	D-AAHI	15 March 1938	Crashed at Augsburg at unknown date
Bf 110 V6	915	D-AUDU		Also designated Bf 110A-0
Bf 110 V7	912	D-AEDO		Also designated Bf 110A-0. W/o 15 November 1938 at Schwasdorf
Bf 110 V8	913	D-AIJO		Also designated Bf 110A-0

Between October 1936 and January 1938, an additional four Bf 110 prototypes joined the flight test programme. On 27 January 1937, the Bf 110 V2 was flown to *E-Stelle* Rechlin for a comprehensive flight test programme, soon being joined by more prototypes. A small batch of Bf 110A-0 service trials aircraft was also completed, the first of these flying for the first time in August 1937. The Bf 110A featured a forward-firing armament consisting of four 7.92-mm MG 17 machine guns, along with a 7.92-mm MG 15 mounted in the rear gunner's compartment. Other design changes implemented in the Bf 110A included lengthening the engine nacelles as well as reducing their depth. The tail wheel was made non-retractable. It had originally been intended to use the 986-hp DB 600 Aa engine for the Bf 110A-0. In the event, this type of engine was deemed unsuitable, being replaced by the 610-hp Jumo 210B instead. This resulted in the Bf 110A being seriously underpowered, achieving a top speed of only 430 kph.

It was intended to use the developed DB 601 A engine for the production examples of the Bf 110. However, as the DB 601 A was still undergoing an extensive test programme, a substitute was found in the lower-powered Jumo 210 Ga engine. As a result, the first production variant, the Bf 110B, was powered by twin Jumo 210s. The first Bf 110B was completed in April 1938, with the first production aircraft rolling off the Augsburg assembly line in June 1938.

Although other new warplanes, including the Bf 109 and Dornier Do 17, were widely publicised, the Bf 110 remained a well-kept secret. The first public appearance of the Bf 110 appears to have been in early September 1938, during the Annual German Army Day and the Nazi Party gathering at Nuremberg. However, the first mention of the Bf 110 in the aeronautical press occurred on 28 September 1938, in the British magazine *The Aeroplane*! The vague story of a new German heavy fighter printed in *The Aeroplane* subsequently found its way to German aviation magazines.

5

Developing the Messerschmitt Bf 110

The basic Bf 110 configuration was also used on the Bf 161 long-range reconnaissance aircraft and the Bf 162 *Schnellbomber*, both of which were direct developments of the basic Bf 110. Although neither aircraft entered series production, their development was closely linked with that of the Bf 110.

By 1935, the *Kampfzerstörer* specification had been abandoned by the RLM. In its place, more specialised aircraft were to be developed. Two of these new aircraft were the Messerschmitt Bf 161 and the Bf 162. Both the Bf 161 and Bf 162 were direct developments of the Bf 110. Although developed in conjunction, priority was given to the Bf 162. According to the RLM specification, the Bf 162 was to be a three-seat light bomber, capable of carrying 800 kg of bombs at a maximum speed of 480 kph. The aircraft was also to be capable of clearing a 20-metre obstacle after an 800-metre take-off run. With the *Schnellbomber* depending on speed to avoid enemy fighters, the defensive armament was reduced to one MG 15 machine gun. The wing structure was similar to the early model Bf 110, albeit being slightly increased in wing area and wingspan. The fuselage was widened to accommodate the crew, with the bombardier sitting slightly behind the pilot beneath a shortened canopy. The internal bomb bay had room for ten SC 50 bombs, with two SC 250 bombs to be carried on external ETC bomb shackles. The front fuselage featured a glazed nose section. Incidentally, the Bf 162 bore a striking resemblance to the later Petlyakov Pe-2.

The first prototype, the Bf 162 V1, was completed in the early summer of 1937. Registered as D-AIXA (W Nr unknown), the Bf 162 V1 was scrapped after the initial flight trials. The second prototype, the Bf 162 V2 (D-AOBE, W Nr 818) joined the flight test programme in September 1937. The third prototype, the Bf 162 V3 (D-AOVI, W Nr 819), did not fly until 20 August 1938.

The Bf 162 was pitted against the Henschel Hs 127 and the Junkers Ju 88 for the role as the Luftwaffe's new *Schnellbomber*. However, the Bf 162 exhibited overall mediocre performance, with the Ju 88 emerging as the winner.

Nevertheless, a propaganda campaign was initiated, with claims that large numbers of Bf 162s were rolling off the production lines for the Luftwaffe. Photographs of two Bf 162s, painted in Luftwaffe camouflage, were widely circulated, with the type also being named 'Jaguar' (this was similar to the Heinkel He 100/He 113 ruse).

In the event, the Bf 162s were used for various tests, with the Bf 162 V3 serving as the test bed for the FDL 131 remote-control armament system intended for the Messerschmitt Me 210.

The Bf 161 retained much of the Bf 110 airframe, including the wings and rear fuselage. The two- or three-man crew sat beneath a shortened (when compared to the Bf 110) canopy. The internal bomb bay could carry either a single vertical camera, or an auxiliary fuel tank. Two MG 15 machine guns were to be operated by a rearward-facing gunner. The first Bf 161 prototype, the Bf 161 V1 (D-AABA, W Nr 811), first flew on 9 March 1938, with Hermann Würster at the helm. Powered by two Jumo 210G engines, the Bf 161 V1 featured a glazed nose section, eventually being evaluated at *E-Stelle* Rechlin in late 1939. Powered by two 980-hp DB 600 Aa engines, the Bf 161 V2 (D-AOFI, W Nr 812) took to the air on 30 August 1938. The aircraft featured a revised nose section but was otherwise similar to the first prototype.

It was soon recognised that the job intended for the Bf 161—i.e., long-range reconnaissance—could just as easily be performed by the Bf 110. As a result, only two Bf 161s were built. The second prototype was subsequently used as a tug for the Messerschmitt Me 163A. In that role, the Bf 162 V2 (coded CE+AT) was used at Augsburg as well as Peenemünde on the Baltic Sea coast.

Messerschmitt Bf 161/162 Technical Data and Performance Characteristics

Type	**Bf 161 V1**	**Bf 162**
Engines	2 × 979-hp Junkers Jumo 210G	2 × 960-hp DB 600 Aa
Wingspan	16.69 m	17.16 m
Length	12.85 m	12.75 m
Height	3.64 m	3.58 m
Wing area	38.5 m²	N/a
Empty weight	4,890 kg	5,810 kg
Maximum weight	N/a	N/a
Maximum speed	440 kph	480 kph
Service ceiling	8,100 m	N/a
Range	870 km	782 km

The Messerschmitt Me 261

Mention must also be made of the Messerschmitt Me 261, which used the basic Bf 110 configuration, albeit on a much grander scale. Construction of the Me 261 began in 1937, with the aircraft being planned to carry the Olympic torch to Tokyo in 1940 in a non-stop flight. Hitler was so enamoured by this notion that the unofficial name of 'Adolfine' was bestowed on the second prototype. However, with the Japanese themselves declaring the Olympic games as forfeited on 16 July 1938, the project was given a low priority.

The first Me 261 prototype did not fly until 23 December 1940, being joined by the second and third prototypes in 1941 and 1943 respectively. With a crew of five, and a wingspan of nearly 27 metres, the Me 261 had the appearance of an enlarged Bf 110. Brief consideration was given to using the Me 261 for ultra-long-range reconnaissance. On 16 April 1943, the Me 261 V3 was flown on a ten-hour sortie. In the event, this was not to be. The first two Me 261 prototypes were damaged in an Allied bomb raid against Lechfeld, with the second prototype eventually being captured by US forces in the spring of 1945.

6

French Interest in the *Zerstörer*

With the French having simultaneously developed its own take on the long-range heavy fighter concept in the shape of the Potez 630/631, it was inevitable that a keen interest was shown in the Bf 110.

During an official visit to Augsburg-Haunstetten in August 1938, French General Joseph Vuillemin was deeply impressed when told about the Bf 110's performance and capabilities. Vuillemin was given a tour of the production line, also witnessing several Bf 110s taking off in rapid succession. However, with only seven Bf 110s having been completed at this time, the Bf 110s simply landed out of sight and were taxied back to the runway for another take-off. The German ruse apparently did work, with Vuillemin being tricked into believing that dozens of Bf 110s were leaving the assembly line every day.

Upon his return to France, Vuillemin initiated a highly secret plan to obtain a Bf 110 by cloak-and-dagger methods for a detailed technical evaluation. This saw two agents from the *Deuxième bureau* (French Intelligence Service) becoming involved in this operation. The plan involved bribing a German pilot to abscond to France in a Bf 110. The pilot in question was Franz-Xaver Öttil, who had earlier received a reprimand for unintentionally crashing into his family's house during a 'buzz' job in a training aircraft. Fired from the Luftwaffe, Öttil somehow managed to secure a job at Messerschmitt on 24 April 1939 as a mechanic.

Three weeks later, on 10 May, Öttil took off from Augsburg-Haunstetten in an early production Bf 110C-1 (W Nr 974). Clad in a mechanic's overall and having no parachute, Öttil sat on a cushion in the Bf 110's bucket seat. Öttil's job had involved taxiing the Bf 110s to the compass and radio direction-finding gear test range. Seeing the Bf 110 leave the ground caused great consternation among the ground crew. Willi Stör, who was in charge of flight testing the factory fresh aircraft, wanted to pursue Öttil in a Bf 109, but no aircraft was immediately available.[1]

Having safely absconded from Augsburg-Haunstetten, Öttil then flew to Bad Wörishofen, where his brother Johann was waiting with the requisite number of fuel drums, climbing into the rear seat after the aircraft had been refuelled.

Unfortunately, Öttil encountered poor weather, with the Bf 110 crashing near the village of Villiers-sous-Chalamont. Both Öttil brothers were killed in the crash.

Naturally, the German authorities demanded that the wreck was to be returned immediately, along with the bodies of Xaver and Johann Öttil. Although the Bf 110 had been written off in the crash, French intelligence did manage to examine one of the relatively undamaged DB 601 engines.

Officially, the Germans attributed the crash to the pilot becoming lost due to poor weather during a training flight.

On 28 June 1939, the RLM relayed a message to the French air *attaché* in Berlin:

> It is more than two months since the accident and we have still not been able to recover our aircraft. We understand perfectly that your technical department has an interest in it and wants to learn about the novelties it may represent but it could have acted with more tact....
>
> Everything that has happened is deeply regrettable. We have the impression that your official services do everything which lies in their power to poison the relations between our two countries.... One of these days that will end in catastrophe...[2]

7
Into Service

As related above, the first production Bf 110Bs were completed in the summer of 1938.

A number of Bf 110Bs were delivered to I./*Lehrgeschwader* 1, where the aircraft were used to develop tactics for the *Zerstörer* units. Although the Bf 110B was considered to have somewhat sluggish flight controls, the aircraft had both a speed comparable to that of contemporary single-seat fighters, as well as a heavy armament. It was thought that the Bf 110 was the perfect tool for the Luftwaffe's *Zerstörer* tactics, including long-range bomber escort and attacking ground targets. Beginning in early 1939, a few Bf 110Bs were also delivered to I./*Zestörergeschwader* 1, *Zerstörergeschwader* 26, and I./*Zerstörergeschwader* 76 for the same purpose. It was soon realised that the Bf 110B lacked the necessary performance, with most aircraft eventually being modified as unarmed trainers for use by the *Zerstörerschulen* (destroyer school) units.

Powered by two DB 601 A engines, the Bf 110C-1 was the first major production variant, with the first examples being delivered in January 1939. Apart from the more powerful (and reliable) engines, the Bf 110C design had been refined. The rectangular wing radiators of the Bf 110B were replaced with more shallow units, with the wingtips being squared off, thus reducing wingspan with some 60 cm. Additionally, the air intakes of the DB 601 A engines were far more streamlined and shallower than those of the earlier Jumo 210 Ga engines.

The first unit to receive Bf 110C-1 was I.(Z)/*Lehrgeschwader* 1. A few months later, I./*Zerstörergeschwader* 1 and I./*Zerstörergeschwader* 76 also began to take delivery of Bf 110C-1s. However, production of the Bf 110C could not keep up with the demands of the Luftwaffe. As a temporary measure, seven *Zerstörer Gruppen* were forced to retain single-seat Bf 109Ds until the early spring of 1940. To increase the production tempo, the Bf 110C also entered production with Focke-Wulf and *Gothaer Waggonfabrik*. Later on, the Bf 110 was also built by Luther, part of the MIAG industrial complex.

8
Blitzkrieg Operations

On 1 September 1939, only three *Gruppen* were fully equipped with Bf 110Cs: I./ZG 1 at Mühlen, with thirty-four aircraft (twenty-seven serviceable); I.(Z)/LG 1 at Jesau, with thirty-three aircraft (thirty-two serviceable); and I./ZG 76 at Ohlau, with thirty-five Bf 110s (thirty-one serviceable)—a total of 102 Bf 110s. These three units were deployed on the Eastern Front, all taking part in the invasion of Poland.

The Polish fighter pilots considered the Bf 110 as a far more dangerous opponent than the Bf 109, having a heavier armament. During the Polish campaign, no less than ninety-four aerial victories were claimed by Bf 110 crews, as opposed to thirteen by the Bf 109 units. The first Bf 110 aerial victory, and, indeed, the first Luftwaffe aerial victory of the war, was *Hauptmann* Schlief who shot down a PZL P.11c fighter on 1 September.[1]

Although outnumbered and outgunned, the Polish fighter pilots bravely fought back, with five Bf 110s being shot down between 2 and 5 September. A sixth Bf 110 was brought down over Osiek Maly airfield on 11 September.

The *Staffelkapitän* of 2./ZG 76, *Oberleutnant* Wolfgang Falck, later wrote:

> We had been briefed to takeoff at 06.00 and escort He 111s of KG 4 to Krakow. In our enthusiasm someone suggested that maybe we should take off early in order to steal an hour of combat on the other *Zerstörer*.
>
> A suggestion was all it took as each pilot raced for his machine in order not to be left behind.
>
> Unfortunately we did not find our bombers until we got over Krakow, happily there was nothing to protect them from, not even flak, just a few little white clouds. After the bombers unloaded we escorted them back to the frontier. As I neared the frontier I could see villages burning and I finally felt that a war had begun. Since our fuel was getting low we turned toward our airfield leaving the bombers behind. As we banked away from the Heinkels I looked down and there was a Heinkel 46 army reconnaissance aircraft looking very lonely down there

> with no protection. I dove down to escort him saying aloud to myself, 'look, we are here, you can do your job under our wings!' All of a sudden he saw me and started to twist and turn like crazy and the gunner blazed away at me. Pulling away I realized I had just gotten my baptism of fire from one of our own aircraft. A few minutes later I saw another aircraft flying. 'Ha! a PZL 23, I can start my score.'
>
> As I tried to gain some height he curved into the sun and as he did I caught a glimpse of red on hi swing—I'm sure he's a Polish aircraft now. We had been briefed that the normal red and white box insignia had the white overpainted with camouflage leaving only the red visible. As I turned into him I opened fire, but fortunately, my marksmanship was no better than the reconnaissance gunner's had been, as he banked to get away I saw it was a Stuka. I then realized that what I had though was a red Polish insignia was actually a red E. I reported this immediately after landing and before long the colored letters on wings of our aircraft were overpainted in black.[2]

On 5 September, I./ZG 76 shot down three PZL.23 *Karas* light bombers, with *Oberleutnant* Falck, *Leutnant* Fahlousen, and *Leutnant* Uellenbeck submitting one victory claim each.

When the Polish campaign ended, only twelve Bf 110s had been written off to all causes. The incredible success of the Bf 110 units appeared to wholly validate the *Zerstörer* concept.

Following outbreak of war on 3 September 1939, no Bf 110s were initially based on the Western Front. However, following the end of the Polish campaign, Bf 110s began to arrive in the west. During the initial stages of the 'Phoney War', Bf 110s of ZG 76 flew '*Sperrflug*' (literally hindrance flights) sorties along the French border.

The first Bf 110 sortie across the frontline occurred on 21 November 1939, when V.(Z)/LG 1 escorted a reconnaissance aircraft west of Reims. Although *Armée de l'Air* fighters intercepted the Luftwaffe aircraft, no losses were recorded on either side.

Two days later, *Lt* Werner Methfessel of V.(F)/LG 1 submitted a claim for a Morane-Saulnier MS 406 fighter, with Methfessel's *Rottenflieger* (wingman) claiming to have damaged a Spitfire.

9

Battle of Heligoland Bight

During December 1939, several RAF daylight armed reconnaissance raids were flown over the Heligoland Bight. The first such raid took place on 3 December 1939, when the RAF sent twenty-four Vickers Wellington bombers over the Heligoland Bight near Wilhelmshaven, where large numbers of *Kriegsmarine* vessels were based. The RAF bombers were detected by a *Freya* radar station at Wangerooge, with eight Bf 110s of I./ZG 26 being scrambled from Jever. However, the Luftwaffe failed to catch the RAF bombers. Incidentally, at the time, the RAF were only allowed to attack naval vessels, and drop leaflets over mainland Germany. If German cities were attacked, it was feared that the Luftwaffe would conduct immediate reprisal raids against British cities.

During a patrol over the North Sea on 6 December, 1./ZG 76 Bf 110s attacked a Do 18 in error, causing 40 per cent damage to the flying boat.

On 14 December, twelve Wellingtons were detected by radar approaching the Heligoland Bight. A number of Bf 109s and four Bf 110s of 2./ZG 26 took off, knocking down five of the Wellingtons. The Bf 110 flown by *Hptm.* Werner Restemeyer sustained 40 per cent damage by return fire. Nevertheless, Restemeyer managed to land back at the airfield.

During the post-raid briefing, the RAF HQ determined that all of the Wellingtons had been downed by *Flak* instead of Luftwaffe fighters! A second raid flown four days later would eventually change this faulty impression.

Believing that the RAF would return, Bf 110s of I./ZG 76 arrived at Bonninghardt on 16 and 17 December to strengthen the aerial defences for the German fleet.

On 18 December, twenty-four Wellingtons were once again despatched to Heligoland Bight. Out of this force, twenty-two reached Heligoland. The thirty-minute battle that ensued was the first major confrontation of the war between the Luftwaffe and RAF's Bomber Command.

No less than twelve Wellingtons were shot down, with nine of these being claimed by Bf 110 crews. Wolfgang Falck noted: 'We flew in the direction of Heligoland and when we sighted the enemy we began climbing. The bombers were quite a distance away and we could see small puffs of smoke as flak burst over Wilhelmshaven as the turned toward England'.[1]

Falck shot down one Wellington, with his rear gunner, *Feldwebel* Fresia, claiming another two. However, the battle was not entirely one-sided, with Falck and Fresia's Bf 110 being hit by return fire: 'With both engines stopped, I glided to the airfield on Wangerooge Island—it was the first and last time that I was a glider pilot'.

No less than thirteen Wellingtons were claimed by I./ZG 76 crews, with two eventually being disallowed. During the post-action briefing, it was determined that when attacking the RAF bombers, the Bf 110 exhibited some distinct advantages over the Bf 109—the 20-mm cannon could hit their targets from a distance of 600 metres, well beyond the range of the Wellington's 0.303-inch machine gun defensive armament.

Luftwaffe pilots claimed to having destroyed no less than thirty-eight Wellingtons, a very large percentage of over-claiming (this was to be a recurring feature of air combat during the war). Eleven Wellingtons had in fact been shot down, with one more ditching during the return flight. Many of the surviving Wellingtons also suffered varying degrees of damage. For the RAF, it was a disaster.

Two of the Bf 110s had suffered 15 per cent damage, with seven more sustaining less than 5 per cent damage.

Following this spectacular success, Messerschmitt paid for a ski vacation in February 1940 at Hirschegg in the Austrian Alps for the pilots involved.

The aftermath of the raid was to prove of profound importance to the war in the air. The RAF realised that daylight raids were highly dangerous, and that the bomber would not always get through as per pre-war doctrine. For the Luftwaffe, the victory over a strong force of RAF bombers (fifty-two bombers were initially believed to have taken part in the raid, with thirty-eight victory claims being submitted) represented a strong case that the Luftwaffe would ensure that no enemy bombers would be able to attack Germany unscathed.

The RAF Fighter Command's first success against the Bf 110 took place on 29 March 1940, when Flt Lt Johnny Walker and Plt Off. Stratton of 1 Sqn damaged the engines of a Bf 110 of 14.(Z)/LG 1 over Bouzonville, north-east of Metz. French anti-aircraft guns then finished off the Bf 110, which crashed near Waldhouse, north of Bitche at 3:10 p.m. The pilot, *Feldwebel* Lindemann, baled out in a wounded state, becoming a prisoner of war, with *Unteroffizier* Radek being killed in the crash.

10

Operation *Weserübung*

For the invasion of Denmark and Norway, code-named Operation *Weserübung* (Weser Exercise), the Bf 110 units were to play a decisive role, being the only fighter able to cope with the distances involved. The *Zerstörer* units initially involved were I./ZG 76 (32 aircraft) and 3./ZG 1 (10), both based at Westerland, and 1./ZG 1 and 3./ZG 1 at Barth with a combined total of twenty-two Bf 110s.

Around 9 a.m. on 8 April, Bf 110s of I./ZG 76 took off from Jever, landing at Westerland on the Isle of Sylt. During the flight, countless naval vessels heading northwards were observed. Upon arrival, the crews were briefed of the impending invasion of Denmark and Norway. I./ZG 76 were to spearhead the invasion, securing the air base at Aalborg before continuing northwards where they were to attack Fornebu airfield outside Oslo before the arrival of troop-laden Ju 52/3ms.

Operation *Weserübung* was to safeguard the supply to the German war industry of high-grade Swedish iron ore, which was shipped from Narvik in northern Norway. Since late 1939, Hitler had grown increasingly concerned that Britain might attempt to seize control of this source of iron ore. Already on 14 December 1939, a decision to invade Denmark and Norway was taken.

During the Winter War between the USSR and Finland, plans to send British and French troops through Norway and Sweden to aid the Finns was rejected by both Norway and Sweden. If the plan, strongly supported by Churchill, had been realised, British troops were to take control of the Swedish iron ore mines, as well as securing Narvik. Another plan, rejected by the Cabinet, was to sow mines in the shipping lanes from Narvik.

Even though the Winter War ended on 13 March, plans for Operation *Weserübung* were set in motion.

It was thought that the invasion force would be met by three Norwegian fighter squadrons with between twenty-seven and thirty-six aircraft, including Gloster Gladiators, Curtiss Hawks, and 'a few elderly Hawker Furies' (this was a gross overestimation, as only seven out of the twelve Gladiators delivered were serviceable, none of the Curtiss Hawks had been fully assembled, and the sole Hawker Fury supplied to Norway having been written off years before).

At 4:15 a.m. on 9 April, German army units crossed into Denmark, meeting little resistance. Two German ships managed to reach Copenhagen unhindered, spearheading the advance into the Danish capital. A few hours later, He 111s of KG 4 escorted by Bf 110s of 3./ZG 1 thundered over Copenhagen, dropping leaflets. One Bf 110 of I./ZG 1 subsequently had to make a forced landing at Skejby Mark due to engine trouble. The remaining Bf 110s landed at Aalborg, having met no opposition. Soon afterwards, the Bf 110s of ZG 76 also arrived at Aalborg.

The eight Bf 110s of 1./ZG 76 had been split into two *Schwärme* (groups of four aircraft), taking off at 5:50 a.m., with the expected flying time to the target being one hour and forty-five minutes. Upon reaching Værløse air base near Copenhagen at 7:30 a.m., the 2./ZG 76 Bf 110s attacked the airfield, with *Hauptmann* Falck shooting down one hapless *Hærens Flyvertrupper* (Army Air Corps) Fokker C.V which had just taken off, its crew being killed. During the six or seven strafing runs, made at five- to ten-minute intervals, one Fokker D.XXI and six Fokker C.Vs were destroyed, with an additional five Fokker D.XXIs, six Fokker C.Vs, and six Gloster Gauntlets being damaged. A Fokker C.V which had taken off at 4:45 a.m. returned to Værløse during the Luftwaffe attack, managing to slip away unseen. One Bf 110 was hit by ground fire, seen with one engine streaming smoke as its crew turned southwards (presumably, this was *Hauptmann* Falck's aircraft, as described below).

Wolfgang Falck later recalled the attack:

> Our job was to cover the KG 4 demonstration flight over Copenhagen, but before that we should clear the airspace of Danish military aircraft or stopping them from taking off. I had two *Staffeln* at my disposal; my third was under the command of I./ZG 76, and would secure the air transports over the Skaggerack, the same as we were to perform later in the day. We took off from Barth at 05.00 heading north across the Baltic Sea at low altitude. We managed to avoid passing over ships, which could have reported our presence. South of Copenhagen, we reached land and set course for Værløse. Shortly afterwards, we attacked the Danish aircraft. One solitary machine managed to get airborne; it was immediately shot down, crashing a short distance from the (airfield).
>
> It was important to stop the Danish aircraft from taking off, in particular the Fokker D.XXIs, which were slower than our aircraft but more manoeuvrable. We attacked the place several times, setting several aircraft on fire. The *Flak* positions returned our fire, with several of our aircraft being hit. After one strafing run, my Bf 110 shook violently; I was thrown toward the top of the canopy with the right engine beginning to run rough. My impression was that I had been struck by a bullet—and in a particularly nasty place. I told my observer, *Feldwebel* Walz, that I would try to reach Barth on one engine. This was successful. During the flight home, I attempted to find out from where I was bleeding, but finally gave up due to the straps and harness. We made a normal landing. I was happily surprised to

> find out that I had not been hit; it had been a case of my imagination. But when my sit-parachute was examined, it was found to be full of holes, with a Danish rifle bullet being nicely embedded. When I flew to Aalborg later the same day, I ventured over Værløse, albeit at a safe altitude this time around.[1]

Following the strafing attacks on Værløse, the Bf 110s were to cover Ju 52/3ms dropping paratroops over Aalborg. Securing the airfield at Aalborg was of vital importance for the invasion of Norway, with the airfield being designated to serve as a staging post for the Ju 52/3ms heading northwards. Bf 110s of ZG 76 also covered the *Wehrmacht* advance across Jutland.

Denmark surrendered later on 9 April. Norway, however, was a different matter. The Bf 110 force was divided into two sections, with 1./ZG 76 heading towards Oslo and 3./ZG 76 to Stavanger.

Due to the expected resistance from Royal Norwegian Army Air Force fighters, 2./ZG 76, led by *Hauptmann* Falck, was to be at the forefront of the invasion force. This was due to 2./ZG 76 having accumulated the largest number of aerial victories. This caused the *Staffelkapitän* of 1./ZG 76, *Oberleutnant* Werner Hansen, to object. Before the war, Hansen had served in the Diplomatic Corps, visiting Norway on several occasions. He claimed to have first-hand experience of Fornebu, as well of Norwegian culture, thus requesting that he lead the sortie. In the end, Hansen's protest was successful.

The three *Staffeln* of I./ZG 76 were given three different targets: 1./ZG 76 was selected to attack Fornebu airport near Oslo; 2./ZG 76 was to attack the Danish airfields at Værløse and Aalborg and then proceed to Norway when these airfields had been secured; and 3./ZG 76 to fly directly to Stavanger-Sola on the Norwegian coast. During the flight northwards, two Bf 110s of 3./ZG 76 were lost in a mid-air collision, with all four crew being killed.

Led by *Oberleutnant* Werner Hansen, the eight Bf 110s of 1./ZG 76 encountered poor weather over Skaggerack. Having crossed the border into Norway, five Gladiators spotted a large formation of Luftwaffe aircraft just after 7 a.m. (LT), consisting of He 111s and 'Do 17s' (it is interesting to note that early in the war, the Bf 110 was frequently misidentified with the Dornier Do 17. Presumably, this was because the Do 17 had received far more attention in the contemporary media than the Bf 110. Also, the basic configuration of both the Do 17 and Bf 110 was generally similar).

Diving down to attack, the Bf 110 flown by *Unteroffizier* Helmut Mütschele and *Gefreiter* Karl Lorey was shot down by Sgt Birger Schye, with the aircraft crashing at Vøyen. Schye was then attacked and shot down by Lt Helmut Lent. Another of the Bf 110s, flown by *Leutnant* Kettling and *Obergefreiter* Volk, had one of its engines put out of action by Lt Krohn. Kettling subsequently managed to land the damaged Bf 110 at Fornebu. A second Bf 110, flown by *Leutnant* Erhard Kort and *Unteroffizier* Bockheimer, was then shot down by Krohn, with both Kort and Bockheimer being killed in the crash.

One of the Bf 110 pilots, Austrian-born Johann Schönherr, later recalled:

> The Norwegian fighters attacked us from an easternly direction. I caught sight of them when they were some 500 metres away from us, and with an altitude advantage of 200 metres. I was part of the second *Schwarm*, flying to the right of the formation heading along the Oslo fiord. We pilots of the second *Schwarm* probably saw the (five) Gladiators before the first *Schwarm* pilots that were flying on the left side. The appearance of the Gladiators must have come as a complete surprise for *Oberleutnant* Hansen. He did not report the attack either by radio or by waggling his wings. When the Gladiators were about 200 metres away, all, or most of the aircraft of the second *Schwarm* dived, while those of the first *Schwarm* continued to fly straight ahead for a few more seconds. As a result, the first Schwarm took the brunt of the attack. The Norwegians fired off some good salvoes during their initial attack.[2]

Having lost three Bf 110s to the Gladiators, the remaining aircraft continued to Fornebu airport outside Oslo to cover the Ju 52/3m transports. Upon arrival at Fornebu, *Oberleutnant* Hansen strafed two Gladiators, setting them on fire before silencing some of the machine gun positions. However, five of the Bf 110s had been hit by ground fire. With fuel almost exhausted, the aircraft had to land at Fornebu. The first to land was *Leutnant* Helmut Lent and *Gefreiter* Walter Kubisch. With only the right engine working, Lent overshot the runway at too high a speed, with the Bf 110 careering off the end of the runway. The undercarriage then collapsed, with the Bf 110 smashing through a fence at the residence of the Theodorsen family.

The remaining Bf 110s managed to get down at Fornebu in one piece. The aircraft were then positioned so that their cannon and machine gun armament would be able to cover the continuous stream of Ju 52/3ms landing. One of the Ju 52/3ms brought the I./ZG 76 maintenance personnel, as well as supplies of ammunition. Work on repairing the shot-through radiators on three of the Bf 110s began immediately (two more of the Bf 110s had had their radios destroyed by ground fire).

During the late afternoon, a RAF Short Sunderland I, serial L2167 of 210 Squadron, overflew Oslo. Lent and Hansen immediately took off in the only two flyable Bf 110s, having little trouble in shooting down the huge flying boat (only one of the Sunderland crew, Sgt Ogwyn Francis George, survived in remarkable fashion, falling without a parachute for about 1,000 metres before landing in a pine tree). After landing back at Fornebu, the Luftwaffe pilots strongly disagreed on which of them that had actually brought down the Sunderland. A compromise was eventually reached, with Lent and Hansen sharing the victory between them.

Led by *Oberleutnant* Gordon Gollob, the eight 3./ZG 76 Bf 110s experienced foggy weather conditions *en route* to Stavanger. Due to the poor weather conditions, Gollob eventually decided to turn back to Fornebu, being followed by three other Bf 110s. Two of the other Bf 110s then collided in mid-air, both crashing into the North Sea, with all four crew being killed. Only two Bf 110s arrived over Stavanger-Sola, strafing the airfield in support of the Ju 52/3ms. Both Bf 110s were forced to land, having exhausted their fuel.

Two days later, on 11 April, additional Bf 110s arrived at Stavanger-Sola, with one Bf 110 suffering a landing accident. For the Germans, the strengthening of the Bf 110 force at Stavanger-Sola proved fortuitous, as the RAF dispatched no less than forty-four Wellingtons against the airfield. Three of the Wellingtons were shot down, with no losses being suffered by 2. and 3./ZG 76.

The following day, 12 April, *Luftflotte* 5 was formed, being commanded by *Generaloberst* Hans-Jürgen Stumpf.

More RAF raids soon followed, with 224 Sqn Hudsons attacking Stavanger-Sola on 14 April, destroying one 2./ZG 76 Bf 110. A second Bf 110, from 3./ZG 76, crashed on take-off during the raid. Three days later, on 17 April, twelve Blenheims of 107 Sqn visited Stavanger-Sola. One Bf 110 struck a bomb crater on take-off, being damaged beyond repair. The Blenheims were met by heavy *Flak*, with the I./ZG 76 Bf 110s shooting down two of the RAF bombers. On this day, I./ZG 76 reported a strength of sixteen Bf 110s at Stavanger-Sola.

With the arrival of eighteen RAF Gladiators at Lake Lesjaskogvann on 24 April, the Luftwaffe attacked in force the following day. During an eight-hour continuous bombardment, thirteen Gladiators and five FAA Blackburn Skuas were destroyed. The net result of the Luftwaffe raids was the British and French decision to withdraw from central Norway and concentrate their efforts around Narvik.

On 26 April, two 3./ZG 76 Bf 110s escorted three He 111s of 2./LG 1, sinking the Norwegian destroyer *Garm*.

During a heavy RAF raid against Bergen, I./ZG 76 Bf 110s were scrambled, flying southwards. Two hours later, RAF Wellingtons arrived over Stavanger-Sola, being met by four Bf 109s and two Bf 110s. The net result of the two raids were two Bf 110s damaged in combat, with one of these being destroyed by fire after the pilot made an emergency landing at Stavanger-Sola. Two more Bf 110s of 3./ZG 76 were also written off.

On 1 May 1940, the Luftwaffe had a total of sixty-four Bf 110Bs (including sixteen under repair), 415 Bf 110Cs (thirty-seven under repair), and ten Bf 110Ds in service.

On 10 May, the Luftwaffe Bf 110 strength in Scandinavia consisted of 1. and 3./ZG 76 at Stavanger-Sola with a total of twenty-five aircraft (sixteen serviceable), and 2./ZG 76 at Aalborg West with eleven Bf 110s (seven serviceable).

Due to the long distances involved during the Norwegian campaign, an auxiliary 1,050-litre capacity fuel tank, known as *Dackelbauch* (literally dachshund belly), was fitted to the belly of some Bf 110D-0s. Although drastically increasing the range of the Bf 110D, the large *Dackelbauch* tank was quite detrimental to the overall performance of the aircraft. It was soon discovered that the jettisoning mechanism did not always work as intended. Another problem was that when released, due to poor ventilation, the *Dackelbauch* was full of highly flammable fumes, which often resulted in the aircraft catching fire in mid-air. Recognising that the *Dackelbauch* had been a rather desperate *ad hoc* measure, the Bf 110 fuel capacity was eventually increased by fitting two 900-litre tanks beneath the wings.

The majority of the sorties flown during the latter stages of the Norwegian campaign consisted of escorting Ju 52/3ms transports and He 111 bombers, with the occasional *Frei Jagd* sorties.

The fighting at Narvik resulted in one Bf 110D-0 inadvertently ending up in Sweden. While escorting Ju 52/3m transports on 24 May, one Bf 110 of 2./ZG 76 flown by *Feldwebel* Neureiter and *Stabsing.* Thönes was forced down on the icy surface of Lake Upmasjaure close to the border with Norway. It would appear that the cause of the forced landing was due to damaged oil lines, making a return flight to Værnes outside Trondheim impossible. With the area around Lake Upmasjaure being virtually uninhabited, the Bf 110 was not detected by Swedish forces. Two days later, a Heinkel He 59 of *Seenotflugkommando* 1 marked with Red Cross insignia landed at Lake Upmasjaure. Attempts were made to set the Bf 110 on fire, with the rear gunner's MG 15 being set up on the shore, spraying the aircraft with bullets. Taking off at 10:45 p.m., the He 59 landed back at Trondheim just over four hours later.

Remarkably, the wreck of the Bf 110 remained undetected until 1946. The wreck was ultimately recovered, and sold to Germany, as related on p. 146.

With British and French forces evacuated from northern Norway, the country surrendered on 8 June.

Although more than twenty Bf 110s had been lost to all causes during Operation *Weserübung*, it is fair to say that the *Zerstörer* units played a decisive role for the German victory. Fitted with the *Dackelbauch* auxiliary fuel tank, the Bf 110D-0 was the only fighter capable of making a return flight from airfields in central Norway to Narvik.

11

Invasion of France and the Low Countries

On 10 May 1940, German forces invaded France and the Low Countries. On this day, 320 Bf 110s (219 serviceable) were serving with Luftwaffe units on the Western Front. These units were: V.(Z)/LG 1 at Mannheim-Sandhofen with thirty-three Bf 110s (twenty-seven serviceable); I./ZG 1 at Kirchhellen, thirty-five (twenty-two); II./ZG 1 at Gelsenkirchen-Buer, thirty-seven (twenty-six); *Stab*/ZG 2 at Darmstadt-Griesheim, three (two); I./ZG 2 at Darmstadt-Griesheim, thirty-two (twenty-two); *Stab*/ZG 26 at Dortmund, three (three); I./ZG 26 at Niedermendig, thirty-four (eleven); II./ZG 26 at Kaarst-Neuss, thirty-five (twenty-five); III./ZG 26 at Krefeld, thirty-seven (thirty); I./ZG 52 at Neuhausen ob Eck, thirty-five (twenty-three); *Stab*/ZG 76 at Cologne-Wahn, three (three); and II./ZG 76 at Cologne-Wahn, thirty-three (twenty-five).

The main tasks of the Bf 110 units were those of bomber escorts and ground strafing airfields and military installations. It was discovered early on that the tactical advantage of the *Zerstörers* was lost during escort sorties. The Luftwaffe bomber crews liked to have the Bf 110s at close range and within sight of the bombers, something which proved to be a highly ineffective use of the *Zerstörers*' capabilities.

On 10 May, several Dutch airfields were attacked including Haamstede, Vlissingen, and De Kooy, with about ten aircraft being destroyed on the ground. Two ancient Royal Netherlands Air Force Fokker C.Vs attempted to strafe Luftwaffe Ju 52/3ms at Waalhaven, both being quickly shot down by Bf 110s.

Also on 10 May, RAF Blenheim squadrons encountered Bf 110s for the first time. During the day, Blenheim squadrons flew a total of thirty-three sorties over the Netherlands, losing no less than eight Blenheims to Bf 110s.

Only two Bf 110s were lost on 10 May, with one aircraft of 4./ZG 1 being brought down by anti-aircraft artillery over Vlissingen. The other aircraft, a Bf 110C-2 of 3./ZG 26, was shot down at 4:40 a.m. by a French fighter.

On 15 May, no less than eleven Bf 110s (two from ZG 1, one from ZG 2, six from ZG 26, and two from ZG 76) were shot down by RAF and *Armée de l'Air* fighters, with several others sustaining damage.

However, it was the evacuation from Dunkirk in late May that the first shadows of doubt of the aircraft's perceived invincibility began to hit the Bf 110 crews. Hans-Joachim Jabs, then serving with II./ZG 76, later wrote of an encounter with the RAF on 29 May:

> Fires were raging all over the city, our Stukas and Heinkels were really pounding it. Two comrades and I had just come through a huge cloud of oily smoke when all of a sudden several Spitfires are in front of us. Out of reflex I hit my firing buttons and two of them go down. One of the Tommies hits the parachute but I don't see if the other pilot got out before his airplane hit the ground. I had not only (scored) my fifth victory, but my sixth victory as well.
>
> It was over Dunkirk however, that we pilots realized that our 110s were not all we thought them to be. Until Dunkirk we *Zerstörer* were the elite, but when we at last met the Spitfire, we began taking large losses. We were too slow and not manoeuvrable enough. When we encountered Spitfires, they would turn into us and attack, one after the other, firing their eight machine guns and then roll over us and then turn and come back at us again. They were like bees and our cockpits were without armour protection. During the Battle of France our *Gruppe* lost 6 machines, but I believe most of them were to Spitfires over Dunkirk.[1]

During the invasion of France and the Low Countries, some sixty Bf 110s were lost, representing about 32 per cent of the initial strength committed.

12
Swiss Interlude

During the Second World War, Switzerland remained fiercely neutral. However, following the German invasion of France, border incursions by Luftwaffe aircraft become more common. In May 1940, 113 border incursions by foreign aircraft were registered, more than twice as many from the previous month. The increased aerial activity around the Swiss border are reflected in that between 16 May and 2 June 1940, no less than five He 111s were brought down by *Schweizer Flugwaffe* Bf 109s.

Reichsmarschall Göring was furious, being adamant that it was necessary to teach the irreverent Swiss a lesson in the might of the Luftwaffe. On the evening of 3 June, *Generalmajor* Ritter von Greim, commander of the *V. Flieger-Division*, arrived at Lachen-Speyerdorf to brief the crews of II./ZG 1 of a 'special mission'. This special mission was to fly alongside the Swiss border and provoke a reaction from the *Schweizer Flugwaffe*. The bait was to be a He 111 of KG 55. Between 9:30 and 11 a.m., the Bf 110s overflew Pruntrut, well inside the Swiss border.

The second attempt took place in the afternoon, with one EKW C-35 biplane being attacked by three Bf 110s at 2:45 p.m. The C-35 crew was extremely lucky to escape. Minutes later, two *Schweizer Flugwaffe* Bf 109s clashed with three Bf 110s (described in the post-action report as 'bombers'), with both Bf 109s suffering damage by return fire. Another flight of Bf 109s spotted eight Bf 110s over La Chaux-de-Fonds, attacking the rearmost aircraft.

Soon afterwards, *Oberleutnant* Rufer attacked a Bf 110C of 6./ZG 1, setting the right engine on fire. The Bf 110 crashed at Grande Combe des Bois in France, with the two crewmembers baling out at too low an altitude, losing their lives. The battle was not all one-sided, though. One of the Swiss Bf 109Ds from a second patrol flight was shot down, with Lt Rudolf Rickenbacher being killed.

This event triggered strong anti-German feelings among the Swiss population. When *Reichsmarshall* Göring sent a wreath to Richenbacher's funeral, held on 7 June, the enraged participants ripped it to shreds.

The following day, 8 June, *Generalmajor* Ritter von Greim sent thirty-two Bf 110s into Swiss airspace. The idea was to provoke the *Schweizer Flugwaffe* into action.

An EKW C-35 that happened to stray into the path of the Bf 110s was quickly shot down, with both crewmembers being killed. The Bf 110s of II./ZG 1 flew in three-vic bomber formation, with the aircraft of 6./ZG 1 providing top cover. Fifteen *Schweizer Flugwaffe* Bf 109Es rose to the challenge, quickly engaging the Luftwaffe Bf 110s.

The first Luftwaffe casualty was Bf 110C-4 (W Nr 2124) of 4./ZG 1, which was shot down at Triengen, west of Zurich. Both crewmembers, *Uffz.* Alois Scholz and *Ogfr* Walter Hoffmann were killed, with the Bf 110 being totally destroyed.

A second Bf 110 of 5./ZG 1 (2N+GN, W Nr 2831) was then shot down, belly landing near Nunningen. The crew, *Fw.* Manfred Dähne and *Ogfr* Herbert Klinke, attempted to remove the rear MG 15 machine gun to destroy the aircraft. Failing in this mission, Dähne and Klinke attempted to escape on foot before being apprehended by the Swiss police. Dähne and Klinke were both repatriated on 28 June, with their Bf 110 being studied by *Schweizer Flugwaffe* experts, not being returned to Germany until 12 September.

The Bf 110 flown by *Oberleutnant* Kadow, the *Staffelkapitän* of 6./ZG 1, sustained heavy damage, with Kadow being severely wounded and the rear gunner, *Unteroffizier* Wunnike, being killed. Kadow nevertheless managed to return to base, with the Bf 110 eventually being declared a write-off.

Although one Bf 109E of the *Schweizer Flugwaffe* had been damaged, with one C-35 shot down and its two crewmembers killed, the net result of the aerial combat on 8 June was that three Bf 110s had been brought down, with three crews being killed.

Intense diplomatic efforts resulted in air combat closer than 5 km from within the Swiss border being banned.

13
The Battle of Britain

Following the surrender of France on 22 June, Great Britain stood alone. The Battle of Britain would officially commence on 10 July, with Luftwaffe aircraft attacking convoys sailing through the English Channel.

As shown during the Battle of France, the Bf 110 was at a disadvantage against the single-seat Hurricane and Spitfire fighters of the RAF, the Bf 110 being less agile as well as lacking in speed. However, the Bf 110 carried a more powerful armament, also having a far better range than the single-seat Bf 109. In order to cope with the RAF fighters, a new tactic consisting of a defensive circle was developed, during which the aircraft flew in a merry-go-round pattern, covering each other from attack.

Although the fixed forward-firing armament could inflict considerable damage to enemy aircraft, the rear gunner's solitary MG 15 machine gun offered little protection. Nevertheless, this particular weapon could, under the right circumstances, prove lethal. Eric 'Winkle' Brown (who subsequently went on to test fly Bf 110s, as well as numerous other captured former Luftwaffe aircraft) later recalled his first impression of the Bf 110 during the summer of 1940:

> The elderly Hawker Hart biplane, with a fellow Fleet Air Arm pilot at the controls, was cruising sedately on a training flight over the tranquil English countryside near Salisbury.... Suddenly, a shark-like Messerschmitt Bf 110 overtook the Hart from behind and out of the sun, its pilot cooly ranging his aircraft alongside, and almost before the unwary FAA pilot knew what was happening, the Messerschmitt's rear gunner had blasted the trainer into oblivion.
>
> This, my first encounter, albeit at a distance, with Willy Messerschmitt's strategic fighter of formidable repute, impressed me profoundly. The rakish lines of the intruder were suggestive of all the predatory characteristics associated with the shark but, more important, that unhappy incident ensured that I took truly to heart three points that were vital for survival in the aerial arena of the first half of the 'forties, or at any other time of hostilities for that matter. A pilot cannot afford to

relax at any stage of a flight however serene his surroundings may seem; his neck must acquire a measure of elasticity in order to maintain a continuous 360 deg look-out, and he must never forget the old World War I maxim of 'Beware of the Hun in the sun!' On reflection, I may owe a lot to *that* particular Bf 110.[1]

The initial clashes between the Bf 110 crews and RAF fighters over the Channel became something of an eye-opener for the Luftwaffe pilots.

Oberleutnant Wolfgang Falck, by now promoted to *Gruppenkommendeur* of I./ZG 1, later recalled an escort sortie over the Channel:

It was the worst mission we had. I was the only one to come back and my machine had over 40 holes in it, my aircraft was so shot up I had to hold the stick in both hands. We were escorting bombers attacking shipping along the coast of England. In the distance we could see the Spitfires climbing to get altitude and position on us but we couldn't go after them since we had to stay with the bombers and wait for the Tommies to attack. When they did it was a slaughter—we just weren't manoeuvrable or fast enough to dogfight with them. There was nothing we could do, my comrades were falling in flames all around me. After being sprayed by gunfire several times I dove for the water with a Spitfire right on my tail. Flying so low I was almost hitting the waves I headed for the French Coast with my machine almost out of control: weaving back and forth I tried to gain some height so we could bail out but every time I came up a little, a stream of tracers went by. My cannons were empty so I couldn't fight back even if I could get into position to fire. I kept yelling at my *Bordfunker* to reload, but he couldn't. Pressed in the corner with four or five Gs pulling on him from my zigzagging, he could do little except fire sporadically at the Spitfires. As long as I kept close to the water the tommies couldn't hit me but I didn't know how long I could keep my crate in the air; my throttle was shot out and fuel was streaming out of holes in my wings.

Finally I crossed the coast line and started dodging around sand dunes, houses and trees but they stayed right behind me, but [were] not able to hit me. Not knowing how long I could keep my machine in the air I wanted to pull up and bail out, but every time I gained a little altitude tracers would go whizzing by.

Crack! Something snapped in my wing, '...it's going to be a miracle if I can keep this off the ground!' I said aloud. Heading north with my escort still on my tail I flew right on the ground toward St. Trond. All of a sudden in front of my machine was a raised guard with a British soldier riding along on a bicycle, his flat little helmet silhouetted against the sky. He was riding along probably thinking of his wife or girl friend when he glances to his right and see me coming right at him. He rode his bicycle right off the road into mid-air as I pulled up to miss him. No tracers, the Spits were gone. After being so close to death I began laughing, thinking on the Tommies [*sic*] face, laughing so hard I almost lost control of the aircraft. I could almost hear what the poor bicycle rider must have been thinking.

> 'The whole bloody German Air Force making a ground attack against one lonely bicycle rider'.
>
> When I set down at St. Trond, *General* Kesselring was there. Pale and shaken, I must have been a sight because years and years later when I met Kesselring he said 'Hello Falck, do you remember when you came back from that mission at St. Trond?'[2]

On 10 July 1940, the official start of the Battle of Britain, the Luftwaffe had a total of 237 Bf 110s available, serving with V./LG 1, ZG 2, ZG 26, ZG 76, and *Erprobungsgruppe 210*. The latter unit had been formed on 1 July 1940, consisting of two *Staffeln* of Bf 110s and one of Bf 109s. Although officially formed for the purpose of evaluating the Messerschmitt Me 210 (which, incidentally, would not enter service until 1942), *Erprobungsgruppe* 210 were to develop *Jagdbomber* (fighter bomber) tactics, flying numerous low-level raids against heavily defended targets such as convoys, airfields, radar stations, and naval bases. The tactics employed by *Erprobungsgruppe* 210 consisted of bomb-carrying Bf 109s making a single low-level pass before climbing to provide cover for the following Bf 110s. Although *Erprobungsgruppe* 210 was mainly equipped with Bf 110C-4s, the unit also had three Bf 110C-6s. The latter variant was armed with a 30-mm MK 101 cannon and used for ground strafing. Another unit to fly ground attack sorties during the latter stages of the Battle of Britain was V.(Z)/LG 1.

The first part of the battle consisted of attacks on convoys in the English Channel, with thirty Bf 110s of ZG 26 attacking the convoy 'Bread' on 10 July. The convoy raids would continue until 8 August. The first day saw three Bf 110s of 8./ZG 26 being shot down off Folkestone. Another two Bf 110s of III./ZG 26 were damaged by RAF fighters, with the gunner of one aircraft baling out over the Channel.

The following day, 11 July, four Bf 110s of 9./ZG 76 were shot down, with five of the crew members being killed or missing. One of the pilots killed was *Oblt* Hans-Joachim Göring, a nephew of *Reichsmarschall* Hermann Göring.

On 13 July, one Bf 110 of *Erprobungsgruppe* 210 sustained 45 per cent damage in a clash with RAF fighters. The crew nevertheless managed to nurse the Bf 110 back to St Omer. The unit's first fatal loss occurred five days later, when a Bf 110 crashed near Antwerp during a routine check flight.

On 16 July, Hitler issued the Führer Directive No. 16, which involved an amphibious landing in southern England. This was called Operation *Seelöwe* (Operation Sea Lion). It was estimated that an invasion could be implemented in late September, at the earliest. Within the German High Command, there were severe doubts if an invasion of the British Isles would succeed. Even if the Luftwaffe were to achieve aerial superiority of the RAF, there was simply not enough transport aircraft available following the huge losses of Ju 52/3ms in Norway and the Netherlands. Additionally, *Grossamiral* (Grand Admiral) Erich Raeder believed that the *Kriegsmarine* was unable to match the quantitatively superior

Royal Navy, with the battleships *Bismarck* and *Tirpitz* still under construction. Also, the *Kriegsmarine*'s capability for amphibious landings was severely lacking.

Nevertheless, a military invasion of Britain was seen as a last resort if a peace settlement could not be reached. On 19 July, Hitler made an 'appeal to reason', stating that a rejection of his olive branch to the British would mean the end of Britain and the British Empire. Churchill rejected the suggestion of peace negotiations outright.

In the event, Hitler would postpone Operation *Seelöwe* indefinitely on 17 September.

If Operation *Seelöwe* had gone ahead, Bf 110s of *Erprobungsgruppe* 210 using *Seilbomben* (rope bombs) would have been sent into action to disable the electrical power grid and telephone communications. The *Seilbombe* consisted of cables attached to a fairing fitted beneath the fuselage. The cables could be extended behind and below the aircraft, with the end of each cable being weighted down, with the cables snatching telephone wires. This highly dangerous tactic would have meant flying at extremely low level.[3]

On 21 July, a Bf 110C-4/B of V.(Z)/LG 1 was brought down by RAF fighters. Although this was not the first Bf 110 to end up on British soil, it was discovered that this particular Bf 110 had external bomb racks. Initially, it was believed that the aircraft was a Bf 162 'Jaguar', which, as related above, was widely believed to have entered Luftwaffe service.

On 24 July, one *Erprobungsgruppe* 210 Bf 110 exploded in mid-air during an attack against a convoy off Harwich. It was thought that the aircraft had been brought down by anti-aircraft guns.

On 29 July, eleven Bf 110s of *Erprobungsgruppe* 210, escorted by thirty Bf 110s of ZG 26, attacked a convoy near the Thames Estuary. The brief skirmish saw one Bf 110 heavily damaged by a 151 Sqn Hurricane pilot. Up to this time, the RAF had been unaware of the existence of *Erprobungsgruppe* 210, although there appeared to be mounting evidence of a Bf 110 unit specialising in low-level attacks. The following day, one Bf 110 of 1./*Erprobungsgruppe* 210 was shot down during an attack against a convoy off Harwich.

During July, a total of twenty Bf 110s were lost in combat, including seventeen shot down by RAF fighters. Worse was to come.

It was to be a bad day for the *Zerstörer* units on 8 August. Two Bf 110s of 14.(Z)/LG 1 were shot down over the Channel by RAF fighters, with another four sustaining between 25 and 70 per cent damage. To make matters worse, two Bf 110s of 3./ZG 26 were lost in a mid-air collision.

By early August, the anti-shipping attacks largely came to an end following the Admiralty's decision to avoid sailing through the Channel. The second phase of the battle, called the *Adlerangriff* (Attack of the Eagles) now commenced. Hitler's Directive No. 17, issued on 1 August, included plans for destroying RAF Fighter Command and achieve aerial superiority over southern England in anticipation of the invasion. According to *Reichsmarschall* Göring, the Luftwaffe could achieve this within days, or, in a worst-case scenario, within weeks.

The biggest Luftwaffe raid against targets in southern England thus far took place on 11 August, when the Portland naval facilities being the target. Sixty-one Bf 110s of I./ZG 2 and II./ZG 2 provided escort for the Luftwaffe bombers. For ZG 2, the Portland raid turned out to be a disaster. Five Bf 110s were lost, with another five suffering 10 to 20 per cent damage.

One priority target was the radar stations along the south coast. During the early hours of 12 August, sixteen Bf 110s of *Erprobungsgruppe* 210 attacked four of the radar stations. Although three of the radar stations were damaged, they were back in action within hours.

The following day, 13 August, became known as *Adlertag* (Day of the Eagles). *Erprobungsgruppe* 210 were to attack two radar stations and RAF Hawkinge and Manston, V.(Z)/LG 1 RAF Detling and Worthy Down, as well as port installations at Portsmouth and Southampton. Aircraft from ZG 2 and ZG 76 were to provide escort for Do 17 and He 111 bombers. Poor intelligence resulted in some airfields used by Coastal Command being attacked.

On 15 August, twenty-nine Bf 110s were lost. One of the pilots killed on this day was the *Gruppenkommendeur* of *Erprobungsgruppe* 210, Swiss-born *Hauptmann* Walter Rubensdörffer. During the day, *Erprobungsgruppe* 210 were very active, flying three separate sorties. The third sortie involved fifteen Bf 110s and eight Bf 109s intended to raid RAF Kenley. By mistake, nearby Croydon airport was attacked instead. With the Bf 109s being forced to return to France after running low on fuel, the Bf 110s were intercepted by Hurricanes of 32 and 111 Squadrons. Over the next fifteen minutes, six Bf 110s were shot down, including the one flown by *Hauptmann* Rubensdörffer.

During the day, aircraft of *Luftflotte* 5, based in Denmark and Norway, joined the battle for the first and, as it turned out, last time. Twenty-one Bf 110s of I./ZG 76 provided escort for sixty-three He 111s attacking targets along the English east coast. To extend the range of the Bf 110s, they were fitted with the cumbersome *Dackelbauch* external fuel tank, making them highly vulnerable to single-seat fighters.

In the event, seven Bf 110s of I./ZG 76 were shot down, including the aircraft flown by the I./ZG 76 *Gruppenkommendeur*, *Hauptmann* Restemeyer. Over southern England, forty Bf 110s of ZG 2 escorted sixty Junkers Ju 88s attacking Worthy Down and Middle Wallop, losing one aircraft shot down over the Channel, while *Erprobungsgruppe* 210 attacked Martlesham Heath, putting the airfield out of commission for two days.

Over the following two days, another twenty-three Bf 110s were shot down. In the long run, such horrendous losses of trained aircrew and aircraft was unsustainable.

The aerial combat on 16 August saw Bf 110s shooting down Flt Lt J. B. Nicholson of 249 Sqn over Southampton. Despite being severely burned, Nicholson continued to attack a Bf 110 before baling out from his Hurricane fighter. For his actions, Nicholson was subsequently awarded with the Victoria Cross.

Between 8 and 18 August, a total of eighty-six Bf 110s were shot down. By this time, a gradual shift in tactics from bomber escort to *Jagdbomber* resulted in the *Zerstörer* units assigning one *Gruppe* for use in the *Jagdbomber* role, with the remaining two *Gruppen* to provide escort duties.

On 31 August, ZG 26 Bf 110s claimed thirteen RAF fighters shot down. In reality, only five Hurricanes were confirmed as lost to the Bf 110s. In return, five Bf 110s were brought down, with another seven being damaged to varying degrees.

On 4 September, the Hawker and Vickers aircraft factories at Brooklands were attacked by a strong force of Bf 110s from *Erprobungsgruppe* 210, LG 1, ZG 2, and I. and II./ZG 76. The Luftwaffe formation was initially identified as consisting of forty Dornier Do 17s, led by between fifteen and twenty Bf 110s. There were some 100 Bf 110s involved in this raid, with thirteen aircraft of *Erprobungsgruppe* 210 making a low-level attack at 1:24 p.m. One single 500-kg bomb exploded in the Vickers machine shop, killing eighty-three and injuring another 419 workers and military personnel. It was, at the time, the most devastating raid against an aircraft factory in Britain. The material damage resulted in two months of production delays.

The RAF claimed to have shot down thirty-four Bf 110s, with another fourteen damaged and four probably damaged/destroyed, as well as three Do 17s, three Junkers Ju 86s, and one Bf 109. In reality, twelve Bf 110s were confirmed as shot down. *Erprobungsgruppe* 210 did not lose a single Bf 110, with the losses being from the following units: 14./LG 1 (three), *Stab* ZG 2 (one), *Stab* ZG 76 (one), II./ZG 76 (two and one 40 per cent damaged), *Stab* ZG 76 (one), and III./ ZG 76 (four).

One of the Bf 110s brought down was flown by *Oblt* Wilhelm Schaefer and *Uffz*. Bendjus of *Stab* ZG 2:

> Because of the trouble I had at the start I followed the *Geschwader* across the Channel straight to England, but the left engine refused to pick up revs properly. The bomb carrying aircraft made their attacks on Brooklands and became involved in a great battle which I could see from afar, I tried to catch up with the rest but couldn't, I still had trouble with my engines.... I was forced down low because I thought this was the safest thing to do. One fighter stayed above me, every time I turned I presented him an easy target. Even though the aircraft had been hit I managed to stay airborne for some time until suddenly the left engine failed. I couldn't maintain control at this height. I cut the ignition on both engines and made for a field ahead [at Mill Hill near Shoreham].[4]

On 7 September, the Luftwaffe attacks against Britain shifted emphasis from RAF Fighter Command airfields to attacking London and other major cities.

Many RAF pilots found the defensive circle tactics (described earlier) employed by the Bf 110 units to be difficult to get to grips with. The defensive circle had been frequently used during the First World War, also resembling the waggon defensive circle against native American Indian attacks. One RAF pilot, Fg Off. Count Manfred Czernin of 17 Sqn, used a hair-raising method against such Bf 110 formations. According to another 17 sqn pilot, Plt Off. H. A. C. Bird-Wilson:

> It was Czernin's firm conviction that the only way to attack them was to carry out a head-on attack and go round in a circle in the opposite direction to the Germans! This may have not been a very successful manoeuvre to shoot down 110s but it usually meant that the formation broke up and thus became easier kills for fellow RAF pilots.[5]

Between 10 July and 31 October, 223 Bf 110s were lost. The Luftwaffe had failed in its primary objective: achieving aerial superiority over the RAF.

Night bomb raids on British cities continued until May 1941, by which time emphasis had shifted to the Balkans, North Africa, and the impending invasion of the USSR (incidentally, German historians do not acknowledge that the Battle of Britain ended on 31 October, arguing that the Luftwaffe continued to attack British targets for another seven months. As the Germans were doing the attacking, they are the ones to decide when the battle ended).

During November and December 1940, *Erprobungsgruppe* 210 in particular continued to attack British targets. Nevertheless, the majority of the Bf 110 *Zerstörer* units were gradually withdrawn from the Channel coast, being redeployed to North Africa, the Balkans, and, eventually, the Eastern Front. However, Bf 110s of reconnaissance units continued to make intermittent forays into British airspace.

Interestingly, notes on how to deal with Luftwaffe aircraft, including the Bf 110, were not issued until March 1941. The Air Ministry's Deputy Directorate of Air Tactics had the following to say about the Bf 110:

> The Me 110 is usually treated in a similar manner to the Me 109, but head-on attacks on the former are not recommended. Beam or quarter attacks with bursts aimed just behind the pilot usually have the effect of setting the aircraft on fire. At close range of 100 yards or under, the Me 110 shows a tendency to disintegrate owing to its light construction. It is well to avoid getting in front of this aircraft on account of the heavy forward armament, which can hit at long range. Its rear gun fire has usually been found to be ineffective. The pilot is well armoured against head-on attack, but usually no other armour has been found in the aircraft brought down in this country.[6]

14

Rudolf Hess Flies to Scotland

Among the best known (and still, more than eighty years later, highly controversial) flights during the Second World War occurred on 10 May 1941. On this day, Rudolf Hess, then the deputy *Führer* of the Nazi Party, flew from Augsburg to Scotland in a Bf 110 on what he later stated to his interrogators, a 'flight of peace'. Having the deputy *Führer* unexpectedly arriving on their doorstep was a great coup for the British. Hess remained a prisoner of war until 1945, subsequently being sentenced to life imprisonment at the Nuremberg trials. Hess was brought to Spandau prison in West Berlin, eventually committing suicide on 17 August 1987, aged ninety-three.

Born on 26 April 1894 in Alexandria, Egypt, Rudolf Walter Richard Hess was working as an apprentice in Hamburg when war broke out in 1914. Much against his father's wishes, Hess enrolled in the Imperial German Army, serving in a Bavarian infantry regiment. During a period of convalescence, Hess applied for pilot training. After completing his basic training at *Jastaschule* II to *Jagdstaffel* (*Jasta*) 35b on 16 October 1918, the commander of *Jasta* 35b, Rudolf Stark, later wrote:

> 20.10.1918: Various pilots have joined the *Staffel* and gradually we have crept up to our official strength. Helmo Ludovici is here ... *Leutnant* Hess came the day before him, bringing with him a cheery optimism and a thirst for military deeds. He wanted to fly off and shoot down a victim at once, but it wasn't quite so simple a business as that because Hess is a raw novice, with no experience of the front. I had to break him into his job gradually.
>
> When he realized it was not quite so easy to shoot down an opponent, he wanted to have a go at a balloon. But I could not allow him to go blindly at one of them; it would have meant his certain death.
>
> Hess did not understand that. He cursed a lot, and was really wild with me. That is the spirit I like to see in young pilots; I would rather have them too headstrong than too tame. We can make something out of Hess.[1]

On 10 November, Stark wrote: 'Tomorrow, there will no longer be a *Jagdstaffel* 35. What will happen then? "Business for me," says [Willi] Stoer. "No fear, I could do that too, but I mean to stick to flying," declares Hess'.

The following day, the war ended. The pilots of *Jasta* 35b attempted to return from Gosselies in Belgium to Bavaria in southern Germany, via Metz. During the flight, the pilots went off course, and, low on fuel, had to land on a rough patch of meadow near Trier. Three of their aircraft were damaged, with the local soldiers' council refusing to refuel the remaining aircraft. Fuel was then transferred to two of the fighters.

Rudolf Stark noted: '[On 12 November], Hess and Stoer took off early in the morning. Hess had a forced landing at Mannheim, where he crashed his machine'.[2]

Following the end of the war, Hess joined the Nazi Party on 1 July 1920. Hess became extremely devoted to Adolf Hitler, being involved in the failed Nazi *coup d'état* in Munich on 8 November 1923. Sentenced to eighteen months in jail, Hess shared a cell with Hitler at Landsberg prison. On 30 December 1924, having had his sentence reduced, Hess (Hitler had been released ten days prior) was released from prison. In April 1925, Hess was appointed as Hitler's private secretary, later securing the spot as the Führer's personal adjutant.

On 4 April 1929, Hess obtained a private pilot's licence. Hess subsequently bought a BFW M.23 lightplane, enjoying using scare tactics by buzzing the public gatherings of his political opponents.

Following the Nazi victory in the 1933 elections, Hess was appointed on 21 April as *Stellvertreter des Führers* (deputy *Führer*). On 1 December 1933, Hess was appointed as minister without portfolio, giving him influence over foreign affairs, finance, health, education, and law.

Nevertheless, Hess continued to fly, even securing first place in an air race in 1934. Hess spoke at numerous Nazi rallies, more often than not introducing Hitler to the crowds.

When the Second World War broke out, Hess attempted to join the Luftwaffe. However, Hitler forbade Hess to fly until the war had ended due to the risks involved. This ban was eventually reduced to one year.

By 1940, Hess was becoming increasingly obsessed with the idea of seeking a separate peace treaty with Great Britain. Having met (or so he claimed) the duke of Hamilton during the 1936 Berlin Olympic Games, Hess believed that the duke could possibly serve as a means to end the war on the Western Front.

With Germany about to invade the USSR, securing a peace treaty with Great Britain would make it possible to commit the vast majority of German forces for the impending onslaught in the east.

Hess pleaded with Willy Messerschmitt to allow him to fly a Bf 110, stating that it would serve as relaxation. With Messerschmitt finally having relented, Hess made his first flight in a Bf 110 in early October 1940. His instructor was his old fighter pilot colleague from the First World War, Willi Stör.

The aircraft used for the 10 May 1941 flight, a Bf 110E-1/N coded VJ+OQ (W Nr 3869), had been modified with additional external fuel tanks in order to increase range. The extra fuel tanks added 1,800 litres of fuel to the normal 1,270-litre capacity. An upgraded set of radios was installed as well as a dinghy which could be released from the cockpit by means of a cable. These modifications and upgrades were standard on the Bf 110E-2/N variant. According to Messerschmitt factory records, this particular Bf 110E-1/N was completed in November 1940, with a first test flight being performed between 21 November and 2 December. In the event, this Bf 110 became Hess's personal aircraft.

Prior to his 10 May 1941 flight, Hess had apparently attempted to reach Britain by air on three separate occasions. The first attempt was on 23 December 1940, when Hess had to return to Augsburg after a three-hour flight. During the flight, he had dropped his signal pistol on the cockpit floor, becoming lodged beneath the pilot's seat and jamming the rudder controls. The second attempt took place on 18 January 1941, with Hess returning to Augsburg after three hours and thirty minutes in the air, reporting an errant radio compass. During the third attempt, on 30 April 1941, Hess did not take off, with the flight instructor Helmut Kaden later suggesting that Hess received orders over the radio to remain on the ground (however, it remains uncertain if Hess had actually intended to reach Great Britain during any of these flights, or if they were intended as dress rehearsals, or merely training flights).

Whatever the case, the Bf 110 had been test flown by Helmut Kaden on five occasions: 29 March, 3 April, 9 April, 30 April, and 6 May.

On 10 May 1941, Hess took off from Augsburg-Haunstetten for his fateful flight. The Bf 110 was detected by British radar when it was some 80 km off the coast at an altitude below 3,000 metres, being identified as 'Raid 42'. A Spitfire from 72 Sqn and a 141 Sqn Defiant subsequently failed to intercept the Bf 110.

At 10:23 p.m., Hess's Bf 110 was observed by a Royal Observer Corps post at Embleton, Northumberland. Two minutes later, the Bf 110 was spotted at Chatton, flying at extremely low level. Hess was trying to locate Dungavel House, a hunting lodge and summer retreat for the duke of Hamilton. A small landing strip was adjacent to Dungavel House, but Hess eventually realised that he would be unable to find it in darkness.

Having remained airborne for more than five hours, Hess made a somewhat complicated exit from his Bf 110 at 11:07 p.m. (LT), landing at Floors Farm near Eaglesham. The Bf 110 came down at Bonnyton Moor. The first to arrive on the scene was the farmer David McLean, to which Hess introduced himself in good English as *Hauptmann* Alfred Horn. Hess had suffered a broken ankle, also having hurt his back when landing on British soil (interestingly, Helmut Kaden stated post-war that Hess's parachute was an Irvin of British manufacture).

At the time, the duke of Hamilton was serving in the RAF as a wing commander at RAF Turnhouse. He had, in fact, closely monitored the progress of the Bf 110, being thoroughly disappointed that the fighters sent to intercept the German aircraft had failed in their mission.

The following morning, the duke of Hamilton was awoken with the news that a Luftwaffe pilot named Alfred Horn wished to see him. The meeting took place later the same day, with Hess revealing his identity (he had already been identified by an interrogator) to the duke, pleading to him to work for establishing a peace treaty. In his diary, the duke of Hamilton wrote: 'I have never seen Rudolf Hess, so far as I am aware ... I cannot think why Hess should have singled me from the whole population of Great Britain as the target for his "peace mission"'.[3]

The deputy *Führer*'s arrival on British soil saw Hitler fly into a rage, declaring Hess as a madman. Upon hearing from the duke of Hamilton of Hess's arrival, Churchill quipped: 'Well, Hess or no Hess, I am going to see the Marx Brothers'.[4]

Between 11 and 16 May, the Bf 110 was salvaged by the RAF's 63 Maintenance Unit and brought to Oxford. Although the Bf 110 was armed, no ammunition was carried. Following arrival at Oxford, the wreck was put on public display for one day only. Allegedly, plans to exhibit the Bf 110 at the Tower of London fell through after a visiting American engineer noted that the tyres appeared to have been produced in the US, with the auxiliary fuel tank being marked '100 octane' according to American practice.

During the Nuremburg trials, Hess was sentenced to life imprisonment as a major war criminal. Hess, along with other former Nazi's sentenced at Nuremberg, was sent to Spandau prison in West Berlin. In 1966, all other prisoners had either died or been released, making Hess the sole prisoner in the 600-cell prison.

On 17 August 1987, at the age of ninety-three, Hess committed suicide at Spandau prison.

As described on p. 148, parts of Hess's Bf 110 is preserved by the Imperial War Museum.

15

The Balkans and Greece

Since late 1940, Hitler had attempted to persuade (or, rather bully) Yugoslavia into strengthening the relationship and cooperation with Nazi Germany and other countries within the sphere of influence of the Germany and her allies. Signed on 27 September 1940 by Germany, Italy, and Japan (and subsequently followed by several East European countries), the Tripartite Pact served a way of governing the relationship between the Axis powers.

When Yugoslavia was forced to sign the Tripartite Pact with Germany on 25 March, this resulted in an anti-German *coup d'état* two days later. Another problem for the Axis in the Balkans was the stiff resistance by Greek forces since October 1940 against numerically superior Italian forces. Furious, Hitler ordered the invasion of Greece and Yugoslavia to commence at the earliest possible moment. Between the *coup d'état* and the start of the invasion, Luftwaffe aircraft made several flights over Yugoslav airspace.

Weeks before, the *VIII. Fliegerkorps* had been transferred to Bulgaria in anticipation of a possible invasion. The *VIII. Fliegerkorps* fighter strength included thirty-eight Bf 110s of 7./LG 2 and II./ZG 26. In addition, III./ZG 26 of *X. Fliegerkorps* had recently arrived at Grottaglie in Italy.

Although the *Vazduhoplovstvo Vojske Kraljeve Jugoslavije* (Royal Yugoslav Air Force, VVKJ), included fairly large numbers of modern combat aircraft, including seventy-three Bf 109Es, about forty Hawker Hurricanes, as well as a score of obsolete biplanes, it was thought that the invasion of Yugoslavia would be little more than a formality. Apart from German forces, Hungary and Italy also provided active support for the invasion.

The invasion began on 6 April, with the Bf 110 units flying escort for the bombers as well as performing strafing attacks against airfields. At dawn, seventeen Bf 109s and a solitary Bf 110 (most likely of II./ZG 26) strafed the airfield at Rezanovacka Kosa, destroying a few VVKJ aircraft on the ground. The VVKJ Hawker Fury biplane fighters that managed to take off were at a severe disadvantage against the faster and more heavily armed Luftwaffe fighters. During the battle, eleven Furies were shot down or forced to land. VVKJ pilots claimed to have brought down three Bf 109s and one Bf 110. During a second strafing raid, two II./ZG 26 Bf 110s were lost. The Yugoslavs subsequently discovered the dead body of a Bulgarian officer in the wreck of one of the Bf 110s. It is thought that one of the Bf 110s may have been downed by *Flak* over Skopje.

During the first raid against Belgrade, Bf 110s flew top cover for the Do 17 and He 111 bombers at an altitude of 3,500 metres. VVKJ fighters put up a fierce resistance, with two Bf 110s being claimed as shot down. Another two were brought down by *Flak*, with another Bf 110 being destroyed in a landing accident. III./ZG 26 Bf 110s also provided bomber escort for the raid against Ortijes airfield outside Mostar. *Feldwebel* Richard Heller scored his fifth victory, shooting down a VVKJ Bf 109. The battle was not entirely one-sided, with one Bf 110 being destroyed and another two suffering damage.

The following day, Ju 87s and Bf 110s destroyed a dozen VVKJ aircraft at Lazarevac airfield. At 4 p.m., one Bf 110 was shot down by a VVKJ IK-Z fighter.

On 14 April, a reconnaissance Bf 110 of *Fliegerführer Arad* in Romania flew over Bijeljina airfield in Bosnia-Herzegovina, which was then attacked by twenty-three Bf 110s as well as Bf 109s and Ju 87s. The raid prepared the ground for seventeen Ju 52/3m troop-carrying transports, which landed immediately after the raid, with the troops swiftly capturing the airfield.

Three days later, on 17 April, Yugoslavia surrendered.

When Italy invaded Greece on 28 October 1940, it was thought that the Italian forces would achieve an easy victory. However, determined Greek resistance managed to stop the Italian offensive. Several RAF squadrons equipped with Hawker Hurricanes and Bristol Blenheims were despatched to Greece to augment the relatively small Greek air force. Following the German invasion, one RAF fighter pilot, Sqn Ldr Marmaduke Thomas St John 'Pat' Pattle, scored some twenty victories in two weeks, including three Bf 110s, before being shot down and killed on 20 April.

On 10 April, two Bf 110s of 7.(F)/LG 2 were lost. One of these, flown by *Oberleutnant* Peters, force-landed near Botevgrad in Bulgaria with the gunner being killed in the crash. The second Bf 110 came down near Krainici airfield in Bulgaria. One of these Bf 110s was claimed by Sqn Ldr Pattle. Another Bf 110 of 7.(F)/LG 2 was shot down over Mount Olympus on 13 April.

On 20 April, Bf 110s of II./ZG 26, led by *Oberleutnant* Ralph von Rettburg, attacked Medini airfield. Marcel Comeau of the RAF's 33 Sqn later recalled the impact of the Bf 110 strafing raid:

> Preceded by a terrified assortment of stray dogs racing across the landing ground, the 110 destroyers hit Medini. Bellies scraping the grass, they flashed past as if propelled by the rhythmic thumping of their cannons. Suddenly the aerodrome was alight with Bofors and small-arms fire. A Greek Junkers burst into flames on

> the hangar apron. A Blenheim collapsed suddenly on a broken oleo. The noise was terrific. So low were the Messerschmitts flying that a nearby Bofors sent a burst into another Bofors across the aerodrome, killing the officer in charge. Then they were diving back for a second run in.... Out in the open a bunch of eight Aussie soldiers having a late breakfast alternated between taking mouthfuls of tinned sausage and rifle-potting the aircraft. A dozen columns of smoke arose among the Blenheims.[1]

At 4:45 p.m., II./ZG 26 Bf 110s arrived over Athens. Fifteen Hurricanes of Nos 33 and 80 Sqns rose to the challenge. The intense combat that followed saw Sqn Ldr Pattle pursued and shot down by three Bf 110s. Although eight Bf 110s were claimed by the RAF pilots, Luftwaffe records state that only three were lost.

On 23 April, I. and II./ZG 26 attacked several airfields, including Argos, Medini, Megara, and Hassani. Around 6 p.m., forty Bf 110s of I./ZG 26 arrived over Argos. Two Hurricanes, including one flown by Plt Off. Roald Dahl, had just taken off for a convoy protection sortie. Another five Hurricanes were about to take-off when the Bf 110s arrived over the airfield. The Bf 110s remained over Argos for forty minutes, making repeated strafing runs against aircraft and installations.

At Medini, one II./ZG 26 Bf 110 was brought down by *Flak*.

Three days later, on 26 April, the Corinth Canal was the target for a heavy raid by Ju 88s escorted by between eighty and 100 Bf 110s. The Bf 110 crews also joined in the attack, attacking ground forces. One Bf 110 of 3./ZG 26 was shot down by small arms fire, with *Unteroffizier* Wilhelm Rödel and his gunner being killed.

On 27 April, twenty Bf 110s of I./ZG 26 attacked Australian troops at Markopoulon. Two Bf 110s were lost, with one crashing near Sparta. A third Bf 110 was later shot down in the vicinity of Athens.

On this day, Greece surrendered. At around 9 a.m., a large formation of 200 Luftwaffe aircraft, including twenty-five Bf 110s (as well as twenty-five Italian bombers), performed a victory flypast over the Greek capitol.

During the Yugoslav and Greek campaign of April–May 1941, twenty-three Bf 110s had been lost to all causes.

16

Invasion of Crete

The final British stronghold in the eastern Mediterranean was the island of Crete. By 7 May, II./ZG 26 had arrived at Argos, later being joined by the *Geschwaderstab* and I./ZG 26, with *Major* Johann Schalk being in command. Additionally, 7.(F)/LG 2 and a detachment of *Aufklärungsstaffel XI Fliegerkorps* also flew Bf 110s.

On 11 May, II./ZG 26 performed an initial strafing raid against Heraklion airfield. On the same day, a Bf 110 of *Aufklärungsstaffel XI. Fliegerkorps* was shot down by anti-aircraft artillery over Crete. Three days later, a dozen Bf 110s of II./ZG 26 attacked Crete, losing two of their number, with *Oberleutnant* Sophus Bagooe, a fourteen-victory *Experte* of 5./ZG 26, and his gunner *Oberfeldwebel* Daniel Becker losing their lives. The second Bf 110, 3U+EM of 4./ZG 26 was shot down by anti-aircraft artillery, with *Gefreiter* Adolf Ketterer and *Gefreiter* Hans Bromba surviving to become POWs.

On 16 May, I. and II./ZG 26 sent thirty Bf 110 to attack targets on Crete. Intercepted by RAF fighters, one Bf 110, 3U+SM of 4./ZG 26, was shot down. A second Bf 110 from 2./ZG 26 was brought down by anti-aircraft guns.

The following day, RAF Beaufighters made a dawn attack on Argos. Spotting numerous Bf 110s lined up on the airfield, the Beaufighters destroyed three Bf 110s and damaged ten others of I. and II./ZG 26, with one II./ZG 76 aircraft being damaged as well.

On 18 May, Bf 110s made continuous strafing attacks against Crete, with one aircraft of 6./ZG 26 being shot down by small arms fire. *Leutnant* Heinz Knecht and *Feldwebel* Georg Schulz survived the ditching off shore, becoming POWs.

On 20 May, German forces began an invasion of Crete. On this day, the *VIII. Fliegerkorps* had a total of 716 combat aircraft (514 serviceable), including 114 Bf 110s. A small number of Bf 110s also served with 7.(F)/LG 2 and *Aufklärungsstaffel XI Fliegerkorps*.

On the first day, three Bf 110s of 4./ZG 26 were shot down by ground fire, with four of the crews being killed. The first Bf 110 was 3U+HM, which crashed near Canea, with 3U+AM, flown by the unit's *Staffelkapitän, Oberleutnant* Reinhold

Heubel, crashing into the sea. The third Bf 110, 3U+CN also crashed into the sea, with *Unteroffizier* Otto Stein and *Gefreiter* Dietrich Hermann becoming POWs.

On 21 May, Bf 110s of II./ZG 26 provided for Dornier Do 17 and Junkers Ju 87 bombers attacking Heraklion, with one Bf 110, 3U+LN of 5./ZG 26 being brought down by anti-aircraft artillery. One Bf 110 of *Stab* I./ZG 26, flown by nine-victory *Experte Hauptmann* Wilhelm Makrocki and his forty-seven-year-old gunner *Hauptmann* Heinrich Gisgruber, made a low-level attack on a ship in Suda Bay. Damaged by *Flak*, the Bf 110 crashed into the ship's mast, with Makrocki and Gisgruber both being killed.

A third Bf 110 was also lost on this day, when an aircraft of *Aufklärungsstaffel XI. Fliegerkorps* failed to return.

On 22 May, attacks on ships continued, with 3U+CC of I./ZG 26 and M8+FN of II./ZG 76 being downed by ground fire. During the day, another Bf 110 of II./ZG 76 crashed at Maleme, which had been captured by German forces the previous day.

Support for Junkers Ju 52/3m transports on 23 May saw Bf 110s of I. and II./ZG 26 strafing Heraklion airfield. During the same day, yet another reconnaissance Bf 110, this time of 7.(F)/LG 2 flown by *Oberleutnant* Erich Kessel failed to return.

Despite the huge losses in men and aircraft, German forces continued to make progress against the Commonwealth and Greek troops. On 1 June, the remaining 5,000 Commonwealth troops surrendered to the German forces.

17
Iraqi Venture

Following the end of the First World War, the Ottoman Empire was dissolved. Iraq became a British mandate under the League of Nations, with the Anglo-Iraqi Treaty being signed in 1930. The treaty allowed the RAF to retain two air bases, Habbaniya and Shaiba, with the British still being in control of the country's oil resources. Although Iraq received its formal independence in 1932, anti-British feelings remained in the country.

During the spring of 1941, the German war machine appeared as invincible as it had during the past year and a half. Within little over one month (April to May 1941), Yugoslavia, Greece, and Crete had been conquered, with British forces being pushed back toward the Suez Canal by Rommel's *Afrika Korps*.

On 1 April, the pro-Axis Iraqi politician Rashid Ali el Ghailani seized power in a *coup d'état*, being supported in this venture by four high-ranking Iraqi officers, hoping to remove Iraq from the British sphere of influence.

To this end, Rashid Ali el Ghailani appealed to Germany and Italy for assistance. However, with German forces being overstretched in the Balkans and North Africa, military assistance was not immediately forthcoming. During the weeks following the *coup d'état*, the British strengthened the air and ground units in Iraq, although little could be spared from other fronts.

On 29 April, the RAF base at Habbaniya west of Baghdad was put under siege by Iraqi army units. The resident No. 4 Flying Training School had a number of Hawker Audax biplanes and Airspeed Oxford trainers, none of which were armed. Although small numbers of Bristol Blenheims, Gloster Gladiators, and Vickers Wellingtons had been rushed to Iraq and Habbaniya, the RAF units were opposed by a Royal Iraqi Air Force (RIAF) that, at least on paper, was both quantitatively and qualitatively superior. To make matters worse, the Royal Iraqi Army surrounded Habbaniya, putting the base under siege.

The first RAF bomb raid against the Iraqi troops, using Hawker Audax and Airspeed Oxford trainers quickly modified to carry a small load of bombs, took place on the night of 2 May. Within the next ten days, a large number of Iraqi

Air Force aircraft were destroyed or damaged in RAF bomb raids. An army relief column, consisting of 2,000 troops and 500 vehicles and known as Kingcol, reached Habbaniya on 18 May.

Despite repeated appeals for help from Rashid Ali el Ghailani, German assistance did not arrive in Iraq until 12 May. With Luftwaffe units engaged in Crete, North Africa, and elsewhere, few aircraft (and no ground troops) could be spared for Iraq. Nevertheless, a unit named *Fliegerführer Irak* was hastily organised. Commanded by *Oberst* Werner Junck, *Fliegerführer Irak* consisted of fourteen Bf 110s, seven Heinkel He 111s of 4./KG 4, as well as twenty Junkers Ju 52/3ms and a few Junkers Ju 90 transports. During an intermediary stop at Athens-Tatoi, all aircraft had their Luftwaffe insignia and markings painted over and replaced with RIAF insignia. This was merely a propagandistic measure, with Luftwaffe crews continuing to fly the Bf 110s (and the other aircraft of *Fliegerführer Junck*) instead of Iraqi nationals. The RIAF insignia was to all intents and purposes a flag of convenience.

The Iraqi venture began badly for the Germans. The appointed liaison officer, *Major* Axel von Blomberg, was killed on 11 May by a stray bullet fired from the ground. That von Blomberg had been killed was only discovered when the He 111 that was carrying him had landed in Baghdad. Also on the same day, three of the 4./ZG 76 Bf 110s were intercepted over Syria by Vichy French Air Force fighters. Nevertheless, the following day, a dozen Bf 110s of 4./ZG 76 had arrived at Mosul in northern Iraq, accompanied by two aircraft of ZG 26. The 4./ZG 76 crews included *Oberleutnant* Hobein (*Staffelkapitän*), *Oberleutnant* Herget, *Leutnant* Drewes, *Leutnant* Eisenach, *Leutnant* Froehling, *Oberfeldwebel* Brandsetter, *Oberfeldwebel* Neureiter, *Oberfeldwebel* Piwarz, *Unteroffizier* Hennies, *Unteroffizier* Wenke, *Unteroffizier* Ziegler, and *Oberführer* Bob.

The two-aircraft *Kette* of ZG 26 was led by *Leutnant* Woerner. Upon arrival at Mosul, the Germans were disappointed to find that the airfield lacked proper dispersal areas, camouflage equipment, and virtually no anti-aircraft guns. All support equipment had to be flown in by the Junkers transports.

The first encounter with the RAF took place on 13 May, when a Blenheim of 203 Sqn was attacked over Mosul by a Bf 110. The Blenheim crew managed to avoid being shot down, in spite of the Bf 110 pilot making four attacks against the RAF bomber. Later the same day, another Blenheim crew of 84 Sqn reported observing a Bf 110 in the Mosul area.

On 15 May, the Kingcol relief force was strafed by Bf 110s, which caused some casualties. A second strafing attack occurred on 18 May. On this date, *Fliegerführer Iraq* only had eight bf 110s, four He 111s and two Ju 52/3ms available.

Well aware that the Luftwaffe had arrived at Mosul, a 203 Sqn Blenheim made a solitary attack on 16 May, with the crew later reporting the presence of six Bf 110s, four Bf 109s (no such fighters were part of *Fliegerführer Iraq*), as well as one He 111. When the Blenheim crew made a low-level strafing attack, they came under the attention of a Bf 110.

On 17 May, two Gladiators of 94 Sqn spotted two Bf 110s taking off from Rashid airfield near Baghdad. To the Gladiator pilots' delight, the Luftwaffe pilots picked up the glove, attempting to out-turn the agile RAF fighters. Both Bf 110s were quickly shot down. It is likely that one of the Bf 110s was flown by *Leutnant* Woerner, who was later reported as killed during the Iraqi operations.

One RAF pilot, Tony Dudgeon, later recalled this encounter:

> A day or two later, two patrolling Gladiators were having a look at Raschid airfield in Baghdad. What should they see but two Me-110s taxying out to take off! With cries of joy and far too much enthusiasm they dived down to attack. In their excitement they overshot and missed them completely. However, incredible as it seems, the fast, twin-engined monoplane fighters did not just fly away. They turned and accepted a dog-fight with the slower, single-engined, but extremely manoeuvrable Gladiator biplanes. And, apparently, they had no rear-gunners. This, for the Gladiator pilots, was like giving them money for old rusty cans. Both Me-110s were promptly shot down in flames. We in Habbaniya did not know it, but this good fortune, enthusiastically celebrated, went far beyond a victory over two Messerschmitt fighters.... We now know that, early on, German planners visited their Iraqi counterparts. The absence of rear-gunners in the Me-110s is a powerful indication that the rear seats were occupied by the staff officers who were doing the forward planning. Moreover, the head of the German Mission to Iraq, Major von Blomberg had already been killed. By the time that the Germans had the ensuing confusion sorted out it was too late.[1]

On 19 May, one Bf 110 and a Ju 52/3m were claimed as damaged during a strafing raid against the Vichy French Air Force airfield at Mezze outside Damascus.

The final day involving air combat occurred on 20 May, when Bf 110s clashed with RAF fighters on several occasions. Although no Bf 110s were claimed as shot down, several RAF pilots reported having hit the Luftwaffe aircraft. However, the only aircraft lost in the air was a Hawker Audax biplane, claimed as shot down by future night fighter *Experte* Martin Drewes. During the day, six Bf 110s also strafed Habbaniya, destroying one Blenheim, one DC-2, and two Vickers Valentia transports. On 31 May, an armistice was signed. A total of fourteen Bf 110s of *Fliegerführer Irak* were lost (indeed all of the Bf 110s committed) during the brief campaign, as were five He 111s and some Ju 52/3ms. As described elsewhere, one Bf 110 was subsequently rebuilt to flying condition at RAF Habbaniya.

If the Germans had managed to secure the Iraqi oil fields and shut down the route between the Middle East to India, this would have had far-reaching consequences for the British, and indeed the Allied war effort.

18
North Africa

By early January 1941, a number of Luftwaffe units of the *X. Fliegerkorps* had been deployed to Sicily in anticipation of transfer to North Africa in support of Italian forces. Among these unit were III./ZG 26, which on 12 January counted thirty-four Bf 110s (sixteen serviceable) at Palermo. Most of the Bf 110s serving in North Africa were modified with sand filters, etc., to ease operations. These aircraft were suffixed '*Trop*', indicating tropicalised.

Led by *Major* Karl Kaschka, III./ZG 26 arrived at Benghazi in mid-February 1941. The job ahead for III./ZG 26 included providing escort for Luftwaffe and *Regia Aeronautica* bombers, convoy escort, as well as attacking ground targets.

The North African venture began inauspiciously for III./ZG 26, with one Bf 110E-1 (3U+FR) having to make a forced landing in on the wrong side of the frontline on 14 February. The crew, *Unteroffizier* Lippki and *Unteroffizier* Matthies became POWs.

On 19 February, III./ZG 26 had its first taste of combat in North Africa. While flying escort for Junkers Ju 87 *Stukas*, the Luftwaffe aircraft were intercepted by Hurricanes of 3 RAAF Sqn. One of the Hurricane pilots, John Jackson, later wrote:

> We finished the patrol and got back to Agedabia and found out from Boyd that they had spotted a number of Ju 87s dive-bombing the village just near where we saw them yesterday and, before attacking, Jock had a good look around but could see no other aircraft, so he and Gaty dived to attack—Boyd held back. Jock got a Ju 87 and looked around to see three Messerschmitts on his tail. One came up from under him and set his gravity tank on fire. Anyway he turned and managed to shoot down an Me 110 and then had to force-land with his plane on fire, and luckily got out unhurt. Poor old Gaty was last seen by Boyd in flames, crashing onto the seashore, and evidently he went into the sea as no further trace of him has since been seen. The Me 110s were evidently sitting up above the dive-bombers—we were fortunate yesterday, as they either were not above the Ju 87s or did not see us. The Me 110 is much faster than a Hurricane,

> according to Boyd, and he reckons he held back because he could see it was just murder. I think he should have shared the fight.[1]

Although two Hurricanes had been shot down, the battle had not been entirely one-sided with one Ju 87 and one Bf 110 being lost. The Bf 110 crew (*Leutnant* Alfred Wehmeyer and *Obergefreiter* Wüst) ditched off the coast, spending an uncomfortable twenty-four hours in a dinghy before being rescued.

When operating at low altitude, the RAF fighter pilots experienced little trouble in out-turning the bigger and more cumbersome Bf 110s. However, when outnumbered, the RAF fighters were at a disadvantage. On one such occasion, on 10 April, six Bf 110s shot down a RAF Hurricane.

There were instances of friendly fire. On 16 April, an Italian Fiat CR.42 pilot claimed to have shot down an RAF Blenheim or a Beaufighter near Derna. Instead, the victim was a Bf 110 of III./ZG 26. Four days later, another Bf 110 was destroyed in rather bizarre circumstances when a RAF Blenheim was shot down by *Flak* over Derna airfield. The stricken Blenheim crashed close to a Bf 110, with the latter being damaged beyond economical repair.

A ground-strafing sortie against the besieged garrison at Tobruk on 2 May resulted in two Bf 110s being downed by anti-aircraft artillery. Tobruk continued to be a prime target for the Axis, with *Regia Aeronautica* Ju 87 Stukas attacked the port installations. Two of the escorting Bf 110s were shot down by ground fire. The following day, aerial reconnaissance showed seventeen Bf 109s and four Bf 110s at Gambut airfield. During the subsequent strafing raid, one Bf 110 was claimed as destroyed.

On 17 June, 1 SAAF Sqn encountered a formation of sixteen Bf 109s and Bf 110s. Although two Bf 110s were claimed as shot down, none were, in fact, lost. One possible explanation is that the black exhaust smoke emitted from the DB 601 engines was misinterpreted that the engines were on fire. On the debit side, two Hurricanes were shot down by III./ZG 26 pilots, one by the *Gruppenkommendeur*, *Major* Karl Kaschka, and the second one by *Leutnant* Fritz Schulze-Dickow.

Four days later, Tobruk fell to Axis forces. The road to Cairo and the Suez Canal seemed open to the Axis forces.

During a dive bomber escort sortie during the evening of 15 July, *Oberfeldwebel* Richard Heller claimed to have shot down three Curtiss Tomahawks. This action resulted in Heller being awarded the Knight's Cross. Although three Tomahawks of 2 SAAF Sqn (in the unit's first combat sortie) had indeed suffered damage during the low-level dogfight, none appear to have been shot down.

In August 1941, I./NJG 3 arrived at Derna. Although a dedicated night fighter unit, the Bf 110s were mainly employed for daytime missions, including convoy escort, reconnaissance, patrol flights, and ground strafing. Incidentally, this was not due to the lack of nighttime targets in the skies over North Africa, with RAF Wellingtons flying continuous nighttime raids. In late October, I./NJG 3 returned to Europe.

On 19 September, two Bf 110s of an unknown unit were destroyed on the ground, with another five being damaged.

On 15 November, III./ZG 26 had a total of twenty-six Bf 110s on strength, with eighteen being serviceable. This was far below the regular establishment of thirty-nine aircraft.

III./ZG 26 was not the only Bf 110 unit in North Africa. On 16 November, a Bf 110 of the reconnaissance unit 2.(H)/14 was shot down by 2 SAAF Sqn. However, the Bf 110 had not been flying a combat sortie. Instead, it was being ferried back to Germany when brought down.

On 18 November, Operation Crusader, the first major Allied offensive in the Western Desert, was launched. Although 8./ZG 26 had been joined at Derna by the two other *Staffeln*, the latter units soon transferred to Crete, flying escort for Junkers Ju 52/3 transports.

On 24 November 1941, three Bf 110s of III./ZG 26 were brought down. The crews of two of these Bf 110s were captured, becoming POWs. The third Bf 110 was flown *Oberfeldwebel* Richard Heller, whose *Bordfunker*, *Unteroffizier* Mühlbrodt, later recalled the combat:

> The sun was just rising but already the Bf 110s were hovering over the British columns. Our *Rotte* (a formation consisting of two aircraft) has discovered a new column on the march. Suddenly I see one, two, three, four black dots on the right. They are approaching. I shout: 'Fighters!' My pilot curves in and at the same moment the fighters zoom over us and we can see the blue rings of their cockades. They turn in again. The sky above is full of black specks and I count 12 or more fighters. It seems as if we have fallen right into the midst of a strong formation.
>
> We try to escape in a frantic dive, because it is hopeless to fight such an overwhelming crowd, but we cannot escape. The Curtiss are too high and overtake us in the dive. Our engines scream and I shout to the pilot: 'First attack!' Exactly behind us appears the snout of a Curtiss; a right turn is useless because to [the] left and right of the attacking fighter two more Curtiss are flying. Out of the wings of the Curtiss come flashes of all colours. Then it rattles in our aircraft as if someone were knocking a milk churn. The next Curtiss is attacking, while the first is hovering over us like a satisfied bird. Second attack, so quickly, that I can scarcely warn the pilot. The hail of bullets comes down like a shower. There is no escape. We are in the trap. The fighters relieve each other as if on a shooting range. Both engines stutter, the right one is smoking. We have only one chance; a belly-landing in the desert! I see the ground approaching. At the same moment a Curtiss is closing in for an attack. The Bf 110 glides towards the ground very softly, but the Curtiss is diving at us like a meteor. The cannon and gun burst[s] are whistling around us, splinters whizz through the cabin. Heller holds the stick with the left, and with the right hand holds the gunsight. I myself seize the machine gun, because we will touch down at any moment. While gliding the Bf 110 hits a

> heap of stones, there is a mighty jerk, and I landing between the drum magazines. For a moment I sit benumbed in the cockpit, but then I jump up. It is high time, as from both sides flames are blazing into the cabin. I jump out and run for cover. The Curtiss disappears. Heller's left hand is bleeding, it was hit between [the] thumb and forefinger. I tie up his arm and make a sling. After a short march we are found by German soldiers who take us to the next airfield. We ask about our wingman, but he had more luck and has landed safely at home despite some damage.[2]

On 25 November, 8./ZG 26 lost two Bf 110s, with a Bf 110 of 2.(H)/14 also being brought down near Sidi Omar.

During the Allied advance westward, wounded soldiers were evacuated by air. For this purpose, the RAAF's 1 Air Ambulance Unit used a small number of pre-war four-engined DH.86 transports. On 8 December, Capt. Nel (a South African pilot attached to the unit) had a very lucky escape. Having spotted a Bf 110, Nel turned away sharply, flying directly into the line of fire of five Bf 110s at a range of less than 150 metres. Nevertheless, Nel managed to land at LG.138 in one piece, although several bullet holes were discovered in the fuselage and tail of the DH.86. On the same day, another DH.86 of the 1 Air Ambulance Unit was shot down by *Oberfeldwebel* Helmut Haugk of 7./ZG 26. During the post-action briefing, Haugk misidentified the DH.86 as a Vickers Valentia.

On 8 December, two Bf 110s of III./ZG 26 were shot down. A third aircraft returned to Derna in a damaged state, where the pilot crashed when attempting to land. Both crewmembers were killed.

On Christmas Eve, two Bf 110s of III./ZG 26 crashed near Crete during a ferry flight, with all four crewmembers being posted as missing. One of the pilots was the III./ZG 26 *Gruppenkommendeur*, *Hauptmann* Thomas Steinberger.

Operation Crusader was a major success for the Commonwealth forces, with much territory being regained. Many wrecks of Luftwaffe and *Regia Aeronautica* aircraft were found at various airfields, with eight destroyed Bf 110s being located at Derna, and another five at Benina.

The attrition suffered in combat by III./ZG 26 may be seen from the fact that in mid-January 1942, the unit counted a mere eight Bf 110s on strength, only four of which were serviceable.

While attacking vehicles east of Bir Hacheim on 10 February 1942, one Bf 110 was destroyed when its bomb load exploded prematurely, killing both crewmembers.

On 22 February, 8./ZG 26 returned to North Africa.

On 13 April, six Bf 110s of 7./ZG 26 escorted two *Regia Aeronautica* Savoia-Marchetti SM.82 transports to an abandoned RAF landing ground in eastern Libya. Aboard the transports were sixty German and Italian troops, who destroyed the fuel dump, also discovering a number of derelict Bristol Blenheims. Three of the Bf 110s also landed, with the remaining three providing air cover.

In April and May, III./ZG 26 Bf 110s flew a number of night sorties.

On 27 May, 5 SAAF Sqn (which had recently arrived in Libya) intercepted a force of ten fighters and ten bombers in the Tobruk area. Although the South African pilots initially identified the enemy aircraft as Junkers Ju 87s, which were later amended to *Regia Aeronautica* Fiat BR.20 bombers, and even Dornier Do 215s, it would appear that they had encountered Bf 110s. Although the Bf 110 pilots formed a defensive circle, one was shot down, with another two falling to ground fire.

During a ground-strafing sortie on 1 June, two Bf 110s were brought down by ground fire, with a third aircraft crashed after being hit by shrapnel from an exploding tank.

On 5 July, two Bf 110s were shot down during a large air battle near El Alamein.

On 23 July, nineteen Bf 110s provided escort for thirty Junkers Ju 52/3ms to the Siwa Oasis close to the Libyan border. The Siwa Oasis had previously been abandoned by Commonwealth forces.

On 5 August, III./ZG 26 relocated to Kastelli, Crete, before transferring to Trapani on Sicily during November. On 19 August, III./ZG 26 reported a strength of forty-six Bf 110s. Nevertheless, even though III./ZG 26 had returned to Europe, the unit continued to fly on operations over North Africa.

The arrival of USAAF units in North Africa during the autumn of 1942 saw III./ZG 26 encountering B-24 Liberators. On 11 October, one 7./ZG 26 Bf 110 was shot down north of Tobruk by a USAAF B-24 gunner.

On 23 October 1942, the Battle of El Alamein was launched. The battle was a turning point of the war, resulting in the Axis forces eventually being forced out of North Africa some seven months later.

Between 10 and 16 November, seven Bf 110s of III./ZG 26 had to be intentionally destroyed by retreating German forces. During a Junkers Ju 52/3m escort sortie on 14 November, a dogfight with RAF Spitfires resulted in the loss of one Bf 110 and one Spitfire. The following day, one Bf 110 was shot down by ground fire over Tobruk.

On 10 December, 8./ZG 26 reported a strength of eleven Bf 110s at Tripoli, with only two being serviceable. The following day, two Bf 110s were shot down near the island of Lampedusa, with all four crew being killed. During a separate combat, a Bf 110 encountered, and damaged a RAF Martin Baltimore.

In early 1943, Bf 110G-2s began to supplant the older variants. The first months of 1943 saw an increasing number of USAAF Lockheed P-38 Lightnings being encountered. The number of escort sorties increased, with this involving both Luftwaffe transport aircraft as well as ship's convoys.

On 31 January, two Bf 110s of III./ZG 26 attempted to intervene when two Heinkel He 111s were being attacked by USAAF Lightnings over the Gulf of Tunis. This effort was in vain though, with both Bf 110s being shot down.

The following day, *Leutnant* Paul Bley claimed to have brought down a P-38. It would appear that Bley's victim was a Lockheed F-4, an unarmed photo reconnaissance variant of the P-38.

On 2 February, *Leutnant* Bley claimed a Consolidated B-24 Liberator and a P-38. However, according to USAAF records, no B-24 was lost on this day. One Bf 110 was shot down by P-38s over the Gulf of Tunis.

While escorting two empty tankers back to Italy on 3 February, no less than three Bf 110s were shot down by USAAF P-38s off Cap Bon, with a fourth aircraft being seriously damaged.

The losses in crews and aircraft was not confined to Tunisia, with a USAAF raid against the III./ZG 26 base at Trapani on 16 February resulting in two Bf 110F-2s being damaged.

On 17 March, ten Bf 110s of III./ZG 26 provided escort for a convoy sailing from Trapani to Bizerta. A number of RAF Beaufighters and Beauforts intercepted the convoy. During the ten-minute dogfight, the RAF crews claimed to have damaged six of the Bf 110s, in addition to two probables. However, only one Bf 110 (of 7./ZG 26) was actually lost, the cause being engine failure. The RAF lost one Beaufighter and one Beaufort.

By early April, it seemed certain that the Axis forces were about to be pushed out of North Africa. The number of Luftwaffe and *Regia Aeronautica* transport flights increased rapidly, delivering supplies to Tunisia and bringing back wounded on the return flights. The majority of these transport aircraft consisted of Junkers Ju 52/3ms, along with Messerschmitt Me 323s, with many Italian Savoia SM.82s being used as well. Luftwaffe and *Regia Aeronautica* fighters provided escort for many of these flights, but in many instances, the fighter escort proved unable to protect the slow and lumbering transports due to their small numbers.

On 5 April, the Allies set Operation Flax in motion. This involved intercepting and shooting down as many transport aircraft as possible. On this day, III./ZG 26 escorted a large number of Junkers Ju 52/3ms, losing two Bf 110G-2s to USAAF Lightnings during the desperate fight. In return, four Lightnings were claimed by the Bf 110 crews, including two by *Leutnant* Bley. During a USAAF bomb raid against Trapani, four III./ZG 26 Bf 110s were damaged.

On 11 April, a formation of nineteen Junkers Ju 52/3ms, escorted by four Bf 110s, four Junkers Ju 88s, and a few Bf 109s, was intercepted by USAAF Lightnings north-east of Cap Bon. All nineteen Junkers Ju 52/3ms were shot down, along with two of the Bf 110s. Two P-38 Lightnings were claimed by *Feldwebel* Helmut Netzke and *Feldwebel* Theodor von Kovarbasic.

Two days later, a heavy USAAF raid against Trapani saw one Bf 110F-2 destroyed, with no less than nine further Bf 110s (including eight Bf 110G-2s) suffering varying degrees of damage.

On 17 April, two USAAF Spitfires were claimed as shot down, including one by a 9./ZG 26 crew. However, two Bf 110s were lost in combat during the day.

The events on the following day, 18 April, would become known as the 'Palm Sunday Massacre'. A large formation of more than sixty Junkers Ju 52/3ms, escorted by a few Bf 109s and Bf 110s, saw more than forty of the slow transports being shot down, along with one Bf 110. Another event during this day saw a USAAF raid against Palermo. One of the B-17s was shot down 15 km south-east of Palermo by *Oberleutnant* Paul Herzberg. One of the III./ZG 26 Bf 110s was shot down during the raid.

On 28 April, *Unteroffizier* Röder claimed to have shot down a P-38 Lightning north-west of Marimetto Island. Interestingly, Röder was serving as a *Bordfunker* at the time.

On 13 May, Axis resistance in North Africa came to an end.

Having seen continuous combat for several months, III./ZG 26 remained at Trapani until June 1943 before moving to Ciampino outside Rome.

19

The Eastern Front

A number of Bf 110 units took part in Operation Barbarossa, the German invasion of the USSR. On the first day, 22 June 1941, thirty-one Soviet airfields were attacked, with the Soviet aircraft being lined up wingtip to wingtip as if anticipating an inspection. Numerous aircraft were destroyed during continuous ground-strafing sorties. During the first day, only two Bf 110s were lost.

Two days after the invasion had begun, Luftwaffe Bf 110 strength on the Eastern Front consisted of 249 aircraft, roughly 10 per cent of the total Luftwaffe strength deployed. The Bf 110 units included 173 *Zerstörers* (132 serviceable), and seventy-six reconnaissance aircraft (sixty-two serviceable).

Messerschmitt Bf 110 Units on the Eastern Front, 24 June 1941

Unit	**Total strength**	**Serviceable Aircraft**	**Remarks**
3./*Aufklärungsgruppe* 10	3	3	*Luftflotte* 1, Northern Front. Also operated other types of aircraft
4./*Aufklärungsgruppe* 33	9	9	*Luftflotte* 1, Northern Front
3./*Aufklärungsgruppe* 31	9	9	*Luftflotte* 2, Central Front.
3./*Aufklärungsgruppe* 122	3	3	*Luftflotte* 2, Central Front. Also operated other types of aircraft
3./*Aufklärungsgruppe* 11	6	3	*Luftflotte* 4, Southern Front. Also operated other types of aircraft
2./*Aufklärungsgruppe* 33	9	8	Luftflotte 4, Southern Front
3./*Aufklärungsgruppe* 121	3	3	*Luftflotte* 4, Southern Front. Also operated other types of aircraft
4./*Aufklärungsstaffel* 121	1	0	*Luftflotte* 4, Southern Front. Also operated other types of aircraft
2./*Aufklärungsstaffel* 122	3	1	*Luftflotte* 4, Southern Front. Also operated other types of aircraft

4./Aufklärungsstaffel 122	3	2	*Luftflotte* 4, Southern Front. Also operated other types of aircraft
7./*Lehrgeschwader* 2	9	8	*Luftflotte* 4, Southern Front. Reconnaissance unit
Stab/ZG 26	4	4	*Luftflotte* 2, Central Front
I./ZG 26	38	17	*Luftflotte* 2, Central Front
II./ZG 26	36	30	*Luftflotte* 2, Central Front
Stab/SKG 210	5	4	*Luftflotte* 2, Central Front
I./SKG 210	41	33	*Luftflotte* 2, Central Front
II./SKG 210	37	37	*Luftflotte* 2, Central Front
Stab/St.G. 1	6	3	*Luftflotte* 2, Central Front. Ju 87 dive-bomber unit
Stab/St.G. 2	6	4	*Luftflotte* 2, Central Front. Ju 87 dive-bomber unit
Stab/St.G. 77	6	6	*Luftflotte* 2, Central Front. Ju 87 dive-bomber unit
I./JG 77	12	7	*Luftflotte* 5. Based in Norway and Finland

Although vast numbers of Soviet aircraft were destroyed on the ground, the Bf 110 crews encountered relatively few enemy aircraft in the air. By 19 August, ZG 26 crews claimed to have destroyed a staggering 853 Soviet aircraft on the ground, as well as shooting down 191 aircraft in aerial combat on the Central Front.

Initially based at Herdla in northern Norway, 1.(Z)/JG 77 flew against Russian targets on the Kola peninsula. The missions mainly included providing escort for Ju 87 Stuka dive bombers, locomotive hunting, and the occasional *Frei Jagd* sortie. The first operational loss for the unit occurred on 5 July, when a Bf 110 was shot down by ground fire over Titowka. The wreck and the dead crew were not located until two weeks later. On 30 July, aircraft of HMS *Furious* and HMS *Victorious* attacked Kirkenes and Petsamo in support of Soviet forces. For the British, the raid was a complete disaster, with twelve Fairey Albacore torpedo bombers and four Fairey Fulmar fighters being shot down. Only two Luftwaffe aircraft were lost during the raid, including one Bf 110.

During one train-busting sortie in the Murmansk area on 1 September 1941, three Bf 110s lost their bearings during the return flight to Rovaniemi, straying into Swedish airspace. One aircraft, flown by *Leutnant* Diederich, managed to return to base, with the other two Bf 110s making forced landings in Sweden after running out of fuel. The Bf 110 (LN+KR, W Nr 4113) flown by *Oberfeldwebel* Rudi Reitz and *Gefreiter* Guntram Johann Weigl overturned on landing at Pajala. Reitz and Weigl had to be literally dug out by Swedish army personnel. The aircraft was dismantled and returned to German authorities in Finland on 20 September.

The second Bf 110, flown by *Leutnant* Felix Brandis and *Feldwebel* Albert Harnack, landed intact at Tärendö. Not realising that they had come down in neutral Sweden, Brandis initially asked to make a telephone call to Rovaniemi. When duly informed by a Home Guard unit, Brandis asked to contact the German legation in Stockholm. Brandis and Harnack then surrendered their sidearms, also being kept away from their Bf 110. They were, however, allowed to perform makeshift repairs to the left engine radiator.

All four Germans were allowed to return to Finland two days after their unscheduled arrival in Sweden. Brandis and Harnack's Bf 110 was thoroughly inspected by both *Flygvapnet* and Saab engineers before being dismantled and returned by rail to Finland on 18 September.

By 13 December 1941, the losses inflicted to the *Zerstörer* units had reduced the number of available Bf 110s to a mere forty-four aircraft (twenty-eight serviceable). The sharp reduction in production numbers also meant that attrited aircraft could not be replaced.

Nevertheless, the *Zerstörer* units continued to fly numerous close-air support and ground-attack sorties. A number of reconnaissance units were also equipped with Bf 110s. During one reconnaissance sortie against Grabtsevo airfield on 27 January 1942, one Bf 110 crew of *Aufklärungsgruppe* 3.(F)/11 managed to shoot down a Soviet LaGG-3 fighter. The subsequent aerial photographs showed a large number of Soviet transport aircraft at Grabtsevo. Bf 110s of I./ZG 26 and Dornier Do 17Z bombers of II./KG 3 attacked the airfield, destroying thirteen aircraft (including a dozen Tupolev TB-3s) as well as the fuel dump. Only one Bf 110, flown by the I./ZG 26 *Gruppenkommendeur*, *Hauptmann* Wilhelm Spies, was lost during the raid. A veteran of the Spanish Civil War, Spies had scored a total of twenty victories.

Making rapid advances into Soviet territory meant that numbers of Soviet troops that had ended up behind the German lines continued to fight as partisans. Attacks against Luftwaffe bases were occasionally performed, with six aircraft (including one Bf 110 of 4.(F)/22) being destroyed at Nikolayev, north-west of the Crimean Peninsula.

One major headache for the Germans was the appearance of Soviet night bomb raids, conducted using Polikarpov U-2 biplanes. Often flown by female crews (dubbed *Nachthexen*, i.e. Night Witches by the German troops), these aircraft flew low and slow over the German lines, dropping bombs before disappearing into the night. Due to their slow speed, the Polikarpov U-2s were very difficult to locate and shoot down. Even though the material damage caused during these raids was negligible, the psychological effect was profound. Being awakened through such nuisance raids was bad for morale. Occasionally, the Luftwaffe was able to strike back. On 31 August 1942, a Bf 110 crew of ZG 1 destroyed ten Polikarpov U-2s on the ground at Novo Nikolskoye near Stalingrad.

During the initial assault on Stalingrad in September 1942, nine Bf 110s were lost in action. On 20 November 1942, the *Luftflotte* 4 Order of Battle included the following Bf 110 units:

Unit	Total strength	Serviceable aircraft	Remarks
3.(H)/11	7	7	Reconnaissance unit
7.(H)/LG 2	7	4	Reconnaissance unit
3.(H)/31	5	1	Reconnaissance unit
Stab ZG 1	2	2	
I./ZG 1	32	18	
II./ZG 1	23	13	

Additionally, the Junkers Ju 87 Stuka unit *Stab* St.G.77 operated a few Bf 110s.

With fighting at Stalingrad at its height, Soviet forces began encircling the German and Axis forces. On 23 November 1942, a complete encirclement had been achieved. A German counteroffensive, code-named Operation *Wintergewitter* (Winter Storm), began on 12 December. In the early hours of 12 December, Bf 110s of ZG 1 strafed Abganerovo airfield, claiming eight aircraft destroyed. Within days, Operation *Wintergewitter* ran out of steam. Between 16 and 18 December, ZG 1 lost eleven Bf 110s. Two days prior to the commencement of Operation *Wintergewitter*, two ZG 1 Bf 110s had been shot down by a Soviet female fighter pilot, Yekaterina Budanova.

During the battle for Stalingrad, Bf 110s of ZG 1 remained active until the last days of January 1943. On 30 January, five Bf 110s of I./ZG 1 made a long-range sortie over the city and its surroundings. During the return flight, *Oberleutnant* Eduard Tratt was seriously injured when his Bf 110 crashed.

During the Battle of Kursk, between 5 July and 23 August 1943, Bf 110s formed a minor component of the overall Luftwaffe strength.

Subsequently, several *Nachtjagd* units, called *Nahnachtjagdschwärme* (close night fighter sections) were formed to combat against Soviet night intruders. Bf 110s were among the aircraft operated by these units.

By late 1943, few Bf 110s remained active on the Eastern Front. By this stage, the main focus for the Bf 110 *Nachtjagd* and *Zerstörer* units was to defend Germany against RAF and USAAF heavy bombers.

20

Defending the Reich by Night and Day

The beginnings of a night fighter force had been established already in 1939. On what might be called operational evaluation, Bf 109Ds and Arado Ar 68F biplane fighters were used as *ad hoc* night fighters. Operational experience showed that the Bf 109D, with its narrow undercarriage, was not particularly suited as a night fighter. Although assisted by searchlights, albeit with no guidance from ground radar stations, few enemy aircraft were encountered, and even fewer were shot down.

However, it is interesting to note that the Germans had begun experimenting with night fighters during the First World War.

On 20 August 1918, *Leutnant* Fritz Anders of *Jagdstaffel* 73 shot down a French SPAD fighter during a night sortie. By 25 September, Anders had downed another four aircraft, making him the world's first night fighter ace. Night fighter operations were also conducted on a regular basis in both Britain and France.

However, following the end of the war, the importance of night fighting appears to have been completely lost to the Luftwaffe High Command. According to Joseph Kammhuber, who in 1941 would be appointed as *General der Nachtjagd*, the pre-war attitude was scornful: 'Night fighting! It will never come to that!'[1]

During a meeting in The Hague on 26 June 1940, *Reichsmarschall* Göring appointed *Oberst* Josef Kammhuber to establish a night fighter arm. Wolfgang Falck was to command the first dedicated *Nachtjagdgeschwader*, NJG 1.

Kammhuber intended to develop two different main types of *Nachtjagd* missions; that of *Nahnachtjagd* (short-range defensive night fighters) and *Fernnachtjagd* (long-range offensive night fighters). The *Nahnachtjagd* were to handle the enemy bombers on their way to and from the target, while the *Fernnachtjagd* were to stalk the bombers back to England, and strike at the RAF Bomber Command's airfields, with Kammhuber drawing the parallel of destroying wasps at their nest. One *Gruppe*, II./NJG 1, was formed to fly *Fernnachtjagd* sorties, commencing operations in September 1940 using Dornier Do 17Zs and Junkers Ju 88s. The psychological effect of knowing that the enemy might attack your aircraft prior to landing following an exhausting eight-hour night sortie, or strike at your airfield was considerable. However, due to various reasons, the *Fernnachtjagd* operations ended in 1941, not being revived until the spring of 1944 and March 1945 (albeit briefly).

The *Nahnachtjagd* operations were supported by a network known as *Himmelbett* (Sky Bed), consisting of *Freya* long-range (100-km) radar stations, searchlights, and night fighters. The *Himmelbett* system was divided into sectors along France, the Low Countries and the German North Sea coast, with the night fighters being controlled through *Freya* ground radar stations. To RAF Bomber Command crews, this first line of defence was known as the Kammhuber Line.

The combination of using ground radar and searchlights for locating and intercepting the enemy aircraft was called *Helle Nachtjagd* (illuminated night fighting). Another tactic was the *Dunkle Nachtjagd* (dark night fighting) essentially consisted of ground radar leading the night fighter crew to their target without the use of searchlights. There was also a combination of the two, known as *Kombinierte Nachtjagd* (combined night fighting).

The beginnings of the *Nachtjagd* operations were inauspicious. The first night fighter victory occurred on the night of 19–20 July 1940, when *Oberleutnant* Werner Streib (a future *Nachtjagd Experte*) shot down an RAF Armstrong Whitworth Whitley west of Osnabrück.[2]

Less than a week later, on 25 July 1940, two Bf 110s of 3./NJG 1 were lost. It was believed that one of the Bf 110s, flown by *Leutnant* Pack, had been hit by return fire from an RAF Wellington, with both Pack and his *Bordfunker* losing their lives. The second Bf 110 crashed near Gütersloh after suffering a mid-air collision with a British parachute flare.

Nevertheless, slowly but surely, the *Nachtjagd* units built up both in strength and operational experience. By the end of 1940, forty-two RAF bombers had been claimed as shot down. However, searching for RAF bombers in dark skies over a blacked-out Germany could be likened to the proverbial needle in a haystack. More efficient *Würzburg* radar stations had begun to arrive in late 1940.

Previously, the *Flak* units had been given priority of receiving *Würzburg* radar stations as fire control radar systems.

As the RAF Bomber Command raids against German targets increased in intensity, so did the losses of aircrew and aircraft. In 1941, a total of 427 RAF bombers were lost to the *Nachtjagd* fighters. For Kammhuber, one initial drawback for the development and upkeep of the Himmelbett system was Hitler's insistence of concentrating the available searchlights around the major cities. Although this had an initial detrimental effect on the *Nachtjagd* operations, it proved to be important for the development of airborne radar.

For the *Nachtjagd* crews, *Nachtjagd* operations did involve a high rate of danger to contend with, even if the Bf 110 crews failed to locate any RAF bombers. Among these were hazardous weather conditions, fog rolling out of nowhere, machine-gun fire from RAF bombers, enemy night fighters at work over German airfields, and simple physical and mental fatigue, which could all contribute to tragedy. One of the men who survived all of this was *Oberfeldwebel* Kurt Bundrock, who flew as *Bordfunker* with the NJG 1 *Experte, Hauptmann* Reinhold Knacke (forty-four night victories). Bundrock would later recall his experiences:

> I'd be more than happy to tell you what a typical *Dunkle Nachtjagd* mission looked like before we had on-board radar. We were guided by ground radar over the radio to the general area of the enemy and given information about his altitude and heading. At that point we had to depend solely on our eyes and were at the mercy of visibility and the whims of the enemy pilot. There were times when the first thing we saw were his exhaust flames, while the enormous silhouette of the plane was all but invisible.
>
> Our exhausts were shielded by long flame dampers and were visible only from a position directly behind us. The English, even with flame shields, emitted flames that could on occasion be visible from 100–150 meters.
>
> Turbulence was a good sign that the enemy was near. When our machine began to shake and lurch, we knew that we were behind him and the pilot would release the gun safety and keep his thumb on the trigger, ready to unleash a salvo from our four machine guns and two cannon at any moment.
>
> 'There he is! Three o'clock, three hundred meters!'
>
> Initially we noticed a slight silhouette in the night sky, and then, as we moved in, a more defined outline. Knacke flew his closing approach, keeping some 50 meters below the English plane because it was easier to make out the outline against the sky than the horizon, where it blended in.
>
> The bomber flew in a rocking motion and because of this we were unable to make out the type. At the same time we knew we had to watch out for a tail gunner, a dorsal gunner or both. Once we were certain, we could decide on the appropriate tactics.
>
> In the meantime the pilot's voice came over the headset—'*Short Stirling, Pauke, Pauke!*' [*Pauke, Pauke* being the Luftwaffe codename for I'm attacking.] And ground control would reply—'*Viktor* [Luftwaffe codename for 'Roger'], good luck!'
>
> Knacke began climbing and positioned himself underneath and to the side of the huge machine. The difference in size between the two planes was like that between a small sports car and a tractor-trailer. When we were 50 meters from the Stirling we started to follow his maneuvers and closed in to 30 meters.
>
> 'I hope his bombs don't go off when you hit him, sir,' I said through the throat-mike. Knacke replied calmly, 'I'm going to go for the left wing.' That was reassuring because if the bomber exploded it would take us with it.
>
> The *Leutnant* lifted the nose so fast that it seemed as if something was pushing our tail down.

At the same time a long burst ripped from our machine guns and tore into the left wing between the fuselage and engine where the fuel tanks were. We had gotten dangerously close and Knacke allowed the plane to drop to the right and brought us out of the dive after we had gotten a safe distance from the Stirling.

We saw some embers and sparks and a trail of lightly colored smoke, but there were no flames. The Stirling started to dive to evade us, but we followed it down. At the same time the tail gunner opened up on us and the bomb bay doors opened as the pilot jettisoned his bomb load.

From a slightly higher altitude Knacke loosed off bursts at the right wing, allowing the bullets to tear into the fuselage. The tail gunner was constantly correcting his aim, and when we fired he could see us better. We had the advantage of speed though, and we quickly veered from his starboard to port side and went below his line of sight. The Stirling began to burn, and pieces started to come off, swept along by the slipstream. We circled around at a constant altitude and watched as the bomber plunged earthwards. At the point of impact there was an enormous explosion.

I made a note of the time, wrote a detailed report of the conditions and based on information from ground control I made an estimate as to the wreck's location. Ground control asked if we had seen any parachutes. We replied in the negative.

But it wasn't always that easy. On average a night fighter had to mount two or three attacks. Often during the second or third attack we would take hits ourselves, which made us stand out from the other crews. Knacke was young (born in 1919), very courageous but not crazy or foolhardy. In spite of that, he tended to get too close to the enemy. I think he was afraid that he would miss, since I noticed more than once that he wasn't a very good shot and he had trouble aiming at a moving target.

I remember one such occasion when ground control at Würzburg-Riese on the island of Sylt guided us over the North Sea between Sylt and Heligoland onto a twin engine Whitley bomber. Knacke made his first attack from below and from the side. The only effect was a few defensive maneuvers and a series of tracers from the tail gunner.

During the entire dogfight I kept the transmitter button depressed so that ground control could follow what was going on, allowing them to listen in on the conversation between Knacke and myself. Throughout I kept thinking that it would be good if ground control kept track of the situation. This way they would be able to send a search team to fish us out of the cold waters as soon as possible.

We made our second attack from slightly below and directly behind the enemy. It was unsuccessful.

We couldn't get in close enough due to the defensive fire.

During the third attack we closed from the rear to take out the gunner from a distance of about 80 meters. The Whitley banked into a turn that usually only a fighter plane would make and we knew that a first rate pilot must be flying her. We heard bullets slamming into our kite during the firefight. We made our fourth pass as the Whitley was doing wild aerobatics and a few shots hit her in the belly which caused some ripping but no flames were visible. During the fifth pass we didn't even get one shot off, but something tore into our 'cardboard box,' as we called our planes at the time. We had been conducting these maneuvers at between 1,500 and 2,000 meters. We made our sixth attack, again from behind and from below with the tail gunner still shooting at us. The British pilot decided to try and escape by diving down to wave-top height. This would prevent us from attacking from below and force us to attack from within range of his tail gunner. Our faster plane didn't help either, since the larger crate was surprisingly agile. The sixth attack failed to produce any visible damage, but the Whitley's evasive maneuvers had slowed it down. One of our rounds must have hit them in the fuselage. We dove in from above for the seventh attack under heavy fire. Again the bomber's fire rattled against our Messerschmitt and one of our engines began to cough.

The Englishman began climbing and turned hard on his right wing and almost lost control, but he regained it a moment later and we noticed white smoke coming out of the starboard engine.

Knacke remained quiet and with the port engine starting to splutter, made a wide turn to follow the Whitley. The bomber was to our right and was trailing a medium length banner of white smoke. Knacke turned to follow and the Whitley slowly came into range. The next salvo tore into the area between the fuselage and left engine. The plane flew on like a lethally wounded animal without making any evasive maneuvers. Then we saw a second smoke trail from the right side of the aircraft. The gunners were silent and we had no idea whether they were dead or out of ammunition. The plane plowed on.

During the ninth and last attack there was no defensive reaction of any kind and Knacke hit the left wing with short burst which set off a flash of bright flames. After a short dive the bomber exploded in a bright cloud of fire. We watched as a cloud of light smoke billowed up from the spot where the bomber had impacted the water. The brave crew went down into the depths of the North Sea.

Knacke slowly changed course and headed for Sylt. While still in the turn he had to shut off our port engine, which was coughing and spewing out white smoke. 'We're losing altitude,' he said. 'How much farther to Sylt?' he asked. I replied, 'I think about 80 or 100 kilometers, I'll let you know more precisely in a moment.' I asked ground control for our exact position, since they had been monitoring us the whole time and requested that they notify the naval rescue teams in the area. The officer in charge of fighters told me that a rescue boat was in the vicinity, the airfield was being lit and fire fighters were on standby.

That's when Knacke told me that we were losing power in the starboard engine. Up until that time, I had never considered the possibility that we wouldn't make

In its intended role as a multi-role *Zerstörer*, the Messerschmitt Bf 110 proved unsuccessful in 1940–41. However, the Bf 110 went on to become the most successful night fighter of the war. (*Via Arlanda Flygsamlingar*)

The Potez 630 was a contemporary of the Bf 110. (*Via Arlanda Flygsamlingar*)

The first prototype, the Messerschmitt Bf 110 V1. (*Via Wolfgang Mühlbauer/DEHLA Archives*)

A front view of the Bf 110 V1. (*Via Wolfgang Mühlbauer/DEHLA Archives*)

A rare air-to-air view of the second prototype, the Bf 110 V2. (*Via Wolfgang Mühlbauer/ DEHLA Archives*)

The Bf 110B entered small-scale production in 1938. The second aircraft is the Bf 110 V4, D-AISY. (*Via Wolfgang Mühlbauer/DEHLA Archives*)

Right: A Bf 110B showing off an interesting variation of the shark's mouth. (*Via Neil Page*)

Below: The Bf 110 following the crash at Villiers-sous-Chalamont. (*Via Jean-Louis Roba*)

Left: The burial of Xaver and Johann Öttil. (*Via Jean-Louis Roba*)

Below: A Bf 110B of 5./ZG 26. (*Via Wolfgang Mühlbauer/DEHLA Archives*)

Above: A factory-fresh Bf 110, possibly at Augsburg. (*Via Wolfgang Mühlbauer/DEHLA Archives*)

Below: The Bf 110 (coded M8+FH) flown by *Unteroffizier* Helmut Mütschele and *Gefreiter* Karl Lorey after being shot down at Vøyen. (*Via Bengt Hermansson*)

Future *Nachtjagd Experte* Helmut Lent's Bf 110 seen after the forced landing at Fornebu on 9 April 1940. (*Via Bengt Hermansson*)

Although substantially increasing range, the *Dackelbauch* fuel tank did nothing to improve the aerodynamic qualities of the Bf 110. (*Via Wolfgang Mühlbauer/DEHLA Archives*)

An air-to-air view of a Bf 110 from *Zerstörergeschwader* 2. (*Via Wolfgang Mühlbauer/DEHLA Archives*)

The large shark's mouth insignia of a ZG 76 Bf 110. (*Via Wolfgang Mühlbauer/DEHLA Archives*)

Above: Bf 110 2N+GN of 5./ZG 1 after being shot down by *Schweizer Flugwaffe* fighters on 8 June 1940. (*Via Hans-Heiri Stapfer*)

Below left: Lifting a 500-kg bomb onto a Bf 110 ETC 500 bomb rack. (*Via Wolfgang Mühlbauer/DEHLA Archives*)

Below right: Rearming the MG 17 machine guns of a Bf 110. (*Via Wolfgang Mühlbauer/DEHLA Archives*)

Bf 110 M8+FH of ZG 76 undergoing maintenance. Note the large *Dackelbauch* fuel tank. (*Via Hans-Heiri Stapfer*)

Epitomising the *Blitzkrieg* tactics, a formation of Bf 110s sweep over flat terrain. (*Via Wolfgang Mühlbauer/DEHLA Archives*)

A Bf 110 of I./*Zerstörergeschwader* 52. Note 'Flying Dragon' unit insignia. (*Via Hans-Heiri Stapfer*)

A Bf 110 of ZG 76 photographed in early 1941. (*Via Hans-Heiri Stapfer*)

Bf 110s performing convoy escort over the Mediterranean. (*Via Swedish Aviation Historical Society*)

In this staged propaganda picture, local Bedouins pose in front of a III./ZG 26 Bf 110. (*Via Hans-Heiri Stapfer*)

Aerial reconnaissance over North Africa was performed, in part, by Bf 110s. (*Via Wolfgang Mühlbauer/DEHLA Archives*)

One of many Bf 110s lost by III./ZG 26 during the North African campaign. The aircraft in the foreground is a Junkers Ju 87 Stuka. (*Via Hans-Heiri Stapfer*)

Above left: The end in North Africa. Note the USAAF Spitfires in the background. (*Via Frihedsmuseet*)

Above right: Bf 110s seen during the early stages of Operation Barbarossa. (*Via Wolfgang Mühlbauer/DEHLA Archives*)

Leutnant Felix Brandis's Bf 110 at Tärendö, Sweden, on 1 September 1941. (*Via Arlanda Flygsamlingar*)

Bf 110s of an unidentified *Nachtjagd* unit. (*Via Frihedsmuseet*)

With its radar gear and heavy armament, the Bf 110G excelled as a nightfighter, but proved highly unsuitable for daylight combat. (*Via Wolfgang Mühlbauer/DEHLA Archives*)

A Bf 110G armed with WG 21 air-to-air rockets. (*Via Hans-Heiri Stapfer*)

A three-quarter view of *Leutnant* Johnen's Bf 110 at Dübendorf. (*Via Hans-Heiri Stapfer*)

Another view of *Leutnant* Johnen's Bf 110. (*Via Hans-Heiri Stapfer*)

A close-up of the seventeen victory bars of *Leutnant* Johnen's Bf 110. (*Via Hans-Heiri Stapfer*)

By the end of the war, many Luftwaffe units were forced to conserve fuel in different manners. This included using oxen to tow aircraft on the ground. (*Via Swedish Aviation Historical Society*)

Leutnant Jacobs Bf 110 at Bulltofta. (*Via Bengt Hermansson*)

The wreck of an early model Bf 110 discovered by Soviet forces during their advance westwards. (*Via Carl-Fredrik Geust*)

About ten derelict Bf 110s can been seen in this fascinating picture. Unfortunately, both the location and circumstances are unknown. (*Via Carl-Fredrik Geust*)

The fuselage of a Bf 110G-4 has been loaded onto a trailer, most likely to facilitate a one-way journey to a scrapyard. (*Via Hans-Heiri Stapfer*)

The Trojka-Schlepp proved less than effective in towing the huge Me 321 assault glider aloft. (*Via Wolfgang Mühlbauer/DEHLA Archives*)

A close-up of the tow cable installation. (*Via Wolfgang Mühlbauer/DEHLA Archives*)

Above: The rear cockpit of the *Bordfunker* included a basic flight instrument panel and control column. (*Via Wolfgang Mühlbauer/ DEHLA Archives*)

Left: A view of the Bf 110 'front office'. Note the Revi gunsight. (*Via Wolfgang Mühlbauer/DEHLA Archives*)

Above left: Another view of the Bf 110 front cockpit. (*Via Wolfgang Mühlbauer/DEHLA Archives*)

Above right: A close-up of the external fuel tank. (*Via Frihedsmuseet*)

A Bf 110 fitted with two 900-litre external fuel tanks. Interestingly, the letters 'EGJ' beneath the left wing indicates that this particular Bf 110 was civilian registered. If so, the registration was most likely D-AEGJ. (*Via Wolfgang Mühlbauer/DEHLA Archives*)

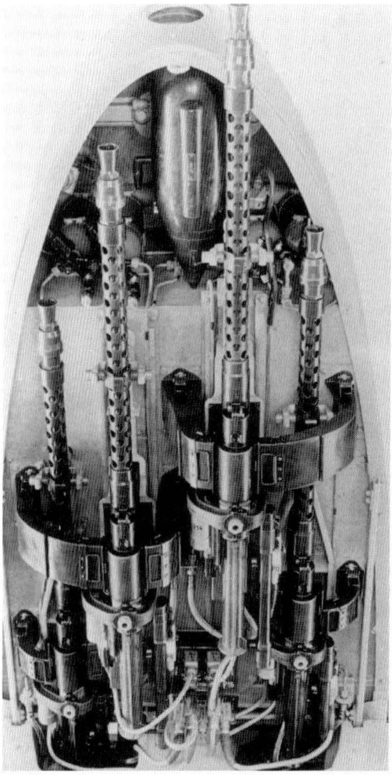

Above left: Quadruple MG 17s were fitted to the upper section of the nose. (*Via Wolfgang Mühlbauer/DEHLA Archives*)

Above right: The front end of a Bf 110. (*Via Frihedsmuseet*)

Above left: The 37-mm BK 3.7 cannon was fitted to some Bf 110G variants. (*Via Wolfgang Mühlbauer/DEHLA Archives*)

Above right: A close-up of the WG 21 twin-rocket tube. (*Via Wolfgang Mühlbauer/DEHLA Archives*)

Above left: The RZ 65 air-to-air rocket was tested on the Bf 110, but not used operationally by Bf 110 units. (*Via Wolfgang Mühlbauer*)

Above right: A close-up of the FuG 220 radar antenna. It is easy to understand why such antennas were known as antlers. (*Via Hans-Heiri Stapfer*)

A very rare picture of the sole *Armée de l'Air* Bf 110. (*Via Jean-Louis Roba*)

Bf 110C-5 5F+CM seen in British hands. (*Via Hans-Heiri Stapfer*)

Seen here during a test flight, this Bf 110 was the former 5F+CM. While flown by the RAF, the aircraft carried the serial number AX772. (*Via Hans-Heiri Stapfer*)

The Belle of Berlin photographed at an unknown location. (*Via Hans-Heiri Stapfer*)

A Bf 110G on display at Farnborough during the autumn of 1945. (*Via Wolfgang Mühlbauer/DEHLA Archives*)

One of the *Regia Aeronautica* Bf 110s photographed at Guidonia. (*Via Gregory Alegi*)

A rare picture of an AAR Bf 110C, coded 2Z+AW (W Nr 944), following a belly landing. Reportedly, this was the only Bf 110 adorned in ARR markings. The 2Z code identifies this as a former NJG 6 aircraft. (*Via Hans-Heiri Stapfer*)

The first of three Bf 110Gs of NJG to make unscheduled arrivals in Switzerland in 1944 was VQ+KL. (*Via Hans-Heiri Stapfer*)

Bf 110G 2Z+OP seen shortly after landing at Dübendorf on 15 March 1944. (*Via Hans-Heiri Stapfer*)

Bf 110G 2Z+OP while undergoing static trials in Switzerland. (*Via Hans-Heiri Stapfer*)

Although of poor quality, this picture nevertheless shows the Bf 110 soon after being captured by the USAAF. Note that the propeller blades are intact. (*Via Hans-Heiri Stapfer*)

A Bf 110 following capture by the USAAF. Note that the propeller and spinner are lying on the ground in front of the aircraft, with the propeller blades being bent, indicating a belly landing. (*Via Hans-Heiri Stapfer*)

One of the Bf 110s exported to the USSR. All of the Bf 110s had temporary civilian registrations applied. This particular Bf 110 was registered as D-OXWO (W Nr 3130). (*Via Carl-Fredrik Geust*)

An unidentified Bf 110 on display in Moscow in 1943. Due to the thin layer of snow visible, the picture was most likely taken in late 1943. Note that the cut-off P beneath the left wing may indicate that the aileron has been replaced while the aircraft was still in Luftwaffe service. (*Via Carl-Fredrik Geust*)

A very rare picture showing a Bf 110G in Soviet markings, apparently in service with the 84 GIAP at Otopeni, Romania, in late 1944. (*Via Carl-Fredrik Geust*)

The fuselage of an unidentified Bf 110 on display at the Frunze Aviation Museum. Note that the painting in the background includes what looks like a Bf 110 on fire. (*Via Carl-Fredrik Geust*)

The unrestored Bf 110F-2 W Nr 5052 on display at Wigram, New Zealand. (*Via Dave McDonald*)

The remains of Rudolf Hess's Bf 110 photographed in 1992. (*Lennart Berns*)

The sole night fighter Bf 110 is preserved with the RAF Museum at Hendon. It is seen here in 2018. (*John Chapman*)

The tail section of Bf 110F-2 W Nr 5096 is one of the components restored. (*Egil Endresen*)

A Bf 110 production line, most likely at Augsburg. (*Via Wolfgang Mühlbauer/DEHLA Archives*)

it back to our airfield. We had flown on one engine before without problems, but what would happen now that the second engine was losing power? What would we do if it seized?

Our position was awful. The starboard engine was still losing power and was starting to splutter. We were slowly, but systematically losing altitude. We could still jump as long as we were above 850 meters and in addition to our life jackets there was a two-man inflatable life raft behind my seat.

Finally the airfield came into sight and we could make out the runway lights at Westerland. 'Maybe we'll be able to make it,' I said hopefully. 'We have to be prepared for the worst,' Knacke replied softly. We were still about 500 meters above the ground and our airspeed was bleeding off perceptibly. The situation was serious.

'I'll try and start the port engine to give a little bit more power and altitude,' stated Knacke as he pressed the starter. The engine coughed, spit out a few flames and gave up in a shudder that vibrated the whole plane. It had given up the ghost.

Altitude: 300 meters. We were slowly approaching the airfield and we could now see the clear outline of the runway. 'If we can make it to the runway, I can belly in,' said Knacke, and added a moment later, 'Bundrock, take a look at this, but move slowly!'

I slowly leaned forward and watched as Knacke moved the stick around as though stirring coffee in a cup. 'For God's sake, what are you doing?' I cried out. 'The stick doesn't work at all. I'm flying with just the elevators and landing flaps,' he replied calmly. At that moment he really impressed me. We had actually made it back to the airfield on one stalling engine. In expectation of the rough landing, I got free of the parachute and stored it between the radio cases and just as we touched down I pulled on the emergency canopy release.

At that moment there was a loud bang, the noise of our impact, grinding and flying dirt until the plane finally came to a stop. An unpleasant hissing finally broke the incredible silence that followed. Knacke shouted 'Run!'

I noticed that the starboard engine was on fire and the flames were getting bigger and brighter and people were running towards us. Cars and fire trucks were speeding in our direction. Knacke jumped out and over the nose, while I headed for the tail and we both ran as fast as we could to get away from the burning plane. It could have exploded at any minute.

It didn't blow up, though, since the firefighters were able to get a layer of foam onto it in the nick of time. With our heads down, we set out on the long walk back to the mess hall. Neither of us said a word.[3]

On the night of 30 May 1942, the RAF sent a force of 1,046 bombers against Cologne. This was the largest night bombing raid so far conducted by the RAF. One II./NJG 1 crew, *Leutnant* Niklas and *Unteroffizier* Wenning, were part of the *Nachtjagd* force on this night:

> In our area we did not have long to wait. At 3,000 metres we encountered the first, which we recognized as a Wellington, 500 metres away. At almost exactly the same time the Tommy spotted us. He made a sudden turn to the right, then turned away from us. We went after him, but his fire was so strong that we could not get into a firing position and we overshot the Wellington.... Again we moved into a position behind the target and, from short range, we pumped shells into the bomber's left wing. It caught fire and we could see the flames. By this time our victim was down to 2,000 metres. Again we closed in. We fired another burst into the fuselage and wings, and the flames burnt brighter. Then we moved out for a while, waiting to see whether it would be necessary to go in again. For a short time the Wellington flew on, the blaze growing the whole time. Then it flipped over and went down, trailing sparks like a comet. Close to the ground it exploded, lighting up the surrounding countryside.

The ground radar station then led Niklas and Wenning toward their next target.

> He was weaving but he did not open fire. Had they seen us? We went straight into the attack. The target grew larger until, suddenly, it seemed enormous. My breath almost stopped: we were going to ram him. From short range we opened fire, hitting him on the wings and on the fuselage. I was about to call out, 'He's on fire!', when suddenly *Leutnant* Niklas shouted, 'I've been hit, breaking off immediately!' I had mistaken the muzzle flash from the rear turret for the glow of hits. We could not bother the Tommy any more—we had our own problems.

Leutnant Niklas had been hit in the left arm and was bleeding profusely. Wenning succeeded in improvising a tourniquet around Niklas's wounded left arm, then directed the pilot back to base at St Trond:

> That was how we flew back to our airfield. *Leutnant* Niklas was almost over the lights before he caught sight of them. It was too late to land on the runway. So, with a sideslip, he tried to get down on the emergency strip. Trees passed just below us. 'We're too low!' *Leutnant* Niklas murmured, 'I can't go on any longer,' and slumped forward. There was a scraping sound and soil was flung against the cabin. We skidded over the ground for what seemed an eternity. I sat there tensely. So this was what a crash landing was like; I had always imagined that it would be different. The crashing and splintering grew louder; there was a jerk—and everything was still. Then *Leutnant* Niklas shouted: 'Let's get out of here!' He had hit his head but had regained consciousness. He leapt from his seat, trying to run and at the same time to release his parachute harness. But it was no good and he fainted. I laid him out gently on the grass, and opened his blood-soaked flying suit. Soon a doctor and others appeared, and they carried him away. I was surrounded by a lot of people, who began to ask questions; I realised how lucky I had been.[4]

With the increased activities of USAAF four-engined heavy bombers, it was decided in January 1943 to involve the *Nachtjagd* units in combatting the Americans by day. The first USAAF raid against Germany took place on 27 January 1943. According to the Luftwaffe High Command, the *Nachtjagd* Bf 110 crews would be effective against USAAF Boeing B-17s and Consolidated B-24s, having better range and heavier armament than the single-seat Bf 109 and Fw 190 fighters. One of the *Nachtjagd* pilots was *Leutnant* Peter Spoden of 5./NJG 5:

> I flew several missions in daylight during the first months of 1944. Only crews with few night victories were selected for these sorties, as the aces were too valuable for the powers that be. We youngsters usually just came into readiness at night, as in the *Himmelbett* night fighting system, the most successful crews were scrambled in the first waves. Nevertheless, those missions were quite exhausting, as we were also at readiness at night.
>
> What's more, we were too slow in daylight with our 110 equipped with *Lichtenstein* [radar] and flame-dampers, and tactically we were at a disadvantage due to our approach from behind. When we came into firing range of the American bombers, it was like flying into a shower! The 109 and 190 on the other hand attacked the *Pulks* [bomber formations] from head-on and out of the sun. Consequently, the losses among our night fighters were horrendous.[5]

In the event, operating dedicated night fighter units against daytime USAAF bomb raids was futile. Fighting by day was completely different to fighting by night. High-performance single-seat fighters such as the P-51 Mustang had little trouble in handling the cumbersome rocket-armed Bf 110s.

But, for the *Nachtjagd* units, the Bf 110 still reigned supreme. However, Kammhuber had been very impressed by the first Luftwaffe dedicated *Nachtjagd* aircraft: the Heinkel He 219. Flying for the first time in November 1942, the performance and capabilities of the He 219 over the Bf 110 resulted in Kammhuber placing large-scale production orders for the aircraft. However, the inspector general for the Luftwaffe, *Generalfeldmarschall* Erhard Milch, had already rejected the He 219 outright. The resulting high-level feud saw less than 300 He 219s completed, with the type never fully replacing the Bf 110 in the *Nachtjagd* role.

In late July and early August 1943, the RAF bombed Hamburg during four consecutive raids. During these raids, a highly effective (and cheap) countermeasure weapon against the German radar was introduced, resulting in drastically reduced Bomber Command losses. Code-named Window, this consisted of small strips of aluminium foil, which when released in large numbers, jammed the German *Würzburg* radar systems. It was virtually impossible to identify the bomber formations from the mass of radar echoes created by Window. Incidentally, this type of radar countermeasure, named *Düppel* by the Germans, was quickly adopted by the Luftwaffe, and used during the so-called Little Blitz during the spring of 1944.

Having rejected the He 219, Milch demanded continued production of the Bf 110. At an RLM conference on 25 August 1943, Erhard Milch stated:

> We must definitely decide on priorities. That means the Bf 109 and Fw 190, and the Bf 110 which bears the brunt of the night fighting. That is why I have said, in the case of the Do 217 for instance, that all aircraft requiring considerable outlay are to be put further down the list. Everything must be staked on the 110. Only the 110 in sufficient numbers can give us the necessary relief at night. Moreover, the 110 can also be used by day. Compared with the other fighter types it has the great advantage of considerably longer range. After the raid on Regensburg, for example, the bombers headed south for Africa. Our twin-engined fighters pursued them to beyond Innsbruck and inflicted quite serious losses. That could not have been achieved with the 109 or the 190 because their limited endurance would have compelled them to land for refuelling and re-arming long before that. Thus the 110 is particularly important for both purposes.[6]

On 15 September 1943, Kammhuber was relieved of his command as *General der Nachtjagd,* officially for his failure at preventing the RAF raids against the industrial centres in the Ruhr Valley, and the devastating raids against Hamburg, being replaced by General Joseph 'Beppo' Schmid.

In 1943, two new *Nachtjagd* tactics were introduced: the *Wilde Sau* (Wild Boar) and the *Zahme Sau* (Tame Boar) respectively. The former involved sending single-engined fighters on *Frei Jagd* night sorties, with the pilots being aided in intercepting the enemy aircraft through searchlights and, amazingly, fires on the ground started through exploding British bombs. The *Wilde Sau* tactic proved largely ineffectual, however.

Zahme Sau consisted of scrambling Bf 110s (mainly), and then have them orbit a radio beacon. When the bomber formations arrived, the night fighters were to formate with the RAF bombers, and by means of establishing continuous radio contact between the night fighter and the ground radio operators, intercept and shoot down the RAF bombers.

A programme of reorganising the *Nachtjagd* forces were implemented almost immediately following Kammhuber's dismissal. Instead of a Central Command, four separate commands were created: *I. Jagdkorps* (covering the Low Countries, large parts of Germany and Denmark), *II. Jagdkorps* (France), *7. Jagddivision* (*Ostmark*, i.e., Austria and the central areas around the Rhineland), and *30. Jagddivision* (single-engined fighters employing *Wilde Sau* tactics). One result was that these four commands operated separately, having little or no interface with other commands.

The operational zenith of the Bf 110's career as a night fighter occurred on the night of 30–31 March 1944. On this night, RAF Bomber Command sent 795 bombers to

Nuremberg. The *Nachtjagd* fighters managed to disperse the bombers, thus avoiding the bomber stream tactics. Little damaged was caused at Nuremberg, with most bombs falling in areas surrounding the city. During the raid, a staggering 95 aircraft were shot down. One of the *Nachtjäger* pilots was *Oberleutnant* Martin Becker, who shot down seven of the RAF bombers. Just eleven Luftwaffe fighters were lost, including one Bf 110. After the war, Becker commented on the raid: 'They seemed to be lining up to be shot down. I just had to stop after the seventh one. I was sick of the killing'.[7]

On 31 May 1944, the Luftwaffe had a total of 471 Bf 110s (326 serviceable). The vast majority of these were serving with night fighter units with *Luftflotte Reich* and *Luftflotte* 3 in France. Only one unit, *Nahaufklärungsgruppe* 2 with the *Luftwaffen Kommando Südost* in the Balkans retained Bf 110s in the reconnaissance role, having a total of twelve aircraft (ten serviceable).

In mid-December 1943, a Bf 110 became the first victim of the recently-introduced P-51 Mustang, with Lt Charles F. Gumm of the 354th Fighter Group. Before the end of the month, another four Bf 110s had been lost to USAAF Mustangs.

During a USAAF raid against Berlin on 6 March 1944, the *Nachtjagd* units, including II./NJG 5, were thrown into battle against the bombers returning to England. One of the Bf 110s was flown by *Leutnant* Peter Spoden:

> [We were] to attack from behind with four aircraft in line abreast. We had discussed this tactic beforehand, because we had been equipped with new rockets which were fixed under our wings. We called these devices *Dödels*. Whilst measuring the distance to target with our *Lichtenstein* we should approach to a distance of 2km [1.2 miles] and then aim for the centre of the combat box. With a successful rocket launch this should lead to the loss of several B-17s.
>
> At a distance of approximately 3km [1.9 miles] from a combat box of twenty or more B-17s, I already saw the first lines of tracer curling towards us, and only moments later I received the first hits in the wings of my aircraft. I was not used to this, as at night one doesn't see the hits in one's own aeroplane, these are only reported to the pilot after the sortie by the groundcrew mechanic.
>
> I gave the order to fire when we were still 2.5km [1.5 miles] distant from the bombers. I pressed the firing button but nothing happened. The rockets had been wrongly loaded, or the electrical system leading to the rockets had been hit. I now fired with all my frontal guns, however I did not observe any hits. Over the R/T I heard my comrades shouting for help, but [I] could not come to their aid as my left engine [had] packed up after being hit. Two of our four night fighter aircraft plunged down into the water. With a lot of difficulty, I made it back to base at Parchim in Mecklenburg. This action took place between Rügen and the Danish coast, in broad daylight.
>
> Another factor that contributed to our losses were the long-range Mustang and Thunderbolt fighters that escorted the bombers in ever increasing numbers

> during early 1944. The 110 was no match for these aircraft, just as had happened with the Spitfire in combat with the 110 during the Battle of Britain in 1940. Due to the heavy losses the daylight missions of the night fighter units were prohibited in April 1944.[8]

The efforts of NJG 5 during the USAAF raid on Berlin were in vain. None of the USAAF bombers were downed, while eight Bf 110Gs were shot down by the P-51 Mustang escort fighters, with a ninth aircraft being seriously damaged.

By early 1944, the Bf 110 was the most numerous type of aircraft of the *Nachtjäger* units. On 31 January 1944, there were 987 night fighters in service, 592 of which were Bf 110s. Although the number of Bf 110s remained fairly constant for the next eight months, the night fighter inventory on 30 September had increased to 1,400 aircraft, including 574 Bf 110s. This was particularly due to the introduction of the Junkers Ju 88G.

21

Swiss Bargain

One very interesting incident, which could have had far-reaching consequences, took place between 28 April and 19 May 1944. When a Bf 110G fitted with the latest radar and *Schräge Musik* landed intact in neutral Switzerland, panic within the RLM and Luftwaffe ensued. Fears that the Bf 110G and its technical secrets would fall into Allied hands ran very high indeed.

When the RAF raided Friedrichshafen on 28 April, one of the Bf 110Gs of NJG 5 that took off in response was flown by *Oberleutnant* Wilhelm Johnen (pilot), *Leutnant* Joachim Kamprath (radio operator), and *Oberfeldwebel* Paul Mahle (gunner). Soon after taking off from Hagenau, two Avro Lancasters (DV192 of 100 Sqn and ND759 of 35 Sqn) were intercepted and shot down in quick succession.

However, when the left engine began to run rough due to lack of oil pressure, Johnen was forced to turn back to base. Inadvertently crossing into Swiss airspace, the crew found themselves caught over Zurich by powerful searchlights. By now, Johnen had turned off the left engine, feathering the propeller. Firing off distress signals and blinded by the searchlights, Johnen was forced to land at Dübendorf just outside Zurich. Immediately following the landing, the crew made several desperate attempts at hiding the secret documents they were carrying, as well as destroy the radar and the whole Bf 110. During the latter attempt, Mahle made a run for the aircraft, jumping up on the wing. While attempting to trigger the explosive charge, the Swiss guards pulled Mahle off the wing by pulling him by his trousers. Mahle's excuse to the Swiss guards was that he was simply going to retrieve some personal effects from the Bf 110 (the crew eventually managed to flush some of the documents they carried with them down the toilet).

Coded C9+EN (W Nr 740055), the Bf 110G-4 was fitted with state-of-the-art radios, including FuG 10, FuG 8, FuG 16, FuG 25, as well as FuG 202 and FuG 220 radar sets. Additionally, the *Schräge Musik* armament (twin cannons fitted in the upper rear fuselage, firing obliquely upwards) was a novelty. Interestingly, *Ofw* Mahle was one of the originators of the *Schräge Musik* armament. To make matters worse, the gunner, *Lt* Kamprath, had brought with him a file containing charts, codes, tables, etc., not required for the sortie. Upon learning of the Bf 110s unscheduled arrival in Switzerland, Hitler flew into a rage, suspecting treason.

The Germans were extremely suspicious that the Swiss would forward information on these highly secret pieces of equipment to the Allies. The Swiss did in fact remove the radar equipment, with this being refitted to the Bf 110 following close examination. In desperation, various plans to destroy the Bf 110 were suggested by the Luftwaffe High Command. These plans included sending a unit of German commandos under the leadership of Otto Skorzeny to Dübendorf to either recover or destroy the Bf 110, or even make a large-scale bomb raid against the air base.

Following some high-level diplomatic wrangling, the Bf 110 was intentionally destroyed on 19 May 1944 in the presence of the German air attaché and *Hauptmann* Friedrich-Wilhelm Brandt, the operations officer of NJG 5 (incidentally, Brandt had discovered to his chagrin that the radar gear had been removed and then reinstalled). Three explosive charges were fitted to the Bf 110, which was then blown up, with the remains subsequently being doused in fuel and burnt.

In their turn, the Swiss were allowed to purchase a dozen Bf 109G-6s, along with license manufacturing rights, the cost being 6 million Swiss Francs in gold. However, as it turned out, these Bf 109Gs suffered from serious manufacturing defects, subsequently being little used by the *Schweizer Flugwaffe*.

With their aircraft blown up, the crew were allowed to return to Germany, flying a night fighting sortie already on 23 May.

Johnen later recalled:

> We were driven to the mess in a Mercedes. A reception seemed to be taking place for, despite the late hour, a hostess in a red dress received us and saw to it that we had food, clothes and quarters for the night. The food was magnificent, but far too rich for our stomachs which had been ruined by wartime fare.... The crew were then interrogated.
>
> The Colonel asked: 'From which airfield did you take off, and what unit do you belong to?' 'Such questions are useless, Colonel,' I replied. 'You will receive no information from me or my crew. We want to get back to Germany as quickly as possible. Please be good enough to notify our military attaché.' The Colonel had presumably expected this reply, for he gave us permission to retire.
>
> From this moment onwards, we were not allowed to communicate with each other. The windows of our sleeping cells were barred and a guard stood outside the door. Thoroughly exhausted, I slumped on my bed and was soon fast asleep. [The] next morning, I needed some time to take in my new surroundings. I did not see my crew all day. The necessary formalities were being carried out and we were taken for further interrogation.
>
> The Swiss were polite and correct, but I could not help feeling a trifle anxious. The second day passed in endless waiting. My companions knocked on the walls

of their respective cells and I devised a plan of escape, for I had no wish to remain in Switzerland. But on the third day of our internment, we were taken by train, under close guard, to Berne.

It was an agreeable surprise when we were given rooms in the Hotel Metropole and the uniformed guards were replaced by a civilian called Fuchs. The German General-consul paid us a visit. We had to get out of our uniforms immediately, for in international Berne they might have given rise to unpleasant incidents. Thus, three night fighters in tattered Luftwaffe uniforms were taken to a store and emerged half an hour later as dapper civilians. The German consul paid for our clothes and gave us a considerable sum of money.

We then wandered round the city like harmless Swiss citizens. Everything that had long since disappeared in Germany was to be had in full measure in the shops. Cinemas, cabarets, dance halls and baths were open until late at night. Released from the tension of war, and revived by the war spring air, we enjoyed our liberty to the full.

At this juncture, just as we were beginning to feel really well, our polite custodian Fuchs told us that within the next few days we were going to be exchanged for three Britishers.[1]

Wilhelm Johnen ended the war with a total of thirty-four night victories. He died in 2002.

Incidentally on 10 September 1944, a USAAF P-51 Mustang strayed into Swiss airspace. Spotting two aircraft, and believing them to be Bf 110s, the USAAF pilot attacked two *Schweizer Flugwaffe* EKW C-3603 light bombers over Pruntrut. Although the C-3603 was a single-engined aircraft, its twin tail and long canopy made it remarkably similar in appearance to the Bf 110. Although both of the C-3603s escaped unscathed, this incident led to new high visibility neutrality markings being introduced for *Schweizer Flugwaffe* aircraft.

22
Italian Interlude

In the summer of 1944, II./NJG 6 made two brief deployments to Italy. The mission was to make freelance sorties in the vicinity of Rome, hunting Allied bombers. However, with no support from the network of radar and other facilities that were available when operating over Germany, the Italian venture was doomed to failure. The first of these deployments only lasted between 4 and 12 May, with the aircraft being based at Ghedi. Allied intelligence were aware of the night fighters, noting ten individual aircraft codes of Bf 110s from *Stab*, 4., 5., and 6./NJG 6. Few sorties were accomplished the unit was ordered back to Germany. Nevertheless, a second deployment to Ghedi began on 29 May. At dusk, the Bf 110s were flown to a forward airfield at Perugia, returning to Ghedi at dawn. On 31 May, the three NJG 6 *Staffeln* had a total of thirteen Bf 110s between them, with eleven being serviceable.

When arriving at Perugia in the early hours of 1 June, three Bf 110s were damaged when hitting bomb craters. Additional problems saw refuelling lasting more than two hours. The sortie was unsuccessful, as was an evening sortie. The aircraft returned to Ghedi shortly after midnight on 2 June. During the evening, nine Bf 110s were flown to Perugia, the last aircraft arriving at 2004 hrs.

The following night turned out to be eventful. Around 12:30 a.m., one Bf 110G-4 (W Nr 720039) was shot down by a RAF Beaufighter from 600 Sqn. The radar operator, *Uffz.* Heinz Schulz, was the only survivor. *Fw.* Helmut Bunje claimed a Wellington shot down south of Rome.

Another Bf 110G-4 (W Nr 720189) was shot down 20 miles east of Lake Bracciano on 4 June, with all three crewmembers perishing. However, later the same day, *Uffz.* Mrusek of 6./NJG 6 returned to his unit. Details about when and where Mrusek's Bf 110 had been lost are lacking, but he knew nothing about the whereabouts of the other two crewmembers. The NJG 6 *Geschwaderkommodore*, *Major* Heinrich Griese, arrived at Ghedi. Griese was fully aware of the limitations of the deployment to Italy. During the evening, seven Bf 110s were flown to Perugia. However, none of the Bf 110s reported any encounters with the enemy before heading back to Ghedi. During the night, the Bf 110 (W Nr 720132) flown by *Oberfeldwebel* Treynogga became lost, with the crew baling out over Graciano. Although two of the crew survived, Treynogga was killed.

During the night of 6 June, a Wellington of 142 Sqn was intercepted by two Bf 110s. However, the Luftwaffe aircraft were driven off by the Wellington's gunners. The following night saw six Bf 110s operate north of Rome. One Bf 110 was damaged when landing back at Perugia. The crew of one RAF Wellington had the unnerving experience of seeing a Bf 110 pass right above them on a reciprocal course.

On 9 June, about ten Bf 110s arrived above the Viterbo area. The crew of a USAAF Beaufighter briefly encountered a Bf 110 over Anzio. Upon returning to Perugia, two Bf 110s suffered 25 per cent damage. No sorties were flown on 10 June due to poor weather. The following night, five Bf 110s were flown from Ghedi to Perugia. Later the same day, orders were received to return to Germany.

On 12 June, six Bf 110s were ferried to Germany. No further Luftwaffe night fighters were to operate in Italian skies.

One burnt-out Bf 110G-4 of II./NJG 6 was subsequently found at Perugia by Allied forces.

23

The End

Since 1944, the Bf 110 had been largely replaced by dedicated night fighter Heinkel He 219s and, in particular, the Junkers Ju 88G. Operational losses of *Nachtjagd* Bf 110s had also risen sharply since the introduction of night intruder D.H.98 Mosquitoes. By 31 December 1944, only some 150 Bf 110 night fighters remained in service. However, the Bf 110 was still a highly potent weapon, capable of inflicting serious losses to RAF's Bomber Command. During a raid against the Lützkendorf synthetic oil refinery, *Hauptmann* Martin Becker of IV./NJG 6 shot down no less than nine Lancasters between 9:53 and 11:37 p.m. This marked the third time that Becker had scored more than five victories during a single sortie. Becker ended the war with fifty-eight victories, making him the tenth highest-scoring *Nachtjäger* pilot.

On 30 March 1945, several *Nachtjagdstaffeln* were disbanded. At this juncture, only three *Nachtjagdstaffeln* and the *Geschwader Stab* Flight of NJG 1 and 7./NJG 6, all serving with *Luftflotte Reich*, were still fully equipped with Bf 110Gs. Other *Staffeln* were operating a mix of Bf 110s, Junkers Ju 88s, and Heinkel He 219s.

Luftwaffe Bf 110 units, 9 April 1945

Unit	Total number of aircraft	Serviceable aircraft	Remarks
Stab NJG 1	29	25	Including Heinkel He 219s
4./NJG 1	16	15	
7./NJG 1	16	14	
10./NJG 1	17	15	
Stab NJG 4	4	4	Including Junkers Ju 88s
Stab NJG 5	16	10	Including Junkers Ju 88s
4./NJG 5	28	25	Including Junkers Ju 88s

7./NJG 5	34	32	Including Heinkel He 219s and Junkers Ju 88s
Stab NJG 6	17	17	Including Junkers Ju 88s
7./NJG 6	15	12	Luftflotte 6
Nahaufklärungsgruppe 13	13	8	Reconnaissance unit, including Focke-Wulf Fw 189s and Siebel Si 204s

During the final months of the war, the breakdown of logistics and the rapidly increasing fuel shortages resulted in the Luftwaffe, including the *Nachtjäger* units, rarely being able to operate effectively against Allied aircraft.

On 15 April, an *E-Stelle* Rechlin test pilot, *Leutnant* Jürgen Schultze decided to seek refuge in Sweden. Upon arrival at Rechlin, Schultze found the air base under attack. One of the very few aircraft to survive the raid undamaged was a Bf 110G-4 (DK+IZ, W Nr 5678). Taking off from Rechlin, Schultze flew to a nearby field, where his wife and mother-in-law were waiting for him. Taking off once more, Schultze and his two passengers arrived at Bulltofta at 9:58 a.m. (LT). All three were subsequently allowed to remain in Sweden. Schultze's Bf 110 had been used in various drop trials, being fitted with register cameras beneath the wings and measuring gear on the wingtips. The aircraft was scrapped in 1946.

On 1 May, a second Bf 110 arrived in Sweden. The pilot, Estonian-born Alexander Siegfried König, had been ordered to fly the personal Bf 110G-4 (G9+AA, W Nr 140655) of *Oberleutnant* H. J. Jabs of *Stab* NJG 1 from a base near Lüneburg to Schleswig on the Danish border. König was accompanied by *Fw.* Fritz Hrachowina (a Czech national). König subsequently belly landed near Hammerlöv in southern Sweden. Both König and Hrachowina were deemed to be civilian refugees, thus avoiding being extradited to the USSR.

The Bf 110 was fitted with FuG 218 *Neptun* radar as well as *Schräge Musik* armament. The aircraft was brought to Bulltofta airport, where it was scrapped. A few parts were sent to the USSR in November 1945.

Few serviceable Bf 110s were among the thousands of Luftwaffe aircraft surrendered in May 1945. In the British Zone alone (north-western Germany, Denmark, and Norway), 4,810 Luftwaffe aircraft were found. In May 1945, a total of forty-five Bf 110s were found in Denmark and twenty-eight in Norway, with a few of the former being selected for evaluation. The others were destroyed by placing explosive charges in the cockpit and engine mounts, with the remains being collected by scrap dealers for disposal.

The scrapping and recycling of former Luftwaffe aircraft continued for several years. In 1951, two German divers recovered a Bf 109 and a Boeing B-17 from Lake *Ammersee* south-west of Munich. Their next haul was to be a Bf 110. At the time, scrap merchants were paying up to 20,000 Deutschmarks for each wreck.

A statistical overview of the number of RAF Bomber Command aircraft shot down by the *Nachtjagd* units between 1940 and 1945, paint a grim picture. The highest number of RAF bombers lost to Luftwaffe night fighters occurred in January 1944, with no less than 308 aircraft being shot down. Until early 1944, the vast majority of *Nachtjagd* victories were claimed by Bf 110 crews.

Nachtjagd Victories by Year

Year	Number of RAF Bomber Command Aircraft Shot Down	Number of Sorties	Remarks
1940	42	1,722	
1941	421	27,101	
1942	687	32,701	
1943	1,816	62,736	
1944	2,235	113,353	
1945	529	44,074	Includes victories over aircraft from RAF Fighter Command, Coastal Command, 2 Tactical Air Force and USAAF

During the war, RAF Bomber Command lost 47,268 aircrew killed in action, with another 9,838 becoming prisoners of war.

24

Other Uses

A few Bf 110s were used for a variety of test purposes. Among these were the gun barbettes intended for the Arado Ar 240 and Me 210, which were tested on a Bf 110C-2/U1.

An attempt in mid-1940 at increasing the range of the Bf 109 involved trials with a Bf 110 towing the Bf 109. Having reached altitude, the Bf 109 pilot turned off his engine and feathered the propeller, thus conserving fuel. The idea was that when the pair reached the combat zone, the Bf 109 would be released. Although successful, this method was not adopted for operational service.

The *DOBBAS Transportgerät* (a collapsible freight container) was tested on a Bf 110E. This could carry up to 1,061 kg of cargo, including a PaK 38 cannon. Fitted beneath the fuselage, it was intended to use the *DOBBAS Transportgerät* on various combat aircraft, thus increasing the air cargo capability of the Luftwaffe. In the event, the *DOBBAS Transportgerät* never entered service.

On 15 March 1942, a Jumo A109-004 A turbojet engine began flight tests, being carried beneath the centre fuselage of a Bf 110.

Glider Tugs

Bf 110s were also frequently used as glider tugs, the most remarkable being the *Troika-Schlepp*, where three Bf 110s towed a Messerschmitt Me 321 assault glider into the air, using a quadruple tow line arrangement. The tow lines were 80, 90, 100, and 100 metres long respectively. Six Bf 110E-1/U1s (including W Nr 4099 and 4100) were provided in anticipation of the initial trials. The Bf 110s were modified by having all armour protection removed, as well as external drop tanks and the rear seat MG 17 machine gun. Twin mirrors were fitted in front of the windscreen, with the fillet plate on one side at the fuselage/wing junction being removed to keep the tow cable as close as possible to the aircraft's centreline. On 1 May, orders were received to modify a further eighty Bf 110s as glider tugs.

However, on 23 May, it was decided that the Heinkel He 111 would be more suitable as a glider tug. This led to the development of the five-engined He 111Z, basically two He 111s joined together by means of a central wing. In the event, Bf 110s had to continue in use as tugs until replaced by He 111Zs.

The first Bf 110/Me 321 *Troika-Schlepp* flight took place on 7 May 1941. The Bf 110s had to take-off using full power, a total of 6,600 hp, with the Me 321 being fitted with Walter HWK RI-202b rocket-assisted take-off (RATO) gear beneath each wing for additional thrust. On one occasion, the RATO gear beneath the starboard wing failed to fire, resulting in an asymmetric take-off. The Me 321 crashed with the loss of the 120 troops aboard. All three Bf 110s also crashed during this horrific accident. One novel idea, which remained on the 'what if' stage, involved mounting one Bf 110 beneath each wing, and one Bf 110 atop the centre fuselage.

Nevertheless, four *Sonderstaffel Großsegler* (Special Assault Glider Squadron) with five Me 321s each as well as between twelve and fifteen Bf 110s tugs each was formed for operations on the Eastern Front. Bf 110s were also used to tow Me 321s during Operation *Beowulf*, the invasion of the Estonian island of Saaremaa on 21 September 1941.

The *Troika-Schlepp* practice was highly dangerous, with a 23 March 1942 report stating that between 50 and 80 per cent of all take-offs ended in accidents.

In the spring of 1941, the Messerschmitt Me 163A V1 (KE+SW) was towed into the air by a Bf 110 at Lechfeld. Initially, no rocket engine was fitted to the Me 163A, with the test gliding flights proceeding later to Augsburg. The Me 163A glider usually released at altitudes between 4,000 and 8,000 metres. Further Bf 110 tug-assisted take-offs with the rocket engine-powered Me 163A included the 2 October 1941 flight when test pilot Heini Dittmar achieved an unofficial world record speed of 1,004 kph (Mach 0.84).

Late in the war, Bf 110s were also employed as tugs by *Jagdgeschwader* 400, towing Messerschmitt Me 163B rocket fighters as an easy way of transfer between bases. As related elsewhere, one such Bf 110 ended up in British hands in May 1945.

On 13 January 1943, two Bf 110 tugs were used to tow the Heinkel He 280 V1 prototype into the air. The weather was very poor, with a blizzard fast approaching. The He 280 had been experimentally fitted with four Argus As 014 pulse jet engines (later used on the V-1 pilotless missile). As the pulse jet engines did not deliver sufficient thrust for a conventional take-off, it was deemed necessary to tow the He 280 into the air. However, the He 280 pilot, Helmut Schenk, discovered that he could not release the tow line. Landing with the tow line still attached to the nose in the blizzard would be highly dangerous. Instead, Schenk chose to use the ejection seat, becoming the first pilot to save his life in this manner.

On 6 May 1944, a Bf 110 tug (Bf 110G-0 W Nr 5188) was used to tow the Blohm & Voss BV 40 glider fighter on its first flight from Wenzendorf. Further flights with the BV 40 were also conducted using a Bf 110 tug.

25

Messerschmitt Bf 110 *Experten*

A large number of pilots scored large numbers of aerial victories while flying Bf 110s. This was especially true of the *Nachtjagd* pilots. What follows are brief biographies over a few of these pilots.

Helmut Lent

Born on 13 June 1918 at Pyrehne, Prussia, into a deeply religious family, Helmut Lent joined the Luftwaffe on 1 April 1936, much against his father's wishes. Lent's primary flight training took place with the *Luftkriegsschule* 2 outside Berlin. His first solo flight, in a Focke-Wulf Fw 44 biplane, occurred on 15 September 1936, with Lent earning his wings on 15 November 1937. This momentous event in any pilot's career had suffered a setback in early 1937 when Lent suffered an accident which kept him grounded for five months. In early 1938, Lent was run over by a car, resulting in a brief hospital stay. Posted to III./JG 132 '*Richtofen*', Lent made his first post-accident flight on 19 July 1938. Just over three months later, on 1 November 1938, III./JG 132 was redesignated as II./JG 141, with Lent being posted to 6./JG 141. Lent flew a number of sorties in during the German annexation of the Sudetenland. On 1 January 1939, II./JG 141 was redesignated as II./ZG 141, eventually becoming I./ZG 76 on 1 May 1939 at Olmütz (present-day Olomouc in the Czech Republic). The first of I./ZG 76 Bf 110s arrived on 7 June 1939.

Lent took part in the invasion of Poland in September 1939, claiming a 'PZL P.24' shot down. On 21 September, Lent was awarded the Iron Cross. During the infamous RAF 18 December 1939 raid against naval vessels in the Heligoland Bight, Lent shot down two Wellingtons. This event saw Lent being singled out by German propaganda, resulting in him becoming a national hero almost overnight. As a result, Lent began to receive loads of fan mail. One of the many women who wrote to Lent eventually became his wife.

On 9 April 1940, Lent force-landed his damaged Bf 110 at Fornebu airport outside Oslo, after claiming one Gladiator shot down. Later the same day, Lent shared in the destruction of an RAF Short Sunderland. On 13 May, Lent was awarded with the Iron Cross 1st Class.

His last daylight aerial victory occurred on 15 June 1940, the victim being an RAF Blenheim of 254 Sqn. Lent participated in the disastrous 15 August 1940 raid against targets in northeastern England. This was Lent's ninety-eighth sortie.

Transferred to 6./NJG 1 as *Staffelkapitän* on 1 October 1940, Lent scored his first nocturnal victory, an RAF Wellington, on 12 May 1941. On 1 July, Lent was appointed as *Staffelkapitän* for 4./NJG 1.

By 30 August, Lent had accumulated twenty-two victories, being awarded with the Knight's Cross. On 1 January 1942, Lent was promoted to *Hauptmann*. During early 1942, Lent flew a Dornier Do 215B-5, achieving the first airborne radar intercept nocturnal victory. On 6 June 1942, Lent was awarded with the Knight's Cross with Oak Leaves.

On 1 January 1943, Lent was promoted to *Major*, becoming the *Geschwaderkommendeur* of NJG 3 in the process. Lent's importance as a night fighter *Experte* resulted in him being awarded with the Knight's Cross with Oak Leaves and Diamonds on 2 August 1943.

On 16 June 1944 at 12:52 a.m., Lent claimed his 100th night victory, an Avro Lancaster. Within eight minutes, Lent had added an additional two Lancasters to his score. Amazingly, Lent had achieved these victories using only fifty-seven rounds of ammunition. His last victory, his 111th, took place on 17 September 1944, the victim being yet another Lancaster.

Subsequently promoted to *Oberstleutnant* (the equivalent of an RAF wing commander), Lent was also awarded with the Knight's Cross with Oak Leaves, Diamonds, and Swords.

On 5 October 1944, Lent was to fly a Junkers Ju 88 from Stade to Paderborn. On approach to Paderborn, the left engine failed, with the Ju 88 hitting power lines. Three of the crew were killed in the crash, with Lent dying from his injuries two days later.

Helmut Lent had accumulated a total of 111 victories, the vast majority at night. He was the second-most successful night fighter pilot of the war.

In 1964, the West German Army air base at Rotenburg was named Lent-Kaserne (Lent Barracks), upon the recommendation of Lent's former commanding officer. However, the policy of naming military barracks after officers who had served during the Nazi regime was controversial. In 2014, the *Bundeswehr* (German armed forces) decreed that Lent's name had to be removed and replaced with a more politically appropriate name. The debate that followed provided both pros and cons for retaining (or renaming) Lent's name for the barracks. In the event, the name Lent-Kaserne was officially changed to the Von Düring-Kaserne (after Johann von Düring) on 8 June 2020.

Heinz-Wolfgang Schnaufer

The foremost night fighter ace of the war was Heinz-Wolfgang Schnaufer. Schnaufer claimed a total of 121 aerial victories, the majority being RAF bombers.

Born at Calw, Würtemberg, on 16 February 1922, Heinz-Wolfgang Schnaufer joined the Luftwaffe on 15 November 1939. Following basic flight training, Schnaufer was posted to 5./NJG 1 in November 1941. Schnaufer first saw action during Operation *Zerberus* (Operation Cerberus) on 11 February 1942. Operation *Zerberus* involved protecting the *Prinz Eugen*, *Gneisenau*, and *Scharnhorst* warships sailing from Brest through the English Channel to Norway, with the Luftwaffe code name being Operation *Donnerkeil* (Operation Thunderbolt).

On 2 June 1942, Schnaufer achieved his first aerial victory, an RAF Halifax. After being guided toward a second bomber by ground control, Schnaufer's Bf 110 was hit by return fire, which set the left engine on fire, damaged the rudder lines, and short-circuited the electrical system. Schnaufer himself was wounded in the left calf. Schnaufer and his *Bordfunker*, Friedrich Rumpelhardt, briefly considered baling out, but Schnaufer managed to nurse the heavily damaged Bf 110 back to Saint Trond. This was the only time that Schnaufer was wounded in combat, as well as his aircraft being hit by enemy fire.

During the following year, Schnaufer's score built up slowly but steadily. On 29 June 1943, Schnaufer shot down three RAF bombers in quick succession. On 13 August, Schnaufer was appointed as *Staffelkapitän* of 12./NJG 1. During the RAF raid against Peenemünde on 17–18 August, Schnaufer had to return to base due to a problematic engine.

With his trusty *Bordfunker* Wilhelm Rumpelhardt having been posted away from NJG 1 for more than a year, Schnaufer flew with different *Bordfunkers* until early October 1943, when Rumpelhardt finally returned. Around this time, a third crew member, a radar operator, was added to the Bf 110. *Unteroffizier* Wilhelm Gänzler became the 'third man' of Schnaufer's crew. When the war ended, Schnaufer, Rumpelhardt, and Gänzler were unique among the *Nachtjäger* crews, being the only crew where all three members had been awarded with the Iron Cross. *Schräge Musik* armament was also added to the Bf 110. It has been estimated that between twenty and thirty of Schnaufer's victories were achieved using *Schräge Musik*.

During a sortie on 15–16 February 1944, Schnaufer suffered appendicitis, being briefly hospitalised. He returned to the air on 19 March. Three weeks earlier, on 1 March, Schnaufer had been appointed as *Gruppenkommendeur* of IV./NJG 1.

During the night of 29 May, Schnaufer downed five four-engined bombers within fourteen minutes for his seventieth to seventy-fourth victories. On 24 June, Schnaufer was awarded the Knight's Cross with Oak Leaves, with the Knight's Cross with Oak Leaves and Swords being awarded just over a month later, on 30 July.

On 21 February 1945, Schnaufer shot down no less than nine Avro Lancasters during two separate sorties. The last seven Lancasters were downed within nineteen minutes, between 8:44 and 9:03 p.m.

Schnaufer's last victories were achieved on 7–8 March 1945. He was then grounded, not being allowed to fly any more combat sorties. Schnaufer was delegated to evaluate the Dornier Do 335 as a potential night fighter. On 9 April 1945, disobeying firm orders, Schnaufer flew one final, unsuccessful combat sortie. His score of 121 victories had been achieved during 164 combat sorties.

Nicknamed 'the Spook of St Trond' by the RAF Bomber Command crews, Schnaufer survived the war, surrendering to British forces at Schleswig-Holstein. Briefly held as a prisoner of war, Schnaufer was released on 4 August 1945. A brief attempt at securing a job as a pilot in South America failed, with Schnaufer deciding to return to the family wine trade business. He died on 15 July 1950 following a car accident outside Bordeaux, France, aged twenty-eight. The Heinz-Schnaufer Straße at Calw is named after Schnaufer.

A fin from Schnaufer's Bf 110 with 121 victory markings is preserved by the Imperial War Museum. A fin from another of Schnaufer's Bf 110s is held by the Australian War Memorial at Canberra.

Werner Streib

Born at Pforzheim on 13 June 1911, Werner Streib initially served with the *Reichswehr* before transferring to the Luftwaffe on 1 October 1935. Assigned as an observer, Streib was eventually transferred to II./JG 132. On 1 November 1938, II./JG 132 was redesignated as I./JG 141, becoming I./ZG 141 on 1 January 1939 before being redesignated as I./ZG 1 on 1 May 1939.

Streib saw action during the invasion of France, shooting down an RAF Blenheim on 10 May 1940. As it turned out, this was to be Strieb's sole daytime victory. On 17 May, Streib was awarded the Iron Cross 2nd Class. The following month, on 6 June, Streib was appointed as *Staffelkapitän* for 2./ZG 1.

With I./ZG 1 being disbanded on 22 June 1940, Streib was transferred to NJG 1. As related earlier, he claimed his first of an eventual total of sixty-seven nocturnal victories on 19–20 July 1940. During this time, Streib was involved in developing an air defence system, eventually known as the *Kammhuber* Line, consisting of *Flak* batteries, radar stations, searchlights, and night fighters. On 7 October, Streib was promoted to *Gruppenkommendeur* of I./NJG 1. Continuing to fly combat sorties, Streib had accumulated a total of nine victories by the end of 1940.

By early 1943, Streib was closely involved with the operational evaluation of the new Heinkel He 219 night fighter. During a sortie in the ninth He 219 prototype on 11–12 June 1943, Streib shot down five four-engined bombers. While landing back at Venlo, the He 219 was destroyed in a crash landing.

On 1 July 1943, Streib was appointed as *Geschwaderkommendeur* of NJG 1. Streib was awarded with the Knight's Cross with Oak Leaves and Swords on 11 March 1944. Later the same month, Streib was promoted *Oberst*, also becoming *Inspektor des Nachtflieger*, a position he held until the end of the war.

Post-war, Streib worked as a farmer. On 16 March 1956, he joined the reconstituted Luftwaffe. Streib retired on 31 March 1966, having served as the *Inspizient Fliegende Verbände* (inspector of flying units).

Werner Streib died on 15 June 1986.

Eduard Tratt

Born at Würzburg on 24 February 1919, Eduard Tratt joined the Luftwaffe in 1937. During the Polish campaign in September 1939, Tratt served with 1./ZG 1. Soon afterwards, Tratt was transferred to *Zerstörergeschwader* 2. During the Battle of France, Tratt claimed three RAF Hurricanes near Dunkirk. During one sortie over southern England, Tratt was wounded in action. Following transfer to 1./*Erprobungsgruppe* 210, Tratt had raised his score to thirteen aircraft by the end of 1940.

By the time of Operation Barbarossa, Tratt was serving with 1./*Erprobungsgruppe* 210. Although the unit was mainly involved in performing ground-attack sorties, Tratt nevertheless managed to shoot down nine Soviet aircraft by the end of 1941. Following the disbandment of 1./*Erprobungsgruppe* 210, Tratt was appointed as *Staffelkapitän* of 4./ZG 26 in January 1942. Two months later, Tratt received command of 6./ZG 26. On 18 February and 27 March, Tratt was wounded in combat.

In April 1942, Tratt was promoted to *Oberleutnant*, also being awarded with the Knight's Cross. During the fight for Stalingrad, Tratt flew a number of ground-attack sorties in support for the encircled 6th Army. On 30 January 1943, Tratt was seriously injured when his Bf 110 (coded RH+YK) crashed north of Rowenki, with Tratt's *Bordfunker*, *Fw.* Paul Rennefahrt, being killed.

After recuperating, Tratt was appointed to command the *Erprobungskommando* 25,a special unit which specialised in the test and evaluation of new aerial weaponry such as air-to-air rockets and cannon armament.

On 11 October 1943, Tratt was appointed as *Gruppenkommendeur* of II./ZG 26. By this time, II./ZG 26 had begun to receive Messerschmitt Me 410s. Tratt flew a number of sorties, knocking down several USAAF heavy bombers.

On 22 February 1944, two days before his twenty-fifth birthday, Tratt was shot down and killed.

With a total score of thirty-eight aerial victories, Eduard Tratt was the highest-scoring *Zerstörer* pilot. Tratt also claimed twenty-six aircraft destroyed on the ground, as well as numerous tanks, road vehicles, and anti-aircraft batteries during 350 sorties.

26
Messerschmitt Bf 110 units

From 1938 until May 1945, Messerschmitt Bf 110s served with a multitude of Luftwaffe units, with the units listed below including the major *Zerstörer* and *Nachtjagd* operators only, as well as a few *Aufklärung* (reconnaissance) units.

During the initial stages of Operation Barbarossa, a number of Bf 110s were attached to three Junkers Ju 87 *Stuka* units, *Stab* St.G 1, 2, and 77, being mainly utilised to take pre-strike and post-strike photographs.

2./*Aufklärungsgruppe* (H)/14

Code 5 F formed on 1 October 1937 at Münster from 2./*Aufklärungsgruppe* 114, becoming 2./*Aufklärungsgruppe* 12 on 1 November 1938. Reformed on the same day as 2./*Aufklärungsgruppe* 18. The unit later became 2./*Aufklärungsgruppe* (H)/14, which was the only one of the four *Staffeln* to operate Bf 110s. In April 1941, 2.(H)/14 arrived at Ain-el-Gazala in Libya. Apart from Bf 110s, the unit also used Bf 109Es in the short-range reconnaissance role. In March and April 1942, 2.(H)/14 had a strength of six Bf 110Es. Two Bf 110s were lost in March 1942, one of which was to enemy action. In April 1942, the unit returned to Germany, in the process becoming wholly equipped with Bf 109s.

Aufklärungsgruppe (F)/33

Code 8 H formed in December 1940 at an unknown location in Germany. Two of the four *Staffeln*, 2.(F)/33 and 4.(F)/33 respectively, operated Bf 110s. By June 1941, 2.(F)/33 was based at Kassel-Rotwesten, moving to Radoskowicze in Poland soon afterwards in anticipation of Operation Barbarossa. In January 1942, 2.(F)/33 returned to Germany, being redesignated as 2.(H)/33 around the same time. Six months later, in July 1942, 2.(H)/33 returned to the Eastern Front, being based at Schatalowsky until April 1943. Between May 1942 and July 1943, 2.(H)/33 was subordinated to *Stab* NAGr. 6, and the *Oberbefehlshaber der Luftwaffe* in August 1943. A final move was then made in April 1943 to Charkiv, with 2.(H)/33 remaining there until disbandment in August 1943 and immediate redesignation as *Stab* II./ZG 76.

Between March 1942 and August 1943, 2(H)/33 lost a total of eighteen Bf 110s, including ten in combat.

The fourth *Staffel*, 4.(F)/33, was based at Nuremberg in May 1941, moving to Tilsit the following month. In December 1941, 4.(F)/33 returned to Germany, being redesignated as 4.(H)/33 the following month. In May 1942, 4.(H)/33 transferred to Siwerskaja, remaining there until August 1943. Between May and October 1942, 4.(H)/33 was subordinated to *Stab* NAGr. 13. Two months later, in December 1942, the unit was subordinated to *Stab* NAGr. 8, remaining so until January 1944, except for a brief period in August 1943, when subordinated to the *Oberbefehlshaber der Luftwaffe*. On 1 April 1944, 4.(H)/33 was renamed 3./NAGr. 14.

Between March 1942 and March 1944, 4.(H)/33 lost thirty Bf 110s, of which eight were non-operational losses.

3./*Aufklärungsgruppe* 121

Formed on 1 October 1936 at Neuhausen, partly from 1.(F)/121. Redesignated on 1 October 1937 as 3./*Aufklärungsgruppe* 11, but reformed on the same day as 2./*Aufklärungsgruppe* 22. 3./Aufklärungsgruppe 121 served during the initial stages of Operation Barbarossa. By the summer of 1942, the Bf 110s had been replaced by Junkers Ju 88Ds.

Erprobungsgruppe 210

Code S 9 formed on 1 July 1940 at Cologne-Ostheim, consisting of three *Staffeln*; of which 1./Erpr.Gr. 210 and 2./Erpr.Gr. 210 were equipped with Bf 110Cs and Bf 110Ds respectively, with 3./Erpr.Gr. 210 flying the Bf 109E. It had originally been intended that the unit was to evaluate the Messerschmitt Me 210 under combat conditions as well as develop suitable tactics, hence the 210 suffix. However, as the Me 210 was still undergoing prolonged flight testing, *Erpr.Gr.* 210 received Bf 110s instead. Moved to Denain on 10 July, attacks on British targets. Calais-Merck was used as a forward airfield. On 22 February 1941, the unit moved to Ursel, continuing on 8 March to Wevelghem and, finally, on 4 April 1941 to Abbeville, remaining there until disbandment on 24 April 1941.

Stab/*Schnellkampfgeschwader* 210

Code S 9, *Schnellkampfgeschwader* 210 (SKG 210) was a direct continuation of the *Erprobungsgruppe* 210. On 24 April 1941, the *Stab*/SKG 210 was formed at Merville. Following a brief stay at Werl, *Stab*/SKG 210 transferred to Radzyn in Poland in anticipation of Operation Barbarossa. The unit remained on the Eastern Front until 26 November 1941, when a move was made to Lechfeld. On 4 January 1942, *Stab*/SKG 210 was reformed as *Stab*/ZG 1.

I./*Schnellkampfgeschwader* 210

Formed on 24 April 1941 at Abbeville from *Erprobungsgruppe* 210. A few weeks later, I./SKG 210 moved to Lippstadt, eventually moving to Radzyn in mid-June prior to Operation Barbarossa. On the first day of Operation Barbarossa, SKG 210 crews claimed the destruction of 344 Soviet aircraft, the vast majority destroyed on the ground for the loss of seven Bf 110s destroyed or damaged. On 2 October 1941, I./SKG 210 returned to Germany, being based at Landsberg-Lech. The unit disbanded on 4 January 1942, being renamed as I./ZG 1. However, 2./SKG 210 remained in Russia until 14 December 1941, presumably operating with II./SKG 210, not returning to Germany until the latter half of December 1941.

II./*Schnellkampfgeschwader* 210

Formed on 24 April 1941 at Stavanger-Sola, Norway, from III./ZG 76. In May 1941, II./SKG 210 moved to Werl, eventually joining *Stab*/SKG 210 and I./SKG 210 at Radzyn in mid-June. II./SKG 210 remained on the Eastern Front until 4 January 1942, when it was redesignated as II./ZG 1 at Bryansk.

6./(Z) *Jagdgeschwader 5*

Code LN, known as the *Eismeer Geschwader*, formed at Kirkenes in northern Norway on 25 January 1942 from 1.(Z)/JG 77. The unit's first *Staffelkapitän* was *Olt* Felix Maria Brandis. On 2 February 1942, Brandis was killed when his Bf 110 (LN+AR, W Nr 2546) crashed at Olanka due to poor weather. On 9 January 1944, the unit moved briefly to Kiestinki before returning to Kirkenes later that month. On 16 February 1944, the unit relocated to Herdla, eventually moving to Trondheim-Lade in May 1944. Redesignated as 10.(Z)/JG 5 on 16 March 1942 and 13.(Z)/JG 5 on 26 June 1942.

On 18 July 1944, 13.(Z)/JG 5 was redesignated as 10./ZG 26.

Between March 1942 and June 1944, 13.(Z)/JG 5 lost a total of twenty-three Bf 110s in combat and another fifty-eight to non-operational causes.

V.(Z)/*Lehrgeschwader* 1

Code L 1, formed at Jesau on 8 October 1939 from I./LG 1, consisting of *Stab*/V.(Z)/LG 1, and three *Staffeln*, 13 to 15.(Z)/LG 1. In November 1939, V.(Z)/LG 1 moved to Mannheim-Sandhofen, remaining there until 13 May 1940. On 17 October 1939, V.(Z)/KG 1 suffered the ignominy of being the first unit to lose a Bf 110 on the Western Front, albeit in a non-operational accident. On 18 May 1940, the unit transferred to Neufchateau, eventually serving during the Battle of France and Battle of Britain. On 1 October 1940, V.(Z)/LG 1 was redesignated as a night fighter unit, I./NJG 3.

Nachtjagdgeschwader 1

Code G 9, *Stab* NJG 1 was formed at Deelen on 22 June 1940. Between March 1942 and December 1944, *Stab* NJG 1 lost a total of thirteen Bf 110s, including eight in combat. I./NJG 1 was formed at Mönchen Gladbach on 22 June 1940 from I./ZG 1. Its most famous commander was *Major* Werner Streib, who served as *Gruppenkommendeur* between 18 October 1940 and 1 July 1943. On 1 July, 1./NJG 1 was redesignated as 5./NJG 1, with a new 1./NJG 1 being formed from 10./ZG 26. Between July and September 1940, 3./NJG 1 operated the Dornier Do 17Z *Kauz* night fighter before converting to the Bf 110, the *Staffel* having transferred to Deelen on 7 September 1940, with a new 3./NJG 1 being raised from 1./ZG 76. In July 1940, I./NJG 1 transferred to Gütersloh, remaining there until March 1941, when the unit moved to Venlo in the Netherlands.

In May 1942, 1./NJG 1 was redesignated 7./NJG 4, a new 1./NJG 1 being formed through the transfer of personnel and aircraft from other *Staffeln* within I./NJG 1. In December 1942, 1./NJG 1 became 10./NJG 5, with a new 1./NJG 1 being formed by transferring personnel and aircraft from I./NJG 1. The first Heinkel He 219s began to arrive in March 1943, gradually replacing the Bf 110s. Between March 1942 and March/April 1944, I./NJG 1 lost thirty-seven Bf 110s in combat and forty-five to other causes. On 31 July 1943, I./NJG 1 had a strength of two Bf 110F-4s and twenty-two Bf 110G-4s.

Stab/Nachtjagdgeschwader 3

Code D 5, formed on 29 September 1941 at Stade from *Stab*/ZG 26. Between March 1942 and June 1944, *Stab*/NJG 3 usually had one or two Bf 110s, being augmented with Junkers Ju 88Cs in the summer of 1943. During this period, *Stab*/NJG 3 lost three Bf 110s, including one in combat.

I./*Nachtjagdgeschwader* 3

Formed on 1 October 1940 at Vechta from V.(Z)/LG 1, consisting of *Stab* I./NJG 3 and 1. to 3./NJG 3 (from 13. to 15./LG 1). From February to October 1941, 1./NJG 3 served in the Mediterranean area, being based on Sicily and then Argos in Greece until May 1941 before moving to Benghazi in Libya later that month. In August 1941, 1./NJG 3 moved to Derna, eventually returning to Vechta in October. The second *Staffel*, 2./NJG 3, ventured briefly to the Smolensk area in February and March 1942. By mid-1942, Dornier Do 217Js began to arrive, followed by Junkers Ju 88s one year later. Nevertheless, Bf 110s remained with I./NJG 3 until December 1944 at least. A total of ninety Bf 110s were lost by I./NJG 3, including fifty-eight in combat. The worst month was February 1944, when nine Bf 110s were lost, eight of which were in combat.

II./*Nachtjagdgeschwader* 3

Formed on 1 September 1941 at Schleswig from the *Zerstörer-Ergänzungsgruppe*. Between September 1941 and 21 January 1944, 4./NJG 3 was based at Westerland on the island of Sylt. On 1 November 1942, a number of crews were transferred to 11./NJG 3. Between March 1942 and April 1944, a total of sixteen Bf 110s were lost, including eleven in combat.

III./*Nachtjagdgeschwader* 3

Formed on 1 November 1941 at Stade from II./ZG 76. Between November 1941 and April 1943, 7./NJG 3 was based at Lüneburg, then moving to Copenhagen-Kastrup, where the unit remained until November 1943. This particular *Staffel* became 4./NJG 5 in December 1942, eventually being reformed in August 1943. Between March 1942 and June 1944, III./NJG 3 lost twenty-eight Bf 110s in combat and another thirty-seven to non-operational causes.

IV./*Nachtjagdgeschwader* 3

Formed in November 1942 at Grove, Denmark, with the *Stab* IV/NJG 3 and 12./NJG 3 being raised from scratch and 10. and 11./NJG 3 being formed from 1. and 9./NJG 2 respectively. Bf 110s formed the main equipment of IV./NJG 3 for a brief period only, between March and June 1944. During this time, ten Bf 110s were lost, of which nine were in combat.

Stab/Nachtjagdgeschwader 4

Code 3 C, later G 9, formed on 18 April 1941 at Metz. In February 1944, the unit moved to Chenay. From June 1942 until May 1943, *Stab*/NJG 4 flew a single Bf 110C-3. In June 1943, this Bf 110 was transferred to another unit, leaving *Stab*/NJG 4 without any aircraft for two months. In August 1943, a Bf 110F-4 was received. Various Bf 110F and Bf 110Gs continued to serve with *Stab*/NJG 4 until December 1944 at least, usually in single numbers. Two Bf 110s were lost, although it seems likely that one of these was, in fact, a Junkers Ju 88.

I./*Nachtjagdgeschwader* 4

Formed in September 1942 at Florennes, Belgium, with the *Stab* I./NJG 4 being raised from scratch, with 1./NJG 4 formed from 9./NJG 1, 2./NJG 4 from 2./NJG 3, and 3./NJG 4 from 9./NJG 4 respectively. Initially, I./NJG 4 was operating a mix of Bf 110s, Dornier Do 217s, and Junkers Ju 88s. In April 1943, 2./NJG 4 was redesignated as 12./NJG 5. The second *Staffel*, 2./NJG 4, was temporarily based at Taveaux in November 1943, moving to Athies in January 1944, remaining there until 16 March 1944. 3./NJG 4 had previously been based at Athies in August and September 1943.

In August 1944, I./NJG 4 moved to Langendiebach. By then, the Bf 110s had been wholly replaced with Junkers Ju 88Gs. Between September 1942 and May

1944, I./NJG 4 lost twenty-two Bf 110s in combat and no less than thirty-seven aircraft in non-operational accidents.

II./*Nachtjagdgeschwader* 4

Formed in April 1942 at Laupheim, with *Stab* II./NJG 4, 4. and 6./NJG 4 being raised from scratch, and 5./NJG 4 being formed from 5./ZG 26. On 1 January 1943, 6./NJG 4 became 11./NJG 4, with a new 6./NJG 4 being formed by transferring personnel and aircraft from other II./NJG 4 *Staffeln*. Remarkably, obsolete Bf 110C and D variants continued in service with II./NJG 4 until late 1943.

There were several temporary deployments, with 5./NJG 4 being based at Dijon between August 1943 until December 1943 at least, with the unit moving to Taveaux on 18 March 1944, remaining there until 7 May. 6./NJG 4 was based at Taveaux between August 1943 and 7 May 1944. Operation Overlord, the Allied invasion of France, resulted in II./NJG 4 retreating back to Germany and Frankfurt in August 1944. During the first three months of 1945, 6./NJG 4 was based at Bad Lippspringe. On 30 March 1945, *Stab* II./NJG 4 as well as 5. and 6./NJG 4 were disbanded, leaving 4./NJG 4 as the sole operational *Staffel* at Gütersloh. By this time, Junkers Ju 88Gs had finally replaced the last remaining Bf 110s.

Between March 1942 and August 1944, II./NJG 4 lost a total of seventy-eight Bf 110s, including thirty-five in combat.

III./*Nachtjagdgeschwader* 4

Formed in May 1942 at Mainz-Finthen, with the *Stab* III./NJG 4 being raised from scratch, and the three *Staffeln*, 7., 8., and 9./NJG 4, being formed from 1./NJG 1, 8./NJG 1, and 4./NJG 1 respectively. From the start, III./NJG 4 flew a mix of Bf 110s and Dornier Do 217s. On 1 October 1943, 8./NJG 4 became 10./NJG 4, with a new 8./NJG 4 being formed through the transfer of crews and aircraft from the other III./NJG 4 *Staffeln*.

In September 1942, III./NJG 4 moved to Juvincourt, remaining there until August 1944. The Allied push into France resulted in III./NJG 4 relocating to Twente in the Netherlands. The stay here lasted barely two months, with III./NJG 4 returning to Mainz-Finthen on 10 September 1944. By this time, the Bf 110s were gradually being replaced by Junkers Ju 88Gs.

Between May 1942 and September 1944, III./NJG 4 lost a total of ninety-seven Bf 110s, of which forty-nine were in combat.

IV./*Nachtjagdgeschwader* 4

Formed on 1 January 1943 at Mainz-Finthen, with *Stab* IV./NJG 4 and 12./NJG 4 being raised from scratch, and 10. and 11./NJG 4 being formed from 8./NJG 4 and 6./NJG 4 respectively. On 1 August 1943, IV./NJG 4 was reformed as I./NJG 6. During its brief existence, IV./NJG 4 lost twelve Bf 110s, of which three were in combat and the rest in non-operational accidents.

Stab/Nachtjagdgeschwader 5

Code C 9, formed on 30 September 1942 at Döberitz, remaining there until March 1944, when the unit was transferred to Deelen. In May 1944, *Stab*/NJG 5 transferred to Athies-Laon in France. Following the invasion of France, the unit moved to Wormditt in August 1944, becoming part of Jagdführer Ostpreussen. At the same time, the Bf 110s were replaced by Ju 88Gs.

I./*Nachtjagdgeschwader 5*

Formed in September 1942 at Stendal from II./ZG 2. The unit remained at Stendal until 4 May 1944, when a move was made to St Dizier. During the autumn of 1943, 3./NJG 5 had been temporarily deployed to Völkenrode. In August 1944, I./NJG 5 transferred to Wormditt as part of Jagdführer Ostpreussen, also reequipping with Ju 88Gs.

II./*Nachtjagdgeschwader 5*

Formed at Parchim in December 1942, with *Stab* II./NJG 5 and 6./NJG 5 being raised from scratch. The remaining two *Staffeln*, 4. and 5./NJG 5, were formed from 7./NJG 3 and 3./NJG 2 respectively. On 10 May 1944, II./NJG 5 was redesignated as III./NJG 6. On the same day, a new II./NJG 5 was formed at Gütersloh from V./NJG 5. The unit remained at Gütersloh until 29 August, with detachments at Twente, Châteaudun, and Hagenau. On 29 August, II./NJG 5 moved to Stendal, with Junkers Ju 88Gs beginning to replace the Bf 110s.

Between October 1942 and October 1944, II./NJG 5 lost a total of ninety-four Bf 110s, including fifty-nine in combat.

III./*Nachtjagdgeschwader 5*

Formed in April 1943 at Neuruppin. III./NJG 5 remained at Neuruppin until March 1944, flying a mix of Bf 110s and Dornier Do 217s. There were detachments at Greifswald, Werneuchen, Königsberg, Parchim, and Mainz-Finthen. In March 1944, III./NJG 5 transferred to Brandis, remaining there for two months only before moving to Athies-Laon in northern France. In April 1944, 7./NJG 5 was disbanded, eventually being reformed in August. With the Allied invasion of France, III./NJG 5 relocated in August 1944 to Wormditt, becoming part of *Jagdführer Ostpreussen*. Soon afterwards, the Bf 110s were replaced by Junkers Ju 88Gs.

Between May 1943 and September 1944, III./NJG 5 lost a total of 104 Bf 110s, of which exactly half were in combat.

IV./*Nachtjagdgeschwader 5*

Formed in December 1942 at Lechfeld and Leipheim as part of *Jagdführer Süddeutschland*, with *Stab* IV./NJG 5, and 10. and 11./NJG 5 being raised from scratch. In January 1943, IV./NJG 5 moved to Insterburg as part of Jagdführer Ostpreussen. In April 1943, 2./NJG 4 was redesignated as 12./NJG 5. Two *Staffeln*,

10./NJG 5 and 12./NJG 5, were transferred to the Eastern Front in January 1943. Six months later, these *Staffeln* moved to Bryansk and Orel respectively, in anticipation of Operation Citadel (i.e., the Battle of Kursk). The following month, 10./NJG 5 and 12./NJG 5 were split up into several detachments, being subordinated to *Luftflotte* 6 in the Smolensk-Bryansk area, and *Luftflotte* 4 in the Poltava-Stalino area in present-day Ukraine.

On 1 August 1943, *Stab* IV./NJG 5 and 10./NJG 5 were redesignated as *Stab* I./NJG 100 and 1./NJG 100 respectively, with both units being reformed at Brandis and Erfurt-Bindersleben on the same day.

Also on 1 August, IV./NJG 5 moved to Brandis, also establishing detachments at Erfurt and Vechta. In May 1944, the unit deployed to Mainz-Finthen, remaining there until August 1944. During this time, a detachment was established at Stubendorf. Yet another move occurred in August 1944, this time to Powunden as part of *Jagdführer Ostpreussen*. Junkers 88Gs began to replace the Bf 110s.

Between October 1942 and December 1944, IV./NJG 5 lost a total of sixty-three Bf 110s, including thirty-two in combat.

V./*Nachtjagdgeschwader* 5

Formed on 11 August 1943 at Insterburg as part of *Jagdführer Ostpreussen*. Nine months later, on 10 May 1944, V./NJG 5 was redesignated as II./NJG 5.

Between September 1943 and March 1944, V./NJG 5 lost a total of fourteen Bf 110s, all to non-operational causes.

In June 1944, a *Schulstaffel* was formed at Königsberg-Neumark, with personnel and aircraft being transferred from other NJG 5 units. The unit flew a mix of Bf 110s and Junkers Ju 88s. In December 1944, the *Schulstaffel* was redesignated as 16./NJG 5. On 1 January 1945, the unit was renamed as *Stabsstaffel*/NJG 5. By 1 May 1945, the *Stabsstaffel*/NJG 5 was based at Lübeck-Blankensee on the Baltic coast.

Nachtjagdgeschwader 6

Code 3 C (until 30 July 1943), 2 Z *Stab*/NJG 6 formed on 15 September 1943 at Schleissheim, flying a mix of Bf 110s and Junkers Ju 88s. In December 1944, Stab/NJG 6 moved to Kitzingen, remaining there until the end of the war. Only one Bf 110 was lost in combat by *Stab*/NJG 6, in May 1944.

I./*Nachtjagdgeschwader* 6

Formed on 1 August 1943 at Mainz-Finthen from IV./NJG 4. In March 1944, I./NJG 6 moved to Illesheim, remaining there for three months before transferring to Neubiberg in Bavaria. During the summer of 1944, detachments were established at Echterdingen and Hailfingen. By this time, I./NJG 6 operated a mix of Bf 110s and Junkers Ju 88Gs. In September 1944, I./NJG 6 moved to Gross Sachenhein, remaining there until the end of the war. On 30 March 1945, I./NJG 6 was reduced to a single *Staffel*, the other units being disbanded.

Between August 1943 and December 1944, I./NJG 6 lost a total of seventy-two Bf 110s, including forty in combat.

II./*Nachtjagdgeschwader 6*

Formed on 15 September 1943 at Neubiberg-Donau. The following month, II./NJG 6 moved to Stuttgart-Echterdingen, remaining there until May 1944. Detachments were also established at Kitzingen and Schwäbisch-Hall. During May and June 1944, a brief sojourn to Ghedi in Italy was made before returning to Stuttgart-Echterdingen. However, during June 1944, II./NJG 6 was briefly based at Venlo in the Netherlands. In September 1944, II./NJG 6 relocated to Schwäbisch-Hall, also beginning to receive Junkers Ju 88Gs.

Between July 1943 and July 1944, II./NJG 6 lost a total of forty-five Bf 110s, of which sixteen were in combat and twenty-nine in non-operational accidents.

III./*Nachtjagdgeschwader 6*

Formed on 10 May 1944 at Hagenau from II./NJG 5. Between June and October 1944, III./NJG 6 was based at Steinamanger in Hungary, returning to Leipheim and Germany during the latter month. III./NJG 5 returned to Hungary soon afterwards, being based at Var until February 1945. With the Red Army push into Hungary, III./NJG 6 transferred to Neubiberg. On 30 March 1945, III./NJG 6 was largely disbanded, with only 7./NJG 6 remaining active. In early May 1945, the unit was based at Bad Aibling.

Between April and December 1944, III./NJG 6 lost a total of twenty-three Bf 110s, including twelve in combat.

IV./*Nachtjagdgeschwader 6*

Formed in May 1943 at Otopeni (10./NJG 6 and 12./NJG 6) and at Zilistea (11./NJG 6) in Romania. There were detachments at Bucharest-Pipera, Focsani, Buzau, Stopeni, and Telish in Bulgaria. IV./NJG 6 rarely operated at night, instead being active against USAAF daylight raids targeting the Romanian oil refineries. Following the Romanian defection from the Axis in late August 1944, IV./NJG 6 moved to Leipheim. Another move, to Schleissheim, was made the following month. While based at Schleissheim, Junkers Ju 88s began to supplant the Bf 110s. Detachments were established at Gevolzhofen, Kitzingen and Ingolstadt. On 30 March 1945, IV./NJG 6 was reduced to only one *Staffel*, 10./NJG 6, the other units being disbanded.

Between July 1943 and December 1944, IV./NJG 6 lost a total of eighty-two Bf 110s, of which exactly half were in combat. The worst month occurred in December 1944, when IV./NJG 6 lost twenty Bf 110s, of which eighteen were in combat.

V./*Nachtjagdgeschwader* 6

Formed in June 1943 at Stuttgart-Echterdingen. The following month, V./NJG 6 was redesignated as III./NJG 2. Three Bf 110s were lost in non-operational accidents during July 1943.

Schulstaffel

Formed on 12 April 1944 at Schleissheim, with personnel and aircraft being transferred from other NJG 6 units. Between 12 April and 26 June 1944, the unit was known as 5.(*Schulstaffel*)/NJG 6. In December 1944, the unit was redesignated as 16./NJG 6, eventually becoming *Stabsstaffel.*/NJG 6 on 1 January 1945.

One Bf 110 was lost in combat in August 1944, with a second aircraft being written off in a non-operational accident in November 1944.

Zerstörergeschwader 1

Code 6 U, later G 9, later 2J, with the nose of the unit's Bf 110s being adorned with a large wasp, ZG 1 was commonly referred to as the *Wespengeschwader* (literally Hornet Wing). Stab/ZG 1 formed at Lechfeld on 4 January 1942 from *Stab*/SKG 210. Between January 1942 and August 1943, *Stab*/ZG 1 was equipped with various Bf 110 variants, with strength varying between one and four aircraft. Between May 1942 and March 1943, *Stab*/ZG 1 served on the Eastern Front, moving to Neubiberg in March 1943. After a brief spell at Montecourvino in the summer of 1943, *Stab*/ZG 1 moved to Lorient in France. Three Bf 110s were lost due to enemy action, with another two being lost in non-operational accidents. In December 1943, *Stab*/ZG 1 re-equipped with Ju 88s. *Stab*/ZG 1 disbanded in July 1944.

I./*Zerstörergeschwader* 1

Formed at Jüterbog-Damm on 1 May 1939 from I./ZG 141. Disbanded at Düsseldorf on 22 June 1940. 1./ZG 1 became *Erprobungsgruppe* 210 at Cologne-Ostheim, with 2./ZG 1 and 3./ZG 1 becoming 2./NJG 1 and 3./NJG 1 respectively. Reformed at Lechfeld on 4 January 1942 from I./SKG 210. In May 1942, I./ZG 1 had a total of forty-four Bf 110s on strength. At the end of May 1942, I./ZG 1 moved to Belgorod, before participating in the fight for Stalingrad until 31 January 1943. I./ZG 1 remained on the Eastern Front until 8 July 1943. The unit then moved to Wunsdorf, eventually being transferred to Lorient on the French Atlantic coast. On 13 October 1943, I./ZG 1 was redesignated as I./ZG 26. The same month, I./ZG 1 was reformed as V./KG 40 becoming part of *Fliegerführer Atlantik*, operating Junkers Ju 88Cs in the maritime strike role. Between April 1942 and September 1943, I./ZG 1 lost eighty-nine Bf 110s in combat, with another fifty-six being lost to other causes.

II./*Zerstörergeschwader* 1

Formed at Fürstenwalde on 15 May 1939 from I./JG 54. Between 21 September 1939 and 1 March 1940, the unit was known as *Jagdgruppe* 101. Initially flying Bf 109s, the first Bf 110s did not arrive until March 1940. On 26 June 1940, II./ZG 1 was redesignated as III./ZG 76. Reformed at Bryansk on 4 January 1942, II./ZG 1 remained on the Eastern Front until March 1943, moving to Trapani on Sicily the following month. II./ZG 1 remained in Italy until early August 1943, being transferred to Lanvéoc in Brittany and *Fliegerführer Atlantik* on 5 August 1943. Between November 1943 and July 1944, II./ZG 1 became part of the 7. *Jagddivision* at Wels. II./ZG 1 suffered huge losses, with 199 Bf 110s being lost in combat between April 1942 and July 1944. Another ninety-one aircraft were lost to various other causes. In July 1943 alone, twenty-four Bf 110Gs were lost, including seventeen in combat, leaving a mere eight aircraft on charge at the end of the month.

III./*Zerstörergeschwader* 1

Formed at Lechfeld in January 1942. III./ZG 1 used Bf 110s for a brief period only between September and November 1942, being based at Bir el Abd in Libya and Trapani in Sicily respectively, with no aircraft being written off.

10./*Zerstörergeschwader* 1

Formed at an unknown location on the Eastern Front in October 1942, 10./ZG 1 flew Bf 110s for almost one year, between October 1942 and July 1943. The unit also operated Bf 109s and Me 210s. Although only one Bf 110 was lost in combat, another eight were destroyed in non-operational accidents.

Zerstörergeschwader 2

Code 2 S *Stab*/ZG 2, formed at Darmstadt-Griesheim on 1 April 1940. In July 1940, *Stab*/ZG 2 moved to Toussous-le-Noble, remaining there until disbanded in September 1940. Reformed at Landsberg-Lech in April 1942. The following month, *Stab*/ZG 2 transferred to Kharkov in the Ukraine. During June and July 1942, the unit was based at Svoboda before returning to Parndorf in Germany in August. The last two Bf 110E-2s were transferred to other Luftwaffe units in October 1942, by which time *Stab*/ZG 2 had been reequipped with Fw 190s. No Bf 110s were lost in combat or in non-operational accidents between April and October 1942.

I./*Zerstörergeschwader* 2

Formed at Bernberg on 1 May 1939 from I./JG 231. Until 30 January 1940, the unit was known as *Jagdgruppe* 102, being equipped with Bf 109Ds. In February 1940, the first Bf 110s were received. I./ZG 2 disbanded in September 1940, with 1./ZG 2 becoming 4./NJG 2 two months later. In April 1942, I./ZG 2 was reformed at Landsberg-Lech from I./ZG 26. Serving on the Eastern Front, I./ZG 2 had a total of forty-one Bf 110s at the end of May. However, twenty-nine Bf 110s were transferred to other units in July 1942, I./ZG 2 being disbanded at Barwenkowo the following month. The personnel and aircraft were redistributed to NJG 4 and III./ZG 1. Between April and August 1942, a total of sixteen Bf 110s were lost to enemy action, with another six to other causes.

II./*Zerstörergeschwader* 2

Code A 2, formed at Freiburg on 26 June 1940 from I./ZG 52. Disbanded in September 1940, with 4./ZG 2 becoming 4./NJG 3. Reformed at Landsberg-Lech and Vienna-Aspern in March 1942, II./ZG 2 transferred to Tschugujew on the Eastern Front two months later. By the end of May 1942, II./ZG 2 had a total of forty-two Bf 110s, which were a mix of older Bf 110Cs to late model Bf 110F-2s. In June, II./ZG 2 moved to Barwenkowo. The Eastern Front sojourn was brief, however, with II./ZG 2 being transferred to Vienna-Neustadt in late July. While here, Messerschmitt Me 210s began to replace the Bf 110s. A total of fifteen Bf 110s had been lost in combat, along with five to other causes. In September 1942, II./ZG 2 was redesignated as I./NJG 5. It would appear that an *Ergänzungsstaffel* also existed between April and July 1942.

Zerstörergeschwader 26

Code U 8 (until 30 June 1941), 3 U ZG 26 was named Horst Wessel after a member of the paramilitary *Sturmabteilung*. Wessel wrote the Nazi hymn *Die Fahne Hoch* (Raise the Flag). After Wessel was killed by Communist sympathisers in 1930, he was elevated to martyr status by the Nazis.

Stab Zerstörergeschwader 26

Formed on 1 May 1939 at Dortmund from *Stab* ZG 142. Initially flying Bf 109Ds, the Bf 110s did not arrive until the early winter of 1939. The unit participated in the invasion of France, relocating to Boos-Rouen in May 1940. The following month, *Stab* ZG 26 moved to Lille, remaining there until November 1940. During that month, the unit transferred to Memmingen. Moving to Hungary in late March 1941, *Stab* ZG 26 took part in the invasion of Yugoslavia and Greece. In June 1941, the unit moved to Suwalki in Poland to participate in Operation Barbarossa. On 25 September 1941, Stab ZG 26 transferred back to Germany, being redesignated as *Stab* NJG 3 at Stade four days later. Stab ZG 26 was reformed at Wunsdorf on 13 October 1943, remaining there until 22 March 1944, when the unit moved to Königsberg. The Bf 110s were replaced by Me 410s. Between March 1943 and March 1944, a total of seven Bf 110s were lost, including two in combat.

I./*Zerstörergeschwader* 26

Formed on 1 May 1939 at Dortmund from I./ZG 142. Disbanded in April 1942, with personnel and aircraft transferred to ZG 1 and ZG 2. Reformed at Bad

Lippspringe on 13 October 1943 from I./ZG 1. On 1 April 1944, I./ZG 26 moved to Fassberg, with Messerschmitt Me 410s replacing the Bf 110s. Between March 1942 and March 1944, I./ZG 26 lost thirty-eight Bf 110s in combat and thirty to non-operational causes.

II./*Zerstörergeschwader* 26

Formed on 1 May 1939 at Werl from II./ZG 142. The *Gruppe* was active during the invasion of France and the Low Countries. Between June and November 1940, II./ZG 26 was based at Crecy-eh-Ponthieu, flying numerous sorties during the Battle of Britain. Following a brief spell at Memmingen, II./ZG 26 transferred to Popesti, Romania, on 18 February 1941, eventually taking part in the invasion of Yugoslavia, Greece, and Crete. Prior to Operation Barbarossa, II./ZG 26 moved to Suwlaki in Poland. The unit was very active on the Eastern Front until the spring of 1942. In March 1942, nine Bf 110s were lost, including five in combat. The following month, II./ZG 26 disbanded at Dugino, with the personnel and eleven B 110s being absorbed by ZG 1 and ZG 2. II./ZG 26 was reformed at Hildesheim on 11 October 1943 from III./ZG 1, receiving Messerschmitt Me 410s in the process.

III./*Zerstörergeschwader* 26

Formed on 1 May 1939 at Lippstadt from III./ZG 142. Equipped with Bf 109Ds, the unit was known as *Jagdgruppe* 126 between 25 September 1939 and 4 February 1940. On the latter date, a move was made to Dortmund, with the first Bf 110s arriving later the same month. III./ZG 26 was active during the invasion of France and the Low Countries, being based at Rouen-Boos from 18 May, eventually moving to Barley-Arques the following month. Bomber escort and ground attack sorties were conducted during the Battle of Britain.

In December 1940, III./ZG 26 moved to Neubiberg, remaining there until early January 1941, when a move was made to Treviso for participation in the North African campaign. With the setbacks in North Africa, III./ZG 26 returned to Sicily in November 1942, remaining at Trapani until June 1943. Later that month, III./ZG 26 transferred to Rome-Ciampino. In early August 1943, the unit returned to Germany, being based at Plantlünne and Wunsdorf, being sent into action against USAAF bombers. On 22 March 1944, a move was made to Königsberg-Devau, with III./ZG 26 to reequip with the Messerschmitt Me 410. It would appear that Bf 110s were retained until June 1944. On 26 September 1944, III./ZG 26 was renamed *Kommando* Nowotny.

Between March 1942 and June 1944, III./ZG 26 lost a staggering 155 Bf 110s in combat, and 130 to non-operational causes. The worst losses occurred in February 1944, when twenty-one Bf 110G-2s were shot down, and another five were lost in accidents.

IV./*Zerstörergeschwader* 26

Formed on 18 July 1944 at Oerlandet, Norway, initially consisting only of two *Staffeln*, 10. and 12./ZG 26, with the former from 13.(Z)/JG 5 and the latter from *Küstenfliegerstaffel Krim*. A Staff Flight, *Stab*/IV./ZG 26 was formed at Oerlandet on 5 September 1944 from *Stab*/SAGr. 126. IV./ZG 26 remained in Norway until disbanding on 23 February 1945, with *Stab*/IV./ZG 26 becoming *Stab*/II./JG 5 and 10./ZG 26 becoming 7./JG 5 respectively.

Zerstörergeschwader 52

Code A 2 ,formed at Illesheim on 1 May 1939 from I./ZG 143, consisting of a *Stab* Flight and three *Staffeln*. Between 24 September 1939 and 6 January 1940, the unit was known as *Jagdgruppe* 152, operating Bf 109Ds. These remained until March 1940, with the initial Bf 110s having begun to arrive the previous month. I./ZG 52 moved from Neuhausen ob Eck to Mannheim in May 1940, relocating to Charleville in France later that month. However, already in June 1940, I./ZG 52 returned to Germany, eventually being redesignated as II./ZG 2 on 26 June 1940.

Zerstörergeschwader 76

Code M 8 *Stab*/ZG 76, formed on 15 April 1940 at Cologne-Wahn, remaining there until July 1940 before moving to Laval. In October 1940, the unit relocated to Stavanger-Sola in Norway. On 1 August 1941, it was reformed as *Stab*/*Jagdfliegerführer* Norwegen. *Stab*/ZG 76 was reformed in August 1943 at Ansbach, eventually moving to Prague on 25 April 1944. The Bf 110s were replaced with Me 410s. Between September 1943 and April 1944, *Stab*/ZG 76 lost five Bf 110s, including two to enemy action.

I./*Zerstörergeschwader* 76

Formed on 1 May 1939 at Olmütz from II./ZG 141. On 16 December *1939*, I./ZG 76 moved to Jever on the German North Sea coast. Between 9 April and June 1940, I./ZG 76 took part in Operation Weserübung, the invasion of Denmark and Norway. On 10 April, I./ZG 76 moved to Stavanger-Sola. The unit remained in Norway until disbanding in September 1940. In August 1943, I./ZG 76 was reformed at Ansbach, with *Stab*/I./ZG 76 being raised from scratch, with the three *Staffeln*, 1., 2., and 3./ZG 76 being reformed from 1./NAGr. 16, 3./NAGr. 12 and *Stabsstaffel*/St.G. 1 respectively. I./ZG 76 served during daylight interceptions of USAAF bombers, eventually moving to Prague on 25 April 1944. Soon after arriving at Prague, the Bf 110s were replaced with Messerschmitt Me 410s.

Between August 1943 and April 1944, I./ZG 76 lost fifty-four Bf 110s in combat and twenty-nine to non-operational causes.

II./*Zerstörergeschwader* 76

Formed on 1 May 1939 at Gablingen. Between 9 September 1939 and 3 February 1940, the unit was known as *Jagdgruppe* 176, flying single-seat Messerschmitt Bf 109Ds. The first Bf 110s began to arrive in February 1940. II./ZG 76 took part in the invasion of France and the Low Countries, moving to Le Mans in late May 1940. The following month, II./ZG 76 relocated to Abbeville, remaining there until September 1940. After a brief spell at Jever, II./ZG 76 participated in the invasion of Greece and Crete, being based at Argos in May and June 1941 before moving to Leeuwarden in the Netherlands the following month. During this time, 4./ZG 76 deployed to Mosul as part of *Fliegerführer Irak*. On 1 November 1941, II./ZG 76 was renamed III./NJG 3.

In August 1943, II./ZG 76 was reformed at Wertheim, with *Stab*/II./ZG 76 being raised from scratch, 4./ZG 76 from 3./NAGr. 4, 5./ZG 76 from 3./NAGr. 11 and 6./ZG 76 from 3./NAGr. 6 respectively. As was the case of other *Zerstörer* units, II./ZG 76 was sent into action against USAAF bombers. The most disastrous month was March 1944, when no less than seventeen Bf 110s were lost in combat, with another seven being written off in accidents. On 25 April 1944, II./ZG 76 moved to Prague, with Messerschmitt Me 410s replacing the Bf 110s. Between October 1943 and April 1944, II./ZG 76 lost thirty-eight Bf 110s in combat, with twenty-eight more being lost to non-operational causes.

III./*Zerstörergeschwader* 76

Formed on 26 June 1940 at Trier-Euren. Four days later, III./ZG 76 moved to Laval, remaining there until October 1940 before transferring to Stavanger-Sola later the same month. III./ZG 76 remained in Norway until 24 April 1941, when the unit was renamed as II./SKG 210.

In November 1943, III./ZG 76 was reformed at Öttingen, with 7./ZG 76 being reformed from 10./ZG 76. *Stab*/III./ZG 76 and the two other *Staffeln*, 8. and 9./ZG 76 were raised from scratch. In the event, the reestablishment of III./ZG 76 was abandoned, with the personnel and aircraft being absorbed by I./ZG 76. Nevertheless, III./ZG 76 did see action, losing a total of thirty Bf 110s between November 1943 and April 1944, including nineteen in combat.

27

Technical Description

The following technical description is inspired by the very detailed 372-page technical assessment performed by Vultee Aircraft, Inc., in 1940–1941. The report not only includes the aircraft itself, but also the engines, armament, flight instruments, generators, electrical wiring, and a wide variety of other ancillary equipment. Interestingly, two of the fuel tanks and one of the oil tanks were subjected to ground-firing tests. It was concluded that the German self-sealing tanks were sub-standard to the similar contemporary US fuel tanks:

> A brief examination will reveal that its designers gave careful attention to the basic factors governing mass production practicability and economy—design simplification; elimination of close limits and clearances; practical assemblies and installations; and a minimum variety of structural shapes and sheet gages—and that this airplane lacks in nothing that a high-grade military airplane should possess. Its performance is good; armament heavy; instruments and controls are adequate.[1]

The Messerschmitt Me 110 is a twin-engined, low-wing, multi-role (day and night fighter, fighter bomber, reconnaissance, and ground attack) aircraft. It is constructed entirely out of metal.

Fuselage

The fuselage is an all-metal, stressed-skin structure, being composed of two symmetrical halves, which are joined vertically along the upper and lower centreline. The construction of the respective main fuselage sections can be performed using vertical jigs, thus providing easy external and internal access for installation of equipment such as electrical wiring, plumbing, and control mechanisms. This method of construction is highly suitable to mass production. Construction of the Bf 110 is similar to that of the Bf 109 single-seat fighter. Two or three (in later variants) crew sit in tandem beneath an enclosed canopy. Entry to the aircraft is through a retractable ladder on the left side of the fuselage. The main armament is fitted to the nose section, with the tail section is fitted to the upper rear section of the fuselage. A detachable bomb rack can be fitted beneath the fuselage.

No heating system is fitted, with the only ventilation for cold air being by means of opening the emergency vision panel, and the sliding panels in the front cockpit. However, there are provisions for electrically heated flying suits for the pilot and rear gunner.

Even though the Bf 110 is a long-range heavy fighter, no evidence could be found regarding the provision of relief tubes.

Tail Section

The tail section consists of a horizontal cantilever stabiliser, elevator, and twin fins/rudders. The control surfaces (rudders and elevator) are fabric-covered. The fabric covering is sewn to cloth-tacking strips attached along the ribs by means of special tubular rivets. Trim tabs are fitted to the respective elevator and rudders. The horizontal stabiliser is attached to the fuselage through three bolts, two at the rear spar and the third at the front, with the latter being connected to the adjustment screw jack mechanism. The horizontal stabiliser is adjustable, being interconnected to the flaps. When the flaps are lowered, the leading edge of the stabiliser is lowered roughly 5 cm, with 4½ degrees of incidence. The vertical fins are interchangeable by means of replacing the tab control support bracket and the rear attachment bracket.

A collapsible dinghy is located in the tail cone, with the release cable being located in the rear gunner's cockpit. The dinghy can be towed towards the front end of the aircraft by means of an external metal cable fitted to the fuselage. The dinghy can then be inflated, with crew presumably using oars or paddles to reach the shore. Unfortunately, this piece of equipment was missing from this particular Bf 110.

Wings

The two wings (left and right) of the monospar type, being attached to the lower centre fuselage at three points: at the leading edge and the upper and lower booms of the main spar. The wings are tapered throughout its length with a squared wingtip. The aspect ratio is 7.3:1. Each wing is constructed out of a centre main spar, with former ribs fitted at 25.4-cm intervals, except where the engine nacelles and undercarriage are fitted, along with lateral stringers 3.5 cm apart. The wings are covered with stressed-skin metal. The slotted flaps, representing 20 per cent of the chord, are hydraulically operated, and can be lowered at speeds up to 250 kph. When the flaps are lowered, the ailerons droop. The ailerons are fabric-covered, being fitted with trim tabs. Handley-Page Type automatic slats are fitted to the outer leading edge of the wings. The aluminium alloy sheet metal varies in thickness, from .32 inches at the wingtips to .82 inches around the engines. The external rivets, with a diameter of a quarter or three-sixteenth inches, are all flush with the outer sheet metal plates, being countersunk. The four main self-sealing fuel tanks (two in each wing) are located forward and aft of the main spar, close to the fuselage attachment point, with access being provided by means of large removable panels on the lower surfaces of the wings, with refuelling caps on the upper surfaces of the wings. The upper area of the fuel tank compartment is strengthened by means of closely spaced chordwise stiffeners and spanwise stringers, which are connected through a number of gussets at specific intervals. Tie-down rings are fitted to the lower surfaces of the wings near the respective wingtip, these being neither streamlined nor removable.

Undercarriage

The undercarriage consists of two hydraulically operated main undercarriage units, which retracts rearwards into the tails of the engine nacelles. When the main undercarriage is raised, two hinged doors close aperture. In an emergency, the undercarriage can be lowered by means of an air-pressure actuation system. The hydraulic wheel brakes are manually operated. A fixed non-retractable tail wheel is also fitted. The wheel well inner fabric lining of the main undercarriage is laced to the surrounding structure, with internal access being provided by means of zippers.

Engines

Two 1,100-hp twelve-cylinder liquid-cooled Daimler-Benz DB 601 A inverted Vee engines, with the cylinders being arranged in two rows of six each. The DB 601 A engine is fitted with fuel injection, and a fluid-drive variable speed supercharger. Although this particular engine is apparently designed for 87-octane fuel, 92-octane fuel has been found in the fuel tanks of captured Luftwaffe aircraft. The induction system includes an automatic, atmospheric-pressure-controlled throttle. The respective engine mounts consist of four sturdy magnesium forgings, attached to the wing front spar. Control rods and bell cranks, as well as piping, end fittings, clamps, and many of the brackets appear to be standard components fitted to other German aircraft. The engine accessories include an electrical inertia starter, with provision for an emergency manual hand crank starter mechanism, a 24V, 1,500-watt generator, a swash-plate driven hydraulic pump, a centrifugal coolant pump, and gravity-fed oil pumps. The exhaust system consists of individual stacks attached to three-stud exhaust flanges.

The VDM propellers are three-blade controllable pitch units, being fully feathered.

Electrical, Hydraulic, and Air Pressure Systems

Hydraulic systems are used for retracting and lowering the undercarriage, and operation of flaps. The electrical system consists of a 24V ungrounded system, with a battery (located in the rear fuselage) and two engine-driven generators providing the necessary power. Compressed air pressure systems are used for charging the machine gun and cannon armament, and the emergency operation of lowering the undercarriage and flaps.

An oxygen system is installed, consisting of eight oxygen bottles fitted to the rear fuselage. No fire extinguishing system has been found, but brackets fitted to the rear cockpit may indicate that fire extinguishers are usually carried aboard the aircraft.

RAF Assessment of the Messerschmitt Bf 110

Eric 'Winkle' Brown flew both the Bf 110C and the later Bf 110G. Brown stated that the Bf 110 had overall 'pleasant characteristics'. Brown later wrote:

> There were many excellent features of German aircraft cockpit layouts that had been standardised, such as systems identification colour schemes. Another was the type of airscrew pitch indicators which were numbered like a clock face, rendering it very simple to set the pitch on any German aircraft. For take-off, for example, the clock pointers were always set at 12 o'clock by moving the electrically-actuated pitch control levers. On the early Bf 110s the clock-type pitch indicators were also mounted on each engine nacelle where they could be seen from the pilot's seat, while the later Bf 110G series had the indicators mounted only on the nacelles and not in the cockpit. All engine instruments were on the starboard of the dashboard, and mixture strength and boost pressure were controlled automatically.
>
> Taxying the Bf 110 was very easy, with good view and ground handling in a crosswind when differential throttling and braking could cope with all conditions. Take-off at 2,600 rpm and 1·3 *atas* of boost was normally effected without recourse to flaps in the earlier production models, but the take-off run was long and 20 deg flap was recommended for the Bf 110G series. During the initial portion of the run directional control was poor, but improved once 120 mph (193 km/h) was attained, this probably being aggravated by the tail heaviness of the aircraft since, with the tail on the ground, the rudders were, of course, considerably blanked by the fuselage and engines. Even with the stick well forward the tail was slow to rise. The take-off of the Bf 110G, with its more powerful DB 605s at 2,800 rpm and 1·42 *atas* of boost coupled with the use of flaps, was markedly improved over that of the Bf 110C.

Once off the ground the flaps were retracted at 500 ft [150 metres], this amount of altitude being necessary for safety because of the considerable nose-down change of trim that accompanied upward flap movement. Speed was then built up to 150 mph [240 km/h] which gave a steep angle and a very good rate of climb at 2,300 rpm and 1·2 *atas* of boost, this being improved on the Bf 110G at 2,600 rpm and 1·3 *atas* of boost. The controls were fairly light, well harmonised and very effective up to 250 mph [400 km/h], but above that speed they began to heavy up, particularly the elevator.... Stability was good fore and aft and directionally, but neutral laterally. Manoeuvrability proved surprisingly good for so large [by contemporary standards] a fighter, but the Bf 110 suffered from the same serious fault as the Bf 109—the automatic slats kept popping out unevenly in tight turns, sighting being ruined by the resultant lateral wobble.

The landing pattern was normally entered at 155 mph [250 km/h] and the undercarriage was fully lowered before the flaps were actuated. The first movement of the flaps caused a large change of nose-up attitude which had to be counteracted by a heavy forward force on the elevators. There was little point in trimming out this force as further flap movement caused a reversal of attitude change with the end result seeing little change of trim required. The ailerons began to droop as the flaps moved, a sudden lightening of their control being evident but no loss in effectiveness being apparent. The approach attitude at 100 mph [160 km/h] was steepish but the view from the cockpit was excellent. As with the Bf 109, care had to be taken not to hold off too high as the automatic slats were activated as the speed decayed and this could cause a wing to drop. The landing run was short as the brakes could be used heavily without any tendency for the tail to rise.[2]

Messerschmitt Bf 110 Technical Data and Performance Characteristics

Variant	Bf 110B-1	Bf 110C-4	Bf 110D	Bf 110E	Bf 110F-2	Bf 110G-4/R3
Engines	2 × DB 600 A	2 × 1,100-hp DB 601 A	2 × 1,100-hp DB 601 A	2 × 1,100-hp DB 601 A	2 × 1,350-hp DB 601 F	2 × 1,475-hp DB 605 B-1
Wingspan	16.9 m	16.28 m	16.3 m	16.3 m	16.28 m	16.28 m
Length	12.8 m	12.10 m	12.1 m	12.1 m	12.07 m	13.05 m
Height	N/a	3.50 m	3.50 m	3.50 m	4.00 m	4.18 m
Wing area	39.3 m²	38.37 m²	38.50 m²	38.50 m²	38.50 m²	38.50 m²
Max speed	455 kph at 4,000 m	561 kph at 7,000 m	510 kph at 5,000 m	510 kph at 5,000 m	570 kph at 5,400 m	550 kph (with radar)
Cruise speed	320 kph	380 kph at 3,000 m	380 kph at 3,000 m	380 kph at 3,000 m	400 kph at 6,000 m	450 at 9,300 m
Empty weight	N/a	5,200 kg	5,200 kg	5,200 kg	5,600 kg	5,094 kg
Maximum weight	5,650 kg	8,900 kg	8,900 kg	8,900 kg	6,750 kg as Zerstörer 9,340 kg as Jagdbomber	9,370 kg
Range, economic cruise speed	1,700 km	1,300 km	1,300 km	1,300 km	800 km without external fuel tanks	850 km with external fuel tanks
Armament	4 × 20-mm MG FF cannons, 3 × MG 17 machine guns, one 7.9-mm MG 15	4 × 7.9-mm MG 17, 2 × 20-mm MG FF, one 7.9-mm MG 15	4 × 7.9-mm MG 17, 2 × 20-mm MG FF, one 7.9-mm MG 15	4 × 7.9-mm MG 17, 2 × 20-mm MG FF, one 7.9-mm MG 15	4 × 7.9-mm MG 17, 2 × 20-mm MG FF, one 7.9-mm MG 15	2 × 7.9-mm MG 17, 2 × 20-mm MG 151, 2 × 20-mm MG FF, one 7.92-mm MG 81

28

Messerschmitt Bf 110 Variants

Bf 110A-0: Pre-series variant, powered by two 610-hp Jumo 210B engines.

Bf 110B-0: Pre-series variant, powered by two Jumo 210G engines. Featured revised nose section.

Bf 110B-1: Production variant, armed with two 20-mm MG FF cannons and four 7.92-mm MG 17 machine guns.

Bf 110B-2: Reconnaissance variant, with one camera replacing the MG FF cannon.

Bf 110B-3: Unarmed advanced trainer, modified from earlier variants. Retrofitted with improved radio flight instruments.

Bf 110C-0: Pre-production series, armed with two 20-mm MG FF cannons and four 7.92-mm MG 17 machine guns and one 7.92-mm MG 15 machine gun in the rear cockpit. Powered by two 1,100-hp DB 601 A-1 engines.

Bf 110C-1: *Zerstörer*, identical to Bf 110C-0 First major production variant.

Bf 110C-2: Fitted with revised electrical system, and *Telefunken* FuG 10 radio.

Bf 110C-3: Reconnaissance variant. Armed with improved 20-mm MG FF cannon (no external breech fairing), otherwise essentially similar to the Bf 110C-2.

Bf 110C-4: Powered by DB 601 A-1 engines, as well as featuring increased armour protection around the cockpit. Otherwise similar to the Bf 110C-2.

Bf 110C-4/B: *Jagdbomber*, ability to carry two 250-kg bombs beneath fuselage, powered by DB 601N engines. Fitted with Revi C12d gunsight. Ability to fly 45-degree dive bomber sorties. Operated by *Erprobungsgruppe* 210 against British targets.

Bf 110C-5: Reconnaissance variant, MG FF cannon deleted.

Bf 110C-6: Intended for bomber interception. Three Bf 110C-6s armed with one MK 101 cannon during the Battle of Britain. However, the armament mostly consisted of a 30-mm MK 103 cannon in ventral fairing, replacing the two 20-mm MG FF cannons.

Bf 110C-7: *Jagdbomber* featuring strengthened undercarriage and ability to carry two 500-kg bombs. Powered by DB 601 N engines.

Umrust-Bausätze

U1: Glider tug.
U2: Space for a third crew member.
U3: Increased fuselage and radiator armour protection.
U4: Increased engine armour protection.
U6: Increased coolant armour protection.

Bf 110D-0: Had extended range for operations in Norway, with large external 1,200-litre non-jettisonable belly tank, known as *Dackelbauch*, fitted. MG FF cannon deleted.

Bf 110D-1: External *Dackelbauch* belly tank deleted and replaced with ability to carry two 900-litre external drop tanks (one beneath each wing). MG FF cannon reinstalled.

Bf 110D-2: Ability to carry two 500-kg bombs on fuselage racks. Rear armament consisted of two MG 17s.

Bf 110D-3: Ability to carry bombs and two 300-litre or two 900-litre drop tanks.

Bf 110E-0: Pre-production series, had under-wing bomb racks for a total of four 50-kg bombs, in addition to fuselage bomb racks.

Bf 110E-1: Production variant. Featured extended tail section for stowage of dinghy.

Bf 110E-2: Powered by DB 601N engines. Could carry 2,000 kg of bombs.

Bf 110E-3: Reconnaissance variant, similar to the Bf 110C-5. MG FF cannon armament removed.

Bf 110F-0: Powered by 1,350-hp DB 601 F engines.

Bf 110F-1: Production variant, fitted with increased armour protection. Could carry up to 1,200 kg of bombs. Fitted with 57-mm bullet-resistant windscreen (retrofitted to earlier variants).

Bf 110F-2: Bomber destroyer variant, armed with WG 21 Dodel 21-cm rockets. ETC bomb racks deleted.

Bf 110F-3: Reconnaissance variant. MG FF cannon armament removed.

Bf 110F-4: Night fighter. First variant fitted with airborne radar.

Bf 110G-0: Pre-production variant, powered by DB 605B engines.

Bf 110G-1: *Jagdbomber*, not built.

Bf 110G-2: *Jagdbomber* and *Zerstörer*. Featured a revised tail section and strengthened undercarriage. The rear gunner's single MG 17 machine gun was replaced with twin MG 81Z machine guns. Entered service in January 1943. Sent into action against USAAF daylight raids. Could be modified with different *Rüstsätze* (field conversion kits).

Bf 110G-3: Reconnaissance variant, fitted with one Rb 50/30 and one Rb 70/30 camera. Front armament restricted to four 7.92-mm MG 17 machine guns.

Bf 110G-4: Night fighter, carried a crew of three, pilot, radar operator and gunner. Fitted with FuG 202 or FuG 220 AI radar. Heavy armament usually included *Schräge Musik*. Could be modified with different *Rüstsätze*.

Rüstsätze (Field Conversion Kits)

R1: Fitted with 37-mm Bk 37 (*Flak* 18) cannon in ventral fairing, which required the removal of the MG 151/20 cannons.
R2: Fitted with GM 1 power boost nitrous oxide injection system. The weight of the GM 1 resulted in the nose armament being removed.
R3: The four 7.92-mm MG 17 machine guns were replaced with two 30-mm MK 108 cannons. Ability to carry an ETC 500 bomb rack or a ventral fairing with two 20-mm MG 151/20 cannons.
R4: Combination of the R1 and R3 *Rüstsätzen.*
R5: Fitted with 37-mm Bk 37 (*Flak* 18) cannon or two 20-mm MG 151/20 cannons in a ventral fairing. Ability to carry an ETC 500 bomb rack. Fitted with Nos 1, 2, and 3 GM 1 power boost nitrous oxide injection systems.
R6: Fitted with Nos 2 and 3 GM 1 power boost nitrous oxide injection systems, ability to carry either two 20-mm MG 151/20 cannons in ventral fairing or ETC 500 bomb rack.
R7: Fitted with 30-mm MK 108 cannon and 540-litre fuel tank in the radio operator's compartment.
Umrustbausätze (factory installed conversion kits) for the Bf 110G.
U1: Twin 20-mm MG 151/20 cannons.
U5: FuG 202 and FuG 212 radar.
U6: Combination of U5 with FuG 221 radar.
U7: GM 1 Nitrous oxide power boost, increasing engine power with up to 300 hp during nineteen minutes. Required removal of rear gunners MG 81Z machine guns.
U8: Additional 540-litre fuel capacity.
U9: Replaced nose-mounted MG 17s with twin MK 108 cannons.

Planned Bf 110 Variants

It had been planned to replace the Bf 110G with Me 110H. Although design work on the Me 110H had been initiated in 1941, most of the improvements over the earlier variants, including the more powerful DB 605 engines, were subsequently introduced in the Bf 110G series (incidentally, by 1944, the designation of all Messerschmitt aircraft was changed from Bf to Me, hence the Me 110H). The Me 110H was to be powered by two DB 605 E engines, featuring increased armament consisting of two 30-mm MK 108 cannons and one MK 103 cannon. The proposed Bf 110H was also to be able to carry two 500-kg bombs beneath the fuselage, and four 50-kg bombs beneath the wings. The latter could be replaced by WG 21 '*Dödel*' air-to-air rockets. The Bf 110H was also to feature increased armour protection, as well as other refinements. The Me 110H was to be built by

Gotha, with preliminary design work commencing in late 1943. On 24 February 1944, the Bf 110H prototype was destroyed in an USAAF raid, which resulted in a severe setback for the project. In September 1944, all development work on the Bf 110H ended.

Me 110H-2: *Zerstörer* and multi-role aircraft. Increased wingspan of 18.58 metres with rounded wingtips, lengthened fuselage, retractable tail wheel, additional 115-litre fuel capacity and FuG 220 D radar.
Me 110H-2/R1: *Zerstörer.*
Me 110H-2/R2: *Zerstörer.* Basically similar to Me 110H-2/R1, with the addition of GM-1 nitrous oxide boost.
Me 110H-3: Projected reconnaissance variant, to be fitted with one Rb 50/30 camera and one Rb 75/30 camera.
Me 110H-4: Projected night fighter variant.
Me 110H-4/U7: Projected night fighter variant.
Me 110H-4/U8: Projected night fighter variant.

29

Messerschmitt Bf 110 Armament

Rheinmetall MG 15

A 7.92-mm machine gun with a seventy-five-round double-drum magazine. Total weight 12.4 kg with gunsight and cartridge bag. Rate of fire 1,000–1,050 rpm, and a muzzle velocity of 755 m/s. The MG 15 was the standard flexible-mount machine gun, fitted to the rear cockpit. Replaced by the MG 81Z on the Bf 110G.

Rheinmetall MG 17

A 500-round belt-fed machine gun. Weighing 10.2 kg, the 7.92-mm MG 17 had a rate of fire of 1,180 rpm, and a muzzle velocity of 950 m/s. Four fixed forward-firing MG 17s were fitted to the lower nose section of the Bf 110B to F variants.

Mauser MG 81

Belt-fed 7.92-mm machine gun weighing 6.35 kg, the MG 81 had a rate of fire of 1,600 rpm, with a muzzle velocity of 885 m/s. Two MG 81s were fitted in a flexible mount to the rear cockpit in the Bf 110G, being designated MG 81Z(willing).

Ikaria Werke Berlin MG FF

Drum-fed 20-mm cannon, with magazines having either thirty, forty-five, sixty, or ninety rounds. A derivative of the Swiss Oerlikon FF, the MG FF entered service in 1936. The FF suffix stands for *Flügel Fest*—i.e., fixed-forward firing. Although considered obsolete already in 1940, it continued in use until the end of the war. Weighing 26.3 kg, the MG FF had a rate of fire of 540 rpm, with a muzzle velocity of 700 m/s. Two MG FFs were the initial standard fixed forward-firing cannon armament of the early series Bf 110. In 1943, two MG FFs were also used in an experimental *Schräge Musik* installation Bf 110C-F, with many others following.

Mauser MG 151/20

Fixed forward-firing 20-mm cannon. Weight 42.5 kg, with a rate of fire of 750 rpm and muzzle velocity of 790 m/s, the MG 151/20 was used the Bf 110G, both as a fixed forward-firing armament in the nose section, as well as in a pod beneath the fuselage.

Rheinmetall-Borsig MK 103

Belt-fed 30-mm automatic cannon. Originally intended both as an anti-tank gun and air-to air weapon, the MK 103 weighed 141 kg, having 440 rpm and muzzle velocity of 860 m/s. Only Bf 110 operational use of the MK 103 was on the Bf 110C-6 bomber interceptor. Planned use included the Bf 110H variants.

Rheinmetall-Borsig MK 108

A 30-mm automatic cannon. Weighing 58 kg, and having 650 rpm, 540 m/s, it was introduced in 1943, and was used both as a fixed-forward firing cannon as well as for the *Schräge Musik* armament. The MK 108 was standard armament for many Luftwaffe aircraft, including the Bf 110G.

Rheinmetall-Borsig BK 3.7

A 37-mm automatic cannon, with BK being short for *Bordkanone* (literally, onboard cannon). Weighing 295 kg with a rate of fire of 160 rpm, and a muzzle velocity of 800–1,140 m/s, the BK 3.7 was an airborne development of the 37-mm *Flak* 18 anti-aircraft gun. One BK 3.7 was carried in a pod beneath the fuselage on the Bf 110G-4/R1, R4, and R5 for use against USAAF bombers. The BK 3.7 carried a total of seventy-two rounds.

Schräge Musik

The type of armament most associated with the Bf 110 is the *Schräge Musik*. Mounted in the upper centre fuselage, the *Schräge Musik* consisted of two machine guns or cannons firing upwards at a forward angle of between 60 and 72 degrees. A rough English translation of *Schräge Musik* is 'strange music, performed at odd time signatures'.

However, the use of such fixed, upward/forward firing armament was not a new invention. During the First World War, RFC B.E.2s were fitted with such armament to counter the nighttime Zeppelin raids. Later on, Sopwith Dolphin fighters were armed with two Lewis machine guns, firing obliquely. Interestingly, the idea of such an armament was also experimentally tested by the German pilot Gerhard Fieseler.

During the late 1920s, the Air Ministry specification F.29/27 called for a fighter to be equipped with a 1.5-inch (37-mm) COW cannon firing upwards resulted in the Vickers Type 161 and Westland COW fighters. Although flight trials were successful, none of the fighters entered production.

Before describing the development and use of the *Schräge Musik*, it might be of interest to describe, very briefly, the almost simultaneous Japanese development of such armament during the Second World War.

In the spring of 1943, the Imperial Japanese Naval Air Force modified a Nakajima J1N1 *Gekko* (code-named Irving) twin-engined fighter with two 20-mm cannons firing downward/forward with two more cannons firing upward/forward.

With USAAF night bombing raids against Rabaoul in New Guinea proving a nuisance, a *Gekko* fighter armed in this manner was to put an end to such raids. During the first sortie on 21 May 1943, one *Gekko* crew claimed to have shot down two B-17 Flying Fortresses. As a result, more *Gekkos* were modified, subsequently being used to combat the USAAF B-29 Superfortress raids over Japan. Other Imperial Japanese Navy and Army aircraft were also fitted with such armament, with varying success. Interestingly, the Japanese had no knowledge of the German *Schräge Musik* development.

In late 1941, *Oberleutnant* Rudolf Schoenert, then serving with 4./NJG 2, put forward the idea of fitting two machine guns firing upward/forward in a night fighter. A year later, flight and firing tests were made using a Dornier Do 17Z-10. Although the tests were successful, official interest was lukewarm. This particular type of armament was named *Schräge Musik*, which roughly translates as weird music played at odd time signatures. Having discussed the matter with *General der Nachtjagd* Josef Kammhuber in July 1943, Schoenert obtained authorisation to fit *Schräge Musik* armament to three Dornier Do 217Js. By this time, Schoenert had been promoted to *Gruppenkommendeur* of II./NJG 5. Closely involved in the development of *Schräge Musik* was an armourer of II./NJG 5, *Oberfeldwebel* Mahle, who fitted two 20-mm MG FF/M cannons to a Bf 110. The installation also included an optical reflector gun sight fitted to a roll bar, with the crosshair being projected against the cabin ceiling.

Already in May 1943, Schoenert had shot down a RAF bomber using *Schräge Musik*. During the last five months of 1943, Schoenert shot down another eighteen aircraft. The first operational use of *Schräge Musik* occurred during the night of 17–18 August 1943, during a RAF raid against Peenemünde. It was erroneously presumed that many of the bombers lost had been downed by *Flak*.

The Luftwaffe managed to keep *Schräge Musik* secret until late 1943, with a complete understanding of its effectiveness not being realised by the Allies until after the war had ended.

By mid-1944, about 30 per cent of all *Nachtjäger* aircraft were fitted with *Schräge Musik*. However, factory installation of *Schräge Musik* did not commence until the later summer/early autumn of 1944.

Wurfgranate 21 (W.Gr.21) '*Dödel*'

Introduced in late 1943 as an air-to-air weapon against USAAF heavy bombers, the *Wurfgranate* 21 consisted of 21-cm rocket tubes, firing 112-kg heavy unguided grenades, aimed by the pilot through a Revi 16B gunsight and fired electrically. It was nicknamed '*Dödel*', meaning fool.

Armament tested on the Bf 110

Rheinmetall-Borsig MK 101

This 30-mm cannon was tested on a Bf 110B-0 (D-AAPY). The cannon was intended for use against tanks and ships. The MK 101 was primarily used on the Henschel Hs 129, but also saw brief use on the Bf 110C-4 with *Erprobungsgruppe* 210.

Rheinmetall-Borsig RZ 65 (Föhn)

Air-to-air rocket. Developed in 1941, the RZ 65 was a rocket powered by a rocket engine. Despite promising trials, the RZ 65 was never used operationally on the Bf 110.

30

Airborne Intercept Radars

FuG 202 Lichtenstein BC

Developed by Telefunken, the FuG 202 search radar was developed from the Lichtenstein B high-altitude radio altimeter. Entering operational trials in August 1941, the FuG 202 Lichtenstein BC became the first mass-produced airborne intercept (AI) radar, weighing 24 kg (not including the antennas). Operating at the 490 MHz frequency band, having an output of 1.5 kW, the FuG 202 BC had a range of 3,500 to 200 metres, with a 65-degree search angle. The radar included four nose-mounted antennas, each of which had four dipoles with reflectors. The radar operator had three screens, providing range, azimuth, and elevation. On 9 May 1943, a Junkers Ju 88R-1 fitted with FuG 202 Lichtenstein BC radar defected to Britain, revealing its secrets (the Ju 88 is now preserved with the RAF Museum). The FuG 202 BC was rendered largely useless in the summer of 1943 through the introduction of Window. Consisting of small strips of aluminium foil, Window resulted in a mass of radar echoes, making it almost impossible to identify the RAF bombers.

FuG 212 Lichtenstein C-1

Developed by Telefunken and introduced in February 1943, the FuG 212 C-1 eventually replaced the FuG 202 BC. The whole weight, including antennas, was brought down to 60 kg. Operating at the 420–480 MHz frequency bands, the FuG 212 C-1 featured longer range and wider search angles. The radar screen display had two cathode-ray indicators. It remained in production for five months only, between June and November 1943.

FuG 218 Neptun IV

Introduced in January 1945 and developed jointly by Siemens and the Flugfunk Forschungsanstalt (Aviation Radio Research Establishment). Combined AI search radar and tail-mounted warning radar. Operated in the 158–187 MHz frequencies, having a range of between 5,000 and 120 metres, with a 120-degree search angle.

FuG 220 Lichtenstein SN-2

Introduced in September 1942, the FuG 220 was developed by Telefunken from the FuG 213 Lichtenstein S air-to-surface vessel (ASV) radar. It operated at 90 MHz, with a range of 900 metres. It was not affected in the same manner as the earlier FuG 202 BC and FuG 212 C-1 radars. The FuG 220 SN-2 required considerably larger antennas (usually referred to as *Hirschgeweih*, stag's antlers), which reduced overall performance. As had been the case with the FuG 202 BC, the British learned the secrets of the FuG 220 SN-2 through a Junkers Ju 88G-1 of 7./NJG 2, which landed by mistake at Woodbridge on 13 July 1944.

31

Foreign Operators

Apart from the Luftwaffe, Bf 110s saw service with a number of other air arms. These included some of Germany's allies, including Hungary, Italy, and Romania. Several other countries attempted to purchase Bf 110s, but for various reasons, none were delivered. Some sources claim that four Bf 110 prototypes were sent to Spain for combat evaluation prior to the end of the Spanish Civil War in March 1939. However, this is without foundation.

In May 1941, fourteen Bf 110s were adorned in Royal Iraqi Air Force colours for operations in support of Iraqi Prime Minister Rashid Ali. The story of these aircraft are told elsewhere in this book.

Requested, but Not Delivered

According to an April 1944 list for new aircraft to be delivered until 1 July 1945, the *Suomen Ilmavoimat* (Finnish Air Force) expected to take delivery of ninety Bf 110s (including thirty night fighters), with the first nine expected to arrive in October 1944. In the summer of 1944, a number of *Suomen Ilmavoimat* pilots were sent to Germany to undergo night fighting training. In the event, no Bf 110s were delivered to Finland, as a peace treaty with the USSR came into force on 4 September 1944.

The Americans erroneously believed that Bf 110s were flown by the Imperial Japanese Naval Air Force, even going as far as allotting the code name *Doc* for Japanese-flown Bf 110s. Post-combat reports by American pilots included the occasional mention of encountering Bf 110s. One such combat took place on 13 June 1942, when American Volunteer Group (AVG) pilot Bob Neale reported having encountered a variant of the Bf 110 during a raid against Kweilin. The type of aircraft encountered by Neale was, in fact, the Kawasaki Ki-45 *Toryu* (code-named Nick). No Bf 110s reached Japan, though.

In mid-1944, the *Slovenské Vzdušne Zbraně* (Slovakian Air Force, SVZ) planned to form a fighter squadron equipped with Bf 110s. Due to the Slovakian uprising in

August 1944, and the subsequent German occupation, no Bf 110s were delivered to the SVZ.

Flygvapnet (Swedish Air Force) made several attempts at acquiring Bf 110s in 1940–41, at one point seeking to purchase no less than 144 aircraft. A manufacturing licence for the Bf 110 was also sought, but this was refused by the RLM. Reportedly, one Swedish pilot, Fred Lambert-Müller was allowed to test fly a Bf 110 on 12 December 1940 as a way of saying *Vielen Dank* (thank you) after he had ferried a Focke-Wulf Fw 58 *Weihe* that had been interned in Sweden back to Kastrup in Denmark.

Fortuitously, a Bf 110E-1 of 1.(Z)/JG 77 which had force-landed in northern Sweden on 1 September 1941 was examined in great detail. Incidentally, the still-born Saab L 24 was of generally similar configuration to the Bf 110, although the former was to be fitted with a tri-cycle undercarriage.

The *Schweizer Flugwaffe* (Swiss Air Force) also showed interest in acquiring Bf 110s. On 16 September 1938, a Bf 110 was demonstrated to a Swiss delegation visiting Augsburg. In his report, the commander of the *Schweizer Flugwaffe, Oberstdivisionär* Hans Bandi, concluded that the Bf 110 indeed was the world's best aircraft in its class. This visit resulted in orders being placed for Bf 108s and Bf 109s, with no apparent interest being shown in the Bf 110. However, on 21 March 1939, the Swiss requested delivery of forty Bf 110s. This was turned down, as the Bf 110 was not yet cleared for export. In March 1943, renewed contact with Messerschmitt included the request for between twenty and thirty Bf 110 *Zerstörers*. None were delivered, though.

Nevertheless, a single Bf 110G was evaluated, albeit not flown, by the *Schweizer Flugwaffe*. That particular aircraft had been interned in March 1944.

Yugoslavia showed interest in acquiring Bf 110s, but export permission was curtly refused. Nevertheless, one Bf 110D was used in April 1941, albeit very briefly, by the VVKJ.

A number of other air arms, including the RAF and the USAAF, evaluated captured Bf 110s. One Bf 110 saw service with the *Armée de l'Air* in 1944–45. Interestingly, the Soviet Air Arm used Bf 110s operationally against the Luftwaffe.

In November 1945, the Danish government requested the transfer of two Bf 110s for instructional purposes. Nothing further is known, so it is presumed that this request was turned down.

It must be said that the British did not in any way encourage the post-war use of former Luftwaffe aircraft within their zone of influence, ensuring that all combat aircraft such as Bf 110s, Bf 109s, Fw 190s, etc., were reduced to scrap.

Non-Luftwaffe Bf 110 Operators

Croatia

In February 1945, two Bf 110G-4s were handed over to the *Hrvatska Zrakoplovna Izobrazbena Skupina* (Croatian Air Force Training Group, HZIS), at Wiener Neustadt. None of these Bf 110s saw service, with one being destroyed at Zagreb in an air raid and the second one being flown to Klagenfurt at the end of the war.

France

As related earlier, the French had made an unsuccessful attempt before the war to acquire a Bf 110 by cloak-and-dagger methods. During the final push to remove the German forces from French territory in 1944–45, several Luftwaffe aircraft were captured, and pressed into service with the *Armée de l'Air*. Among these was one Bf 110 day fighter variant (former identity unknown). The aircraft had been captured at La Martinerie airfield, 230 km south of Paris. The Bf 110, serial number 3, was on charge with GB I/34 *Bearn*, also being reported to have served with *Escadron de Ravitaillement en vol 2/93 Aunis* and GR III/33 *Perigord*. The Bf 110 was rarely flown, usually carrying VIPs aloft. The aircraft was subsequently transferred to the CEV test establishment at Brétigny, presumably being scrapped shortly afterwards.

Great Britain

On 21 July 1940, a Bf 110C-5 5F+CM (W Nr 2177) of *Aufklärungsgruppe* 14 (4.(F)14) was shot down by 238 Sqn Hurricanes. Deemed repairable, parts of another Bf 110C-5, coded 2N+EP (W Nr unknown) which had been shot down at Povington Heath on 11 July 1940 was used in the rebuild to airworthy condition. This work was carried out at RAE Farnborough.

Issued with the RAF serial number AX772, the Bf 110 flew for the first time in British hands on 25 October 1940. Between October 1940 and October 1941, AX772 accumulated 26:55 hours in the air. Most of the flight testing concerned handling and performance characteristics. On 13 October 1941, AX772 was transferred to the Air Fighting Defence Unit (AFDU) at Duxford. Some months late, on 5 March 1942, the Bf 110 was transferred to No. 1426 Flight, based at Tangmere, which operated a number of different former Luftwaffe aircraft for evaluation purposes, also touring RAF and USAAF bases to assist in recognition of Luftwaffe aircraft. Remaining on charge with No. 1426 Flight until 1 November 1945, the Bf 110 was then transferred to 47 MU at Sealand, although it appears likely that the aircraft remained at Tangmere until early 1946. Sadly, this historic Bf 110 was scrapped at 34 MU Sleap in late 1947 to early 1948.

One Bf 110D (W Nr 4035) of 4./ZG 76 which had come down near Fallujah, Iraq, in May 1941was restored to flying condition. The story of this particular aircraft and its recovery included some hair-raising moments.

After an abandoned aircraft had been observed about 50 km south-east of RAF Habbaniya, an RAF intelligence officer, Grp Capt. James Pelly-Fry, argued for the recovery of the aircraft. It was thought that the aircraft was a Bf 110. On 1 June, two armoured vehicles accompanied by a Tiger Moth, located the Bf 110. Pelly-Fry then began inspecting the downed aircraft:

> Some sixth sense prompted me to tell everybody to keep well back whilst I walked up to the aircraft. The Germans fitted a self-destruct system; often also capable of being used as a booby trap.
>
> Fortunately, what I was looking for was on the ground underneath the tailplane; a 'black box' with the simple inscription '4Kg' painted on the side. About 9lb of explosive set to go. I could see the wiring from the thing disappearing into the fuselage.
>
> By now the troops were well aware of the implications—and so was I. Whilst I carefully examined the sinister black box and then walked right round the machine almost on tip-toe, the lads took up the extraordinary Red Indian habit of circulating around and around at a respectable distance. Well, nothing to it now. Wire cutters severed the leads, a final look around, and then with the adrenalin flowing like crazy, I climbed onto the wing and peered into the cockpits. Sure enough, all had been set to blow up when the first chap opened the pilot's sliding roof.
>
> When no further booby traps had been seen, the lads moved in—very warily I confess. Nothing at all to indicate why that Bf 110 had force-landed—this from the preliminary inspection. We never did find out. Also seen were the footprints of the crew going across the desert in an easterly direction. Again, we never found out what happened to them, although on the return flight we searched as best we could.[1]

The following day, the Bf 110 was lifted, and the undercarriage lowered. The aircraft was then towed to Habbaniya. Using the spares inventory left behind at Mosul by the Germans, work of returning the Bf 110 to airworthy condition proceeded swiftly.

Named *Belle of Berlin*, the Bf 110 was air-tested at RAF Habbaniya on 5 September 1941 by Sqn Ldr Al Bocking (11 Sqn). Additional flights were made on 11 and 14 September, after which the Bf 110 was ferried to Heliopolis in Egypt. By 16 December, the Bf 110 was on charge with 267 Squadron, with the squadron codes KW being painted on the aircraft. According to RAF records, a Bf 110 was taken on charge in the Middle East on 1 January 1942, being assigned the serial number HK846. In all likelihood, HK846 was *Belle of Berlin*.

Over three and a half months, the Bf 110 accumulated 23:05 hrs in the air. Among the pilots given the opportunity to fly the Bf 110 were Tony Dudgeon and James Pelly-Fry. In March 1942, the aircraft was most likely transferred to 89 Squadron. It is said to have remained with this unit until October 1942 (incidentally, published photographs of a Bf 110 in RAF markings carrying the code letter G possibly show *Belle of Berlin*. Hypothetically, the G code could have been short for German).

It was then decided to fly the Bf 110 to South Africa. However, during the ferry flight south, with Flt Lt Alec Noon at the controls, the aircraft was damaged beyond repair when attempting to land at Atbara, Sudan. The cause was due to the undercarriage having failed to lock in the down position.

Post-war, one Bf 110G (W Nr 180850) was selected for preservation by the Air Historical Branch (AHB). By January 1946, the aircraft arrived at 47 MU Sealand. Later transferred to RAF Stanmore Park for care-taking by the German Air Force Equipment Centre (GAFEC), it was used as set dressing for the movie *Angels One Five*, shot at RAF Kenley in 1952. Apparently, the Bf 110 was in poor condition, being scrapped soon after the filming ended.

Immediately following the end of the war, a total of seven late-model Bf 110Gs were allocated Air Ministry (AM) serial numbers. One of these, AM 34, still survive with the RAF Museum. The history of this particular Bf 110 can be found on p. 148.

AM15 Bf 110G-4/R8 3C+BA (W Nr 180560) of NJG 4. Fitted with FuG 218 radar. Surrendered at Eggebek, and ferried to Schleswig on 14 June 1945, continuing to Britain 23 June. Transferred to the Fighter Interception Development Squadron/Night Fighter Leader School of the Central Fighter Establishment at Tangmere. Most likely present at RAE Farnborough on 13 December 1945. The Bf 110 was struck off charge on 30 May 1946 and subsequently scrapped. Erroneously, this aircraft has been attributed as having been personal aircraft of *Major* Schnaufer, NJG 4's *Geschwaderkommodore*.

AM 30 Bf 110G-4/R3 D5+DK (W Nr 730037) of I./NJG 3. Surrendered at Grove, Denmark. Fitted with FuG 202 and FuG 220 radars. A publicity photo, showing former Luftwaffe personnel painting RAF insignia and 'AIR MINISTRY 30' on the aircraft has appeared in many publications. The Bf 110 arrived at Farnborough on 12 September 1945, being on static display during the German Aircraft Exhibition held at Farnborough in October–November 1945. Noted dumped at Farnborough on 15 December 1946, and presumed scrapped shortly afterwards.

AM 34 Bf 110G-4/R6 D5+RL (W Nr 730301) of I./NJG 3. Surrendered at Grove, Denmark. Fitted with FuG 220 radar. Left Grove on 1 August 1945, being ferried to Schleswig by Sqn Ldr Ian Sommerville. Preserved at RAF Museum (see p. 148).

AM 38 Bf 110G-4/R8 D5+DM (W Nr 180551) of II./NJG 3. Surrendered at Copenhagen-Kastrup, Denmark. Apparently, this particular Bf 110 was not flown to Britain.

AM 85 Bf 110G-5/R1 (W Nr 420031). Possibly surrendered at Eggebek. As with AM 15 (see above), it has been alleged that this Bf 110 had been the personal mount of Major Heinz Wolfgang Schnaufer. This remains unsubstantiated, though. On 28 July, the Bf 110 was ferried from Schleswig to Farnborough by Flt Lt Edwards. On

2 August, a brief test flight was made. The next day, the Bf 110 made a return flight Farnborough–Northolt–Farnborough. The final flight appears to have occurred on 9 August, when US test pilot Jack Woolams ferried the Bf 110 to 6 MU Brize Norton. The aircraft was struck off charge at Brize Norton on 14 August 1947.

AM 86 Bf 110G. Precise information is lacking on this particular Bf 110. Although ferried from Knokke in Belgium to RAF Manston on 18 October 1945, it seems that the aircraft did not reach RAE Farnborough.

AM 88 Bf 110G. No unit, code, or W Nr known. Possibly used by JG 400 to tow Me 163 rocket fighters on ferry flights. Such aircraft were known as *Doppelschlepp* tugs. Air tested at Husum (a former JG 400 base), on 23 October 1945 by Sqn Ldr McCarthy (this may, incidentally, have been the last flight of a Bf 110). Nothing further known.

Hungary

During the night of 4–5 September 1942, Soviet bombers unexpectedly raided Budapest for the first time. A second raid followed on 9–10 September. These raids sent shock waves through the Hungarian High Command. As the *Magyar Kiralyi Honved Legierö* (Royal Hungarian Home Defence Air Force, MKHL), lacked night fighters, an urgent request was despatched to Berlin. In the end, the Commander of an MKHL long-range reconnaissance squadron, *Ezredes* (Colonel) Edgár Kekz, managed to persuade his old friend, *Reichsmarschall* Hermann Göring, to supply night fighters to Hungary.

According to German sources, three 'Bf 110Js' were delivered to the MKHL in 1943. One Bf 110 was photographed at Budapest-Budaörs on 10 July 1943, with three being in service by October 1943. These three aircraft, one Bf 110F-4 and possibly a pair of Bf 110Gs, lacked radar. This meant that any night intercepts had to be assisted by ground control radar, and/or searchlights. The Bf 110s were assigned to the *5/1 éjjeli vadászrepülö-század* (5/1 Night Fighter Squadron), known as *Bagoly* (Owl) and based at *Budapest-Mátyasfold*. A few obsolete Fiat CR.42 biplanes initially served alongside the Bf 110s. Although the serial numbers V.951–953 were allotted to the Bf 110s, it is unclear if these markings were actually painted on the respective aircraft.

With Hungary having acquired a manufacturing licence for the Me 210, an *Ausbildungskommando-Zerstörer* (Heavy Fighter Training Unit, ABK-Z) for the training of MKHL aircrew was established in May 1943. Based at Budapest-Ferihegy and led by *Oberleutnant* Hans-Arnim Weirich, the ABK-Z had about twenty-five Bf 110C-4s. As the Bf 110s lacked dual controls, some of the training was performed using MKHL Fw 58 Weihe's. The major stumbling block between the German instructors and the Hungarian pilots was the language barrier. Nevertheless, most of the Hungarians had a working knowledge of German, ably assisting their colleagues during the training schedule. There was only one minor accident during this time. When taking off, one MKHL pilot forgot to open the fuel valve of the port engine. The Bf 110 was slightly damaged in the ensuing forced landing.

In 1942, an MKHL ground training unit was formed at *Újvidék* (present-day Novi Sad in Serbia). The following year, two Bf 110s and two Me 210s were delivered to this unit.

By 9 March 1944, Hungarian-built Me 210Ca's, modified as night fighters, had entered service with the 5/1 NFS. However, the 5/1 NFS only saw combat during day-time operations, with little success. Responsibility for night fighter operations over Hungary remained with the Luftwaffe.

On 19 March 1944, German forces occupied Hungary. This was due to the Hungarian leader, Admiral Miklos Horthy, having conducted secret peace talks with the Allies. Nevertheless, MKHL operations were not affected. In May 1944, a night fighter training course, led by Luftwaffe instructors, began at Tápiószentmerton. Three early model Bf 110s were used. On 23 September 1944, an initial group of fourteen MKHL personnel were sent to Ohlau (present-day Oława in Poland) for Bf 110G-4 conversion training with the resident NJG 102. The MKHL crews became known as 6./NJG 102. One pilot, *Szakaszvezetö* (Sergeant) József Zimmermann, strayed across the frontline, becoming a POW after making a forced landing on the Soviet side.

In October 1944, the 5/1 NFS was renamed as the *101. éjjeli vadászszázad* (101 Night Fighter Squadron). Its commanding officer, *Százados* Adam Krúdy, was charged with treason, being replaced by *Százados* János Hollós.

Having completed their training, the first group of MKHL crews returned to Hungary. A second group of pilots and radar operators arrived at Ohlau in late December 1944. In mid-January 1945, the conversion training was transferred to Prague-Kbely. However, few flights were undertaken, partly due to a severe lack of fuel. During one training sortie, one crew ended up on the Soviet side. Although taken prisoner, they eventually managed to cross the frontline and return to their unit.

Around this time, the 101 NFS was based at Csorna in western Hungary. A total of twelve Bf 110G-4s were delivered. These Bf 110s were finished in MKHL markings, with the serial numbers M.101 to 112 being allotted. Plans for the establishment of a second night fighter squadron remained unfulfilled. With most of Hungary being occupied by Soviet forces, the 101 NFS moved to Wiener-Neustadt outside Vienna, Austria. Four aircraft were based at Parndorf, with a few sorties being made. The main task of the 101 NFS was to provide escort for transport aircraft delivering supplies to the beleaguered Hungarian capitol. These sorties involved flying at an altitude of between 3,000 and 4,000 metres, lasting between one hour and up to two and a half hours.

Plans to replace the Bf 110G-4s with more effective Junkers Ju 88G or Dornier Do 335 night fighters were not proceeded with. By early April, the remaining Bf 110Gs at Parndorf were burnt to prevent capture. The 101 NFS personnel then marched to Ingolstadt before surrendering to US Army units.

Italy

When Italy declared war on Britain and France on 10 June 1940, the *Regia Aeronautica* (Royal Air Force, RA) had no night fighting capability. Little resources were spent on night fighters until RAF bombers began to pay regular visits to northern Italian cities. As a result, a few Fiat CR.42 and Reggiane Re.2000CN fighters were modified for the nocturnal fighting role. These had little success, though. In January 1942, a delegation led by *Gen.* Attilio Biseo, visited Germany, touring Luftwaffe night fighter units and ground radar installations. The subsequent report included a request for twenty-four Bf 110C-3 night fighters to be delivered as an interim measure, with the indigenous Caproni Ca.331B showing great promise for the future.

Work on an RA night fighter infrastructure commenced on 15 February 1942, when two training units were formed. A bomber unit, the 41° *Stormo*, was to reform as a night fighter unit. The 41° *Stormo* consisted of the 59th and 60th *Gruppi* which had two squadrons each, the 232, 233, 234, and 235 *Squadriglias.*

In June 1942, RA crews left for Germany to undergo training on the Bf 110. Upon their return to Italy the following month, they brought along two used Bf 110C-3s, W Nr 964 and 1358. Also in July 1942, *Generalleutnant* Josef Kammhuber paid a visit to Italy, during which Dornier Do 217J night fighters were offered instead of Bf 110C-3s, as the latter was out of production, as well as obsolete. Two Do 217 sub-variants were be delivered, the Do 217J-1 which lacked radar, and the Do 217J-2 which had radar. A third Bf 110C-3, W Nr 1804, was also to be supplied. The price for the Bf 110s was 374,500 *Reichmark*. Additionally, Kammhuber offered assistance in establishing of a chain of radar ground stations.

Based on the respective *Werk Nummern*, the Bf 110s had originally been built as Bf 110C-1s. All had accumulated a considerable number of flying hours prior to delivery, with W Nr 964 having flown for 300 hours, W Nr 1358 for 254 hours, and W Nr 1804 for 174 hours. The Italian serials were the same as the respective *Werk Nummern*, i.e., M.M.964, M.M.1358, and M.M.1804.

The Italians expressed disappointment that the Bf 110s were augmented with the Do 217J, a converted medium bomber. Reportedly, the RA crews disliked the Do 217Js.

Nevertheless, as the Bf 110C-3s lacked radar, they were virtually useless as night fighters. The trio of Bf 110s were assigned to the 235a *squadriglia*, based at Lonate Pozzolo, along with a few Do 217Js. The first operational sortie was flown on 21 October, with the Bf 110s being ordered to patrol the airspace north of Turin. Only two of the Bf 110s participated, with M.M.964 being unserviceable.

Little information on the operational activities of the 235a *squadriglia* Bf 110s have survived. In February 1943, M.M.1804 was written off in a crash. On 27 June 1943, the two remaining Bf 110s were still listed as operational. However, they were withdrawn from use soon afterwards. Seen in retrospect, the RA night fighting operations failed to stop the RAF raids. Only one success for the German-supplied Do 217s was recorded. On the night of 16–17 July 1943, an RA Do 217J-1 was used to shoot down a 207 Sqn Lancaster (DV 183, coded EM-W), which crashed near Vigevano.

Romania

The *Aeronautica Regâlã Romåna* (Royal Romanian Aeronautics, ARR) operated about twenty-four Bf 110C, D, and Fs in the night fighting role. With Soviet bombers having made intermittent night raids against Bucharest in 1941 and 1942, the ARR High Command decided to form a night fighter squadron. It was also expected that RAF and USAAF bombers would soon arrive over the Romanian capitol. In September 1942, eleven pilots (mostly from *Escadrila 51 vânãtoare*) transferred to Tecuci air base to initiate night fighter training. In early 1943, the new unit, known as *Escadrila 51 vânãtoare de noapte* (51 Night Fighter Squadron), was formed at Bucharest-Pipera. Commanded by *Cãptan aviator* Marin Ghica, the 51 NFS was also known as 12./NJG 6. Together two additional squadrons, Nos 10 and 11, the unit, subsequently renamed *Escadrila 1 vânãtoare de noapte* (1 Night Fighter Group, 1 NFS).

The unit saw action on 1 August 1943 during the large USAAF raid against the oil refineries at Ploesti, with one Bf 110C being lost. On 13 March 1944, Bf 110C 2Z+FW (W Nr 973) was damaged in a landing accident at Zilistea. The *coup d'état* on 23 August 1944 resulted in Romania breaking away from its erstwhile German ally. Clashes between Luftwaffe and ARR aircraft saw two Luftwaffe Bf 110s being shot down on 26 August. About 200 Luftwaffe aircraft were captured by Romanian forces, this number apparently including a few Bf 110s. One former NJG 6 Bf 110 was subsequently used as a high-speed liaison aircraft, being present at Trencin, Slovakia, in April 1945. The ARR Bf 110s were flown in Luftwaffe colours and markings, including *Stammkennzeichen*, although at least one aircraft was adorned with ARR national insignia. No aerial victories were achieved by the ARR Bf 110 crews.

Switzerland

Although the *Schweizer Flugwaffe* (Swiss Air Force) never operated Bf 110s, that type of aircraft nevertheless has a very interesting Swiss connection. On 6 February 1944, a Bf 110G-4/B2 of I./NJG 6, coded VQ+KL (W Nr 5338), belly landed at Cras de Coeuve. Discovering themselves to have arrived in Switzerland, the crew, *Leutnant* Bruno Lange (pilot) and *Obergefreiter* Günther Achterberg (radio operator), immediately hid all documents, also attempting to destroy the FuG 202 radar. This was prevented by Swiss troops that arrived on the scene.

The Bf 110 was then dismantled, and brought to Dübendorf, where it was studied in great detail.

Only five weeks later, on 15 March 1944, another Bf 110G-4 made an unscheduled arrival in Switzerland. This particular Bf 110 was coded 2Z+OP (W

Nr 5547) and belonged to 6./NJG 6. Flown by *Ofw* Helmut Treynogga and *Uffz.* Heinz Schwarz, the Bf 110 was forced to land at Dübendorf at 11:47 p.m. on 15 March 1944. Although the crew were soon repatriated, the Bf 110G remained in Switzerland. The night fighter, and its armament and radar in particular, was studied in great detail by the Swiss. Although the Bf 110 was adorned with *Schweizer Flugwaffe* insignia, it remained firmly grounded. The aircraft was still present at Dübendorf in April 1947, being scrapped soon afterwards.

As described elsewhere, a third Bf 110G also arrived at Dübendorf in 1944. This particular aircraft caused a high-level diplomatic crisis, eventually being blown up at the request of the Germans.

USA

In the autumn of 1940, one 2./*Erprobungsgruppe* 210 Bf 110D, coded S9+CK (W Nr 3341), shot down on 15 August 1940 was sent across the Atlantic to US aircraft manufacturer Vultee. This Bf 110 subsequently became the subject of a very detailed technical assessment. Although the exact fate of the aircraft is unknown, it may be presumed that it was scrapped after having outlived its usefulness.

In early 1943, a former ZG 1 Bf 110D was noted at the USAAF's 12th Air Force Fighter Training School at Constantine, Algeria. Although USAAF markings had been painted on the fuselage and fins/rudders, the ZG 1 *Wespe* insignia still appeared on the nose. It is unclear if this particular Bf 110 was air-tested while in USAAF hands, but it seems likely that at least one test flight was made, possibly resulting in a belly landing.

Although many former Luftwaffe aircraft were taken to the USA following the end of the war for evaluation, this did not include any Bf 110s.

USSR

Although the cooperation between Germany and the USSR can be traced to the early 1920s, the Molotov-Ribbentrop non-aggression pact, signed in August 1939, deepened relations between the countries. A Soviet delegation arrived in Germany, touring factories of various aircraft manufacturers. A German-Soviet trade agreement, signed on 11 February 1940, resulted in orders for the latest German aircraft and miscellaneous aviation technology.

Five Bf 110s as well as replacement engines were among the various aircraft included in the trade agreement. According to a message sent to Stalin and Foreign Secretary Molotov: 'Following an intermediate landing at Welikije Luki, five Messerschmitt Me 110s landed at Moscow's central airport at 1850 hrs on 28 April'.[2]

Upon arrival, the Bf 110s were evaluated at the NII VVS and LII test establishments. An optical flight data recorder was installed in a Bf 110 at the NII VVS. At the LII, one Bf 110 was demonstrated to a member of the Tupolev OKB (construction bureau) Alexandr A. Arkangelskiy (incidentally, the head of the Tupolev OKB, Oleg Tupolev, had earlier been accused of secretly forwarding information of his designs to the Germans, making it possible for Messerschmitt to produce the Bf 110).

Although having a powerful armament, it was thought that the Bf 110 could only operate successfully as a bomber, due to its lack of performance. Nevertheless, the flying qualities were deemed to be excellent: '[The Bf 110] can be flown for quite a long time with hand[s]-off, free, controls.... From the point of view of flying procedures, the aircraft could be flown by pilots of average and below average skills'.[3]

TsAGI subsequently prepared a report on the Bf 110, covering the control surfaces effectiveness, control lever loads, as well as crew comfort and visibility. One Bf 110 was also employed to test the Soviet 23-mm MP-6 experimental cannon.

A second Soviet delegation visited Germany in February–March 1941, placing orders for additional Bf 110s. During this trip, a captured Spitfire and a Curtiss Hawk were demonstrated at an airfield near Berlin. A Russian pilot was allowed to fly both the Spitfire and Hawk, with flight characteristics of the former apparently leaving a particularly good impression.

Following the commencement of the German invasion on 22 June 1941, a special reconnaissance unit, equipped with a dozen German aircraft, including three Bf 110s as well as Dornier Do 215s, Junkers Ju 88s, and Bf 109s, was formed. Commanded by Major Valentin I. Khomyakov (a former Spanish Civil War veteran and NII VVS test pilot), the unit was to fly long-range reconnaissance sorties over German territory. Interestingly, some of the unit's pilots were Spanish, having arrived in the USSR following *Generalissimo* Franco's victory in March 1939. Only a few sorties were flown, though, primarily using the Do 215s.

One Bf 110 forced down near Leningrad in September 1941 by 158 IAP PVO fighter pilot Ivan Ye. Plekhanov was studied by technical personnel. The Bf 110 was named *Ivan's Laboratory*, but it is believed that it was never flown.

In late 1942, one Bf 110 was used by the 750 AP ADD long-range bomber regiment to fly clandestine sorties. Flown by Senior Lieutenant Vyacheslav G. Opalev and Yevgeni Okorokov, one Luftwaffe Ju 88 had been shot down on the first sortie. About ten sorties were flown before the Bf 110 was shot down in error over Tula by Soviet *Flak*, with Opalev managing to bale out safely. Other captured Bf 110s are said to have been used for similar purposes.

A Bf 110 was included in a huge exhibition of captured German hardware, held at *Park Kultury* (Culture Park) in Moscow in late June 1943.

One former Romanian Bf 110 was painted in Soviet Red Star insignia, and test flown by the 83 GIAP at Otopeni in late 1944. One Bf 110G-4/R4 coded G9+AA (W Nr 140655) which had landed in Sweden was subsequently transferred dismantled to the USSR on 8 November 1945.

Yugoslavia

Although the Yugoslavian Air Force, the *Vazduhoplovstvo Vojske Kraljeve Jugoslavije* (Royal Yugoslav Air Force, VVKJ), attempted to acquire Bf 110s in 1939–40, none were delivered. The *Reichsluftfahrtministerium* curtly replied that the Bf 110 was not intended for export. On 1 April 1941, a Luftwaffe Bf 110C-4 landed at Kraljevo due to navigational error.

The three Germans aboard stated that following take-off from Vienna, they had become disorientated due to poor weather. Instead of arriving at the intended destination, Turnu Severin in Romania, they landed at Kraljevo at 6:30 p.m. Instead of immediately returning the Bf 110 to the Luftwaffe, orders were received to disassemble the aeroplane for a detailed technical assessment. Less than one week later, on 6 April, the Germans invaded Yugoslavia.

The following day, the Bf 110 was transferred to Belgrade, and then to Veliki Radinci. Prior to the flight, the Bf 110 was painted in VVKJ camouflage. Nevertheless, Yugoslav anti-aircraft artillery opened fire on the Bf 110. Upon touching down at Veliki Radinci, the pilot discovered that the brakes were inoperable. The aircraft never flew again, being deliberately burnt on 12 April to prevent it from being captured by the Germans. Unfortunately, the identity of this particular Bf 110C-4 remains unknown. Nor are any photographs of the Bf 110 known. Allegedly, it carried the *Haifisch* (shark's mouth) insignia on the nose when it landed at Kraljevo, thus indicating a ZG 76 aircraft.

One of the two Bf 110s delivered to Croatia survived the war but was not used by the post-war Yugoslav Air Force.

32

Preservation

Only a few Bf 110s has survived. Considering the large numbers lost during the war, and the (almost) wholesale scrapping of former Luftwaffe aircraft in the immediate post-war era, this is hardly surprising. The best-known preserved aircraft is a Bf 110G on display at the RAF Museum. For many years, it was the only one of its kind on display.

During the early 1950s, the fuselage of a Bf 110 was on display at the Frunze Aviation Museum in Moscow. It is presumed that this aircraft was later scrapped at an undetermined date.

Following the breakdown of the USSR in 1991, many former Luftwaffe aircraft, including a few Bf 110s, were recovered from crash sites in Russia. One such Bf 110 was completely restored and put on display at the Berlin Technical Museum. Other Bf 110s recovered from Russia are under restoration or in storage in Germany, Italy, and Norway, with a full-scale replica containing many original components being on display in Denmark. With the Russian-Ukrainian conflict, and the resulting sanctions against the former nation, it appears unlikely that further wrecks of former Luftwaffe aircraft will be recovered on behalf of western aviation museums and collectors.

Reportedly, an intact Bf 110 still resides in a lake in northern Germany, where it was dumped following the end of the war.

Although some efforts to restore a Bf 110 to airworthiness have been initiated, none has, so far, been returned to the air. Given the amount of work necessary, as well as money, it seems likely that no Bf 110 will be returned to airworthy condition.

Small parts from three Bf 110s, W Nr 5637 (partly burnt), 73510, and 110155, are stored at Tikkakoski with the Finnish Air Force Museum. Parts also survive in Austria, Norway, and Russia.

Denmark

A remarkable Bf 110G replica containing a fair amount of original components can be found at Gilleleje, Denmark. The replica is the work of the gardener Henrik Mortensen. In the early 1990s, Mortensen acquired an original instrument panel from a Bf 110. Not content with this, he began construction of a cockpit section which eventually grew into a forward fuselage. An original, albeit damaged left wing was then added. Missing components were built out of sheet metal and glass fibre. The aircraft has been placed in a diorama setting, with parts of a Luftwaffe *Nachtjagd* base having been reconstructed.

Germany

Since the 1990s, several Bf 110s have been returned to Germany, although only one has been restored for static museum display.

Technikmuseum Speyer, Speyer

The wings of an early production Bf 110D-0 (W Nr 3154) are on display at Sinsheim. This particular Bf 110 has an interesting history. Serving with 2./ZG 76 as NO+DS during Operation Weserübung, the Bf 110 suffered damage from RAF Gladiators on 24 May 1940. With damaged oil lines, the crew, *Fw.* Neureiter and *Stabsing*. Thönes, had to belly land on the ice on Lake Upmasjaure in northern Sweden. Neureiter and Thönes subsequently removed the rear-mounted MG 15, firing into the fuselage in order to disable the aircraft. Two days later, a Heinkel He 59 of *Seenotkommando* 1 landed on the thawing ice, successfully rescuing the Bf 110 crew. When the ice melted, the Bf 110 sank. The wreck lay undisturbed until 1946, when it was discovered by fishermen. Several attempts at recovering the Bf 110 were subsequently made, but it was not until 1995 that the aircraft was finally recovered. Tentative plans to keep the Bf 110 in Sweden for museum purposes came to nothing, and the wreck was sold to Germany. Both wings, stabiliser, and part of the fuselage are on display in an unrestored state at the Technikmuseum at Speyer.

Deutsches Technikmuseum, Berlin

W Nr 5052
StkZ TI+LE
LN+NR

Completed in August 1942, this Bf 110F-2 *trop* was delivered to 13./(Z)JG 5. It would appear that this particular Bf 110 was modified from Bf 110C-1 W Nr 3084.

During a raid against the Murmansk railway on 11 January 1943, the Bf 110 sustained damage from ground fire. With a damaged starboard engine, and one fuel tank set on fire, a belly landing was made on the frozen surface of Lake Pyavozero. The crew, *Lt* Helmut Ziegenhagen and *Uffz.* Franz Kirchmayer, were lightly injured, being located by a Finnish army patrol the following day. Ziegenhagen and Kirchmayer were then picked up by a Luftwaffe Fi 156 *Storch*.

When the ice melted, the Bf 110 sank to a depth of two metres, remaining there until discovered in the early 1990s. In late 1992, the Bf 110 was recovered by means of a Mil Mi-6 helicopter on behalf of British enthusiast Jim Pearce, and transported to Britain, arriving at Pearce's Sussex workshop in December. Upon close inspection, it was discovered that the aircraft was in very good condition, with a restoration to airworthiness being one option. In the event, the aircraft, along with the other Bf 110 wrecks owned by Pearce, was sold to Tim Wallis of the Alpine Fighter Collection in New Zealand. In April 1994, the Bf 110 arrived in New Zealand. However, it was subsequently sold to the Technikmuseum Berlin, with parts from other Bf 110s being used to restore the Bf 110F-2.

The Bf 110 was restored to static condition at Friedrichshafen, being rolled-out on 16 September 2000 following eighteen months of restoration work.

The museum also has components of Bf 110E-2 W Nr 4502 and Bf 110C-4 W Nr 3235 (LN+ER of 1./(Z)JG 77, both recovered in Russia and obtained in 1994 by the Alpine Fighter Collection in New Zealand. Both eventually ended up with the Technikmuseum in Berlin.

W Nr 3235 LN+ER of 1./(Z)JG 77 was lost near Murmansk on 5 July 1941. Both crew, *Lt* Weyergang and *Uffz.* Triggers, were killed. In 1992, major components of this Bf 110, including both engines, and parts of the wings and fuselage were obtained by Jim Pearce. Sold to the Alpine Fighter Collection, and then to Technikmuseum, Berlin. Parts incorporated in the static restoration of W Nr 5052.

W Nr 4502 M8+ZE A was a replacement aircraft, transferred from IV./ZG 76 to 10.(Z)/JG 5 On 11 March 1942, the Bf 110 was shot down by Russian fighter during a raid against Murmaschi airfield near Murmansk, 25 miles west of Murmaschi. Emil Gross was badly wounded and Gerhard Sarodnik was slightly injured. The badly wounded Gross pleaded to Sarodnik to perform a mercy killing, believing this to be a much better option than spending time in a Soviet POW camp. In the event, both Gross and Sarodnik were rescued the following day by a Fi 156 *Storch*. Both Gross and Sarodnik survived the war. Although souvenir hunters paid the occasional visit to the wreck of the Bf 110, it lay mostly undisturbed. In 1992, Jim Pearce managed to obtain the Bf 110. Unfortunately, the aircraft sustained damage during the recovery, with the windscreen and one of the fins being stolen *en route* to the UK. The Alpine Fighter Collection then bought the Bf 110.

Great Britain

Imperial War Museum, Duxford

Possibly the most historic Bf 110 to survive (albeit consisting only of an incomplete and battered fuselage and various other, smaller parts) is Bf 110E-1/N VJ+OQ (W Nr 3869). This particular aircraft was used by Rudolf Hess on his infamous flight to Britain on 10 May 1941. Preserved by the Imperial War Museum, a 5.3-metre section of the rear fuselage and one DB 601A engine can be seen at Duxford (the second DB 601 A engine is preserved by the RAF Museum at Hendon). Other smaller parts from Hess's Bf 110 kept by the IWM includes a section showing the *Balkenkreutz* national insignia, cut from the rear fuselage, on display at IWM North Stretford. An aneroid altimeter and temperature gauge remains in storage.

A section cut from the fuselage, measuring 44 × 58 cm, and hidden away by a farmer following Hess's arrival in Scotland, was sold in 2014 to the US-based The War Museum for a staggering $8,125.

RAF Museum, Hendon

W Nr 730301
D5+RL
AM 34
8479M

For many years, the Bf 110G-4/R6 preserved with the RAF Museum was the only one of its kind on display anywhere in the world. Probably built in 1944, its wartime service is unclear. In May 1945, the Bf 110 was surrendered at Grove (now known as Karup), Denmark. The aircraft carried the code D5+RL, indicating 1./NJG 3. Fitted with a FuG 220b Lichtenstein SN-2 radar, the Bf 110 was one of five selected for evaluation at RAE Farnborough. This particular Bf 110 was allotted the Air Ministry serial AM 34. On 1 August 1945, the Bf 110 was ferried from Grove to Schleswig in northern Germany by Sqn Ldr Ian Somerville. Schleswig was where the operation of organizing the delivery of aircraft selected for evaluation at RAE Farnborough was coordinated. Two days later, Sqn Ldr Joe McCarthy flew the Bf 110 to RAE Farnborough. On 5 September, Eric 'Winkle' Brown ferried the Bf 110 to 6 MU at Brize Norton for storage.

In May 1946, the aircraft was selected for preservation by the Air Historical Branch, with the Bf 110 being transferred to 76 MU at Wroughton for storage. With 76 MU being disbanded shortly afterwards, the aircraft was dispatched to 47 MU at Sealand. By 1949, the aircraft was part of the German Air Force Equipment Centre at RAF Stanmore Park. The Bf 110 may have arrived here already in 1947, due to congestion at Sealand. Later in 1949, the Bf 110 was on temporary display in London. Also in 1949, it was transferred to RAF Andover, where it was intermittently put on public display until moved in July 1957 to 15 MU at Wroughton for storage.

After a brief move to RAF Fulbeck, the Bf 110 moved to RAF Church Fenton in 1960. While here, the aircraft had been repainted in a Luftwaffe night fighter colour scheme by 8 August. Just over a month later, the Bf 110 was once again on the move, this time to RAF Biggin Hill, being put on display for the Battle of Britain open day. The erroneous code 'OL' was applied to the fuselage around this time. The Bf 110 remained at Biggin Hill until January 1968 at least, being consigned to storage at RAF Henlow soon afterwards. In August 1973, the Bf 110 was put on display at RAF St. Athan.

On 16 February 1976, the book-keeping serial number 8479M was allotted. Also in 1976, a programme of restoration was initiated. This involved stripping away all the layers of paint, with the aircraft being finished in a blue/grey camouflage scheme. The correct D5+RL was also applied.

On 7 August 1978, the Bf 110 was roaded to the Battle of Britain Museum at Hendon, which opened to the public on 28 November 1978. However, the Bf 110 remained the property of the Ministry of Defence until formally donated to the RAF Museum on 3 August 1998. In October 2016, the aircraft was dismantled and moved into the nearby Bomber Hall, where it was reassembled on 22 and 23 January 2018. Although the Bf 110 had played an important role during the Battle of Britain, this late-model Bf 110G-4 had served as a night fighter during the latter stages of the war, now being displayed in more appropriate surroundings in the Bomber Hall.

One Bf 110C (W Nr 3115) of I.(Z)JG 77 recovered in Russia in 1992 reportedly remains stored in the UK. This particular Bf 110 was upgraded at an unknown juncture as a B 110E, with the new W Nr 4501 being issued. Additional details are lacking.

Mention must also be made of Bf 110 replicas in Britain.

A Bf 110 mock-up was featured in the 'Late for a Funeral' episode of the 1981 BBC drama *Bergerac*, playing the role of a Bf 110 that had crashed off the coast of Jersey. Also worthy of mention, is the 75 per cent scale replica Bf 110 fuselage constructed for an episode of the BBC television drama *Monarch of the Glen*. Following completion of filming, the fuselage was put on display at Aviemore Ski Lodge. However, when a visitor complained about the swastika insignia, the fuselage was promptly removed. It was then briefly displayed at the lower station of Cairngom Mountain Railway. The fuselage is currently on display at the Kent Battle of Britain Museum at Hawkinge.

Italy

One Bf 110C-4 (W Nr 3577) originally recovered from Russia is owned by an Italian enthusiast. Coded H8+FM of the reconnaissance unit 4./H33, the Bf 110 was lost in action over northern Russia on 1 July 1942. The three crew were posted as missing in action. The Bf 110 was recovered in 1993 by Russian military personnel and members of the Russian Geographical Society on behalf of Canadian enthusiast Jeet Mahal. Mahal eventually sold the aircraft to the Italian-based Aeronautical Restoration Association. Tentative plans to restore the Bf 110 to airworthiness did not reach fruition, with the aircraft remaining in storage near Varese. In November 2022, it was announced that the Bf 110 had been sold to Mario Federighi of the *Archivio Storico Federighi*. Following conservation, the Bf 110 will be put on display at Federighi's private collection of historical aircraft located near Pisa. There are no plans to restore the Bf 110, which, incidentally, is the one of its kind in private ownership.

Norway

Major sections of a Bf 110F-2 (W Nr 5096) are kept by the *Flyhistorisk Museum* at Stavanger-Sola. During the latter part of its service career, this particular Bf 110 served with 13.(Z)/JG 5, being coded LN+DR. On 10 February 1943, the aircraft was damaged by Soviet ground fire, with the pilot making a belly landing at Kemijärvi in Finland. With damage being estimated at 15 per cent, the Bf 110 was quickly repaired. However, the Bf 110 was lost on 23 July 1943. The crew, *Obfw.* Karl Becker (pilot) and *Uffz.* Ottmar Werz (radio operator/gunner), had taken off (most likely from Kirkenes) for a naval escort sortie off Nordkap. Encountering Soviet P-39 Airacobras, the Bf 110 was shot down south-west of the Makkaur lighthouse. With Werz sensing that the Bf 110 was diving vertically, he baled out over the sea. Werz was subsequently picked up by a *Kriegsmarine* vessel, commanded by an old school mate of his, *Kapitänleutnant* Bebermeyer.

Unknown to Werz, Becker regained control of the Bf 110, force-landing close to Makkaur lighthouse near Båtsfjord. The wreck was left at the crash site, with the cockpit section eventually being blown up by German troops. Presumably, this took place during the German retreat from northern Norway in late 1944 to early 1945. The wreck was also known to the local population, which stripped off useful parts. In 1984, the newly-established *Flyhistorisk Museum* at Stavanger-Sola became aware of the existence of the wreck. With Luftwaffe Bf 110s having operated from Stavanger-Sola during the war, plans were set in motion to recover the wreck. Permission to recover the Bf 110 was obtained from Norwegian authorities. However, the biggest stumbling blocks were finances, and the inaccessibility of the wreck site. In the event, a successful recovery was eventually achieved, with the Bf 110 being loaded aboard a ship. However, this ship was rerouted, with the wreck being loaded aboard another ship while at sea! Nevertheless, the Bf 110 arrived at Tananger harbour for onwards transportation to Stavanger-Sola.

Although several sections have since been restored, including the empennage and both wings, these remain in storage.

Russia

The tail section and one wing of a former 13.(Z)/JG 5 Bf 110F is on display at the Victory Museum in Moscow. Coded LN+AR (W Nr 5020), the Bf 110 was lost on 9 February 1943 in an emergency landing 10 km south of Alakurtti, Finland, while returning to Kemijärvi. The crew, *Uffz.* Otto Weissenburger and *Uffz.* Wilhelm Pfeiffer, were both injured in the forced landing. The area had been ceded to the USSR following the end of the Winter War on 13 March 1940, but occupied by Finnish and German forces following the commencement of Operation Barbarossa. However, Alakurtti subsequently became a part of the Murmansk Oblast following the peace treaty between Finland and the USSR. The wreck was recovered during the 1990s. Restored and painted in Luftwaffe colours, the parts are on display in an outdoor setting, being subjected to the harsh Russian climate.

APPENDIX

Messerschmitt Bf 110 Production

Although exact production totals for the Bf 110 are missing, it is fairly safe to say that between 5,000 and 6,170 were built between 1936 and 1945. Trying to establish a correct production total is an almost impossible task. This is due to the lack of contemporary documentation, and the often-contradictory information contained within surviving records.

Taking to the air for the first time in 1936, the Messerschmitt Bf 110 remained in production until almost the very end of the war. When its planned replacement, the Messerschmitt Me 210 proved itself to be a severely sub-standard combat aircraft, the Bf 110 had to be reinstated in series production. Indeed, by late 1942, Bf 110 production had been substantially increased.

Apart from BFW/Messerschmitt, the Bf 110 was also manufactured by three other companies: Focke-Wulf, Gothaer Waggonfabrik AG, and the Mühlen und Industriebau Aktiengesellschaft (MIAG), or rather its subsidiary Luther. It would appear that a fair number of older airframes were reworked as new variants, receiving a new *Werk Nummer* in the process. This complicates the question of the actual number of aircraft produced. If a damaged aircraft is upgraded during the subsequent weeks or months of refurbishment, and, as a result, a new aircraft emerges, does that account for one, or two different Bf 110s? For instance, in his book *History of the German Night Fighter Force 1917–1945*, Gebhard Aders states that in 1941, 280 Bf 110s were 'rebuilt'. Aders also records the production numbers for the Bf 110 *Nachtjäger* aircraft as being 594 (1941, excluding rebuilt aircraft, but including *Zerstörers*), 501 (1942, including *Zerstörers*), 789 (1943), 1,397 (1944), and fifty-four (1945) for a total of 3,335 aircraft.

Three other published sources are *Warplanes of the Third Reich* by William Green, German *Aircraft of the Second World War* by J. R. Smith and Anthony Kay, and *Messerschmitt* by Armand van Ishhoven provide widely different production numbers. It must be emphasised that all of the above books were published in the 1970s. Although excellent by the standards of the day, much new information has since come to light. Green states that 6,150 Bf 110s were built, while Smith and Kay claim a slightly lower total: 5,873.

In his book *Messerschmitt*, published in 1975, Armand van Ishoven states that 3,028 fighters, 2,240 night fighters, and 494 reconnaissance Bf 110s were built between 1939 and 1945, which give a total of 4,974 aircraft.

German aviation historian Gerhard Lang states that a total of 6,043 Bf 110s were built, adding that other sources claim production totals amounting to 5,930, or 6,031 or 6,170 aircraft. Interestingly, Lang does not mention reworked (i.e., modifying older Bf 110s into new, upgraded variants) aircraft.

The first production variant was the Bf 110B, with a total of eighty-seven being completed, including three Bf 110B-0s and twenty-two Bf 110B-1s by BFW and sixty-two Bf 110B-1s by Gotha. Two assembly lines were eventually established by Gotha for Bf 110 production, at Gotha and at Fürth respectively.

By late 1938, two Bf 110Bs on average were rolling off the Augsburg-Haunstetten assembly line every week. Introduced in 1939, the Bf 110C became the first major production variant. Between September and December 1939, 156 Bf 110Cs were completed. Focke-Wulf at Bremen and MIAG, with its subsidiary Luther, joining the production programme in late 1939. Located at Brunswick, Luther ended production of the Fw 58 *Weihe* light transport to give way to the Bf 110. Luther went on to almost exclusively producing the Bf 110 during the war.

In the spring of 1940, the first Bf 110Ds began to reach Luftwaffe units, with a few Bf 110D-0 seeing service in Norway.

By 1 May 1940, a total of 644 Bf 110s had been delivered to the Luftwaffe, including eighty-seven Bf 110Bs, 525 Bf 110Cs, and thirty-two Bf 110Ds. By the end of the year, 1,231 Bf 110s had been completed. Two new basic variants, the Bf 110E and Bf 110F, were introduced in 1941. In this year, Focke-Wulf terminated production of the Bf 110, having delivered some 247 aircraft. By early 1942, Bf 110 production had virtually come to an end. This can be seen from the fact that in February 1942, Gotha and Luther delivered a mere four Bf 110s between them. In the event, Bf 110 production had to be reinstated. Between March and December 1942, 577 Bf 110s were completed, with a peak of eighty-four in November. Out of these, a total of 468 were built by Gotha and Luther, with Messerschmitt dropping out of the production programme completely in 1942.

The first Bf 110Gs were delivered in early 1942, this eventually becoming the most-produced basic variant. Gotha built nearly 3,000 Bf 110Gs, with Luther adding at least 500 more. During 1943, Bf 110 production was substantially increased, with a total of 1,509 aircraft being completed. Out of these were 438 Bf 110G-4s by Gotha, and 424 Bf 110G-2s and sixty Bf 110G-2/R3 by Luther. During the first three months of 1944, Gotha delivered sixty-two Bf 110G-2/R6, forty-two Bf 110G-4/R3, forty-nine Bf 110G-4/R6, and eighty-nine Bf 110G-4/R7 for a total of 242 aircraft. During the same period, Luther completed one Bf 110G-2 (end of production), sixteen Bf 110G-2/R5, ten Bf 110G-2/R6, and thirty-six Bf 110G-2/R7 for a total of sixty-three aircraft. The dip in production in February 1944, was due to the USAAF's concentrated attacks against German aircraft production (known as 'Big Week'), with the Luther factory at Brunswick sustaining heavy damage during this campaign.

Given the increasing obsolescence of the Bf 110, and the gradual breakdown of the German aircraft industry, it would appear that less than fifty Bf 110s were completed in the first months of 1945.

Endnotes

Chapter 5

1 van Ishoven, Armand, *Messerschmitt Bf 110 at War* (1985), p. 9f.
2 *Ibid.*, p. 11.

Chapter 7

1 To prevent further attempts of unauthorised flights, a huge steel clamp was fitted to the Bf 110's tail section. This meant that the aircraft could only be taxied, even at full engine rpm, but not flown. The only ones having a key for the steel clamp were the test pilots.
2 van Ishoven, Armand *Messerschmitt Bf 110 at War* (1985), p. 14.

Chapter 9

1 Franks, Norman, *Aircraft versus Aircraft. The Illustrated Story of Fighter Pilot Combat from 1914 to the Present Day* (1998), p. 70.
2 Campbell, Jerry L., *Messerschmitt Bf 110 Zerstörer in action* (1977), p. 11.

Chapter 10

1 Campbell, Jerry L., *Messerschmitt Bf 110 Zerstörer in action* (1977), p. 13.

Chapter 11

1 Helme, J. *Flyvehistorisk Tidskrift* No. 2/1970, pp. 3-9 (Kongelig Dansk Aeroklub Flyvehistorisk Sektion, 1970).
2 Guhnfeldt, Cato, *Fornebu 9. April* (1990), p. 153f.

Chapter 12

1 Campbell, Jerry L., *Messerschmitt Bf 110 Zerstörer in action* (1977) p. 21. It would appear that the six Spitfires lost in combat by the RAF on this day, all were brought down by Bf 109s.

Chapter 14

1 Brown, Eric, *The Bf 110...Hermann's Destroyer* (1973), p. 177.
2 Campbell, Jerry L., *Messerschmitt Bf 110 Zerstörer in action* (1977), p. 22.
3 Interestingly, essentially the same tactic was employed by the Israeli Air Force during the Suez War in 1956, when P-51 Mustangs fitted with cables were sent to destroy the Egyptian lines of communications in the Sinai peninsula.
4 Parry, Simon, *Circle of Death September 4th, 1940* (1990), p. 393.
5 Franks, Norman, *Aircraft versus Aircraft. The Illustrated Story of Fighter Pilot Combat from 1914 to the Present Day* (1998), p. 90f.

6 *Ibid.*, p. 92. Around the same time, the Air Ministry issued its Pamphlet 114C, *Instructions for Flying the Messerschmitt 110.*

Chapter 15

1 When interviewed by World War One historian Bruno Schmäling, Helmo Ludovici and Rudolf Stark both agreed that Hess was a 'strange person'. However, being a fellow pilot, Hess was accepted by his colleagues. He was also regarded as a bit of a loner, with a tendency for fanaticism. E-mail to the author from Bruno Schmäling 12 September 2022.
2 E-mail to the author from Greg VanWyngarden 11 September 2022. In 1932, Rudolf Stark published his wartime diary *Die Jagdstaffel unsere Heimat* (translated into English the following year as *Wing's of War: an Airman's Diary of the Last Year of World War One*).
3 Nesbit, R., *The Flight of Rudolf Hess* December 1986, p. 630.
4 *Ibid*, p. 620. The Marx Brothers movie was *Go West.*

Chapter 16

1 Shores, Christopher, *Air War for Yugoslavia Greece and Crete 1940–41* (1999), p. 265.

Chapter 18

1 Dudgeon, A. G., *The Luck of the Devil* (1985), p. 190f.

Chapter 19

1 Shores, Christopher, *Mediterranean Air War Volume One* (2012), p. 132.
2 *Ibid*, p. 339.

Chapter 21

1 Boiten, Theo, *Nachtjagd The Night Fighter versus Bomber War over the Third Reich 1939–45* (1997), p. 11.
2 By comparison, the first RAF night fighter victory, by a Bristol Blenheim Mk IF fitted with radar, occurred on the night of 2–3 July 1940, with a Dornier Do 17 being shot down.
3 Based on Kurt Bundrock's memoir, *Kampf am nächtlichten Himmel, Einsatzerlebnisse eines Ritterkreuzträgers der Nachtjagd*, Rastatt 1979, pp. 27-30. Translated by Neil Page.
4 Price, Alfred, *Battle over the Reich* (1974), p. 30f.
5 Boiten, Theo, *Nachtjagd The Night Fighter versus Bomber War over the Third Reich 1939–45* (1997), p. 83f.
6 Price, Alfred, *Messerschmitt Bf 110 Night Fighters* (1971), p. 41.
7 Forczyk, Robert, *Bf 110 Vs Lancaster 1942–45* (2013), p. 68.
8 Boiten, Theo, *Nachtjagd The Night Fighter versus Bomber War over the Third Reich 1939–45* (1997), p. 91.

Chapter 22

1 Swiss Shadowplay, www.pressreader.com. Retrieved 12 December 2022.

Chapter 28

1 'Analysis of the Messerschmitt Me-110 Airplane', p. 13.
2 Brown, Eric, *The Bf 110…Hermann's Destroyer* (1973), p. 178f.

Chapter 32

1 Pelly-Fry, James, *The Belle of Berlin* (1982), pp. 216-217.
2 Sobolew, D. A., *Deutsche Spuren in der Sowjetischen Luftfahrtgesichte* (2000), p. 113.
3 Gordon, Yefim, & Rybak, Boris, *Under the Red Star* (1997), p. 82.

Bibliography

Periodicals

Aakra, K., & Dybvig, O., *Messerschmitt Bf 110 I Norge* (Bergen, Norway 1996)
Brown, E., 'The Bf 110...Hermann's Destroyer' in *Air Enthusiast*, Vol. 5 No. 4, October 1973, pp. 177-181 (Leicester: Fine Scroll Limited, 1976)
Gordon, Y., & Rybak, B., 'Under Red Stars' in *FlyPast* August 1997, pp. 81-82 (Key Publishing Ltd, 1987)
Helme, J., '*Luftoperationerne den 9. april 1940*' in *Flyvehistorisk Tidskrift* No. 2/1970, pp. 3-9 (Konglig Dansk Aeroklub Flyvehistorisk Sektion)
Nesbit, R., 'The Flight of Rudolf Hess' in *Aeroplane Monthly*, November and December 1986, pp. 572-575, 587, and 628-631 (Sutton: Business Press International, 1986); 'Hess's Last Flight' in *Aeroplane Monthly*, August 1995, pp. 16-21 (Sutton: Business Press International, 1995)
Parry, S., 'Circle of Death September 4th, 1940' in *Air Pictorial*, October–November 1990, pp. 391-394 (Profile Books Ltd, Ascot 1990)
Pelly-Fry, J., 'The Belle of Berlin' in *Aeroplane Monthly*, April 1982, pp. 216-217 (Sutton: Business Press International, 1982)

Printed Books and Articles

Aders, G., *History of the German Night Fighter Force 1917–1945* (Crécy Books Ltd, 1992)
Bernád, D., & Punka, G., *Hungarian Fighter Colours 1930–1945, Vol. 2* (Sandomierz: STRATUS s.c., Sandomierz, 2014)
Bernád, D., *Rumanian Air Force The Prime Decade, 1938–1947* (Carrollton: Squadron/Signal Publications, Inc., 1999)
Boiten, T., *Nachtjagd The Night Fighter versus Bomber War over the Third Reich 1939–45* (Marlborough: The Crowood Press Ltd, 1997)
Bridgman, L., (ed.), *Jane's All the World's Aircraft 1945–46 edition* (London: Sampson Low, Marston & Company, Ltd, 1946)
Bundrock, K., *Kampf am nächtlichten Himmel, Einsatzerlebnisse eines Ritterkreuzträgers der Nachtjagd* (Rastatt: 1979)
Butler, P., *War Prizes* (Hinckley: Midland Counties Publications, 1998)
Campbell, J. L., *Messerschmitt Bf 110 Zerstörer in action* (Carrollton: Squadron/Signal publications, Inc, 1977)
Cornwell, P. D., *The Battle of France: Then and Now* (London, UK, ATB Books 1993)
Cynk, J. B., *Polish Aircraft 1893–1939* (London: Putnam & Company Limited, 1971)
Dudgeon, A. G., *The Luck of the Devil* (Shrewsbury: Airlife Publishing Ltd, 1985)
Ethell, J. L., & Price, A., *Target Berlin Mission 250: 6 March 1944* (London: Arms and Armour Press, 1981)
Forczyk, R., *Bf 110 Vs Lancaster 1942–45* (Oxford: Osprey Publishing, 2013)

Franks, N., *Aircraft versus Aircraft. The Illustrated Story of Fighter Pilot Combat From 1914 to the Present Day* (London: Grub Street, 1998)
Geust, C.-F., *Under the Red Star* (Shrewsbury: Airlife Publishing Ltd, 1993)
Green, W., *Warplanes of the Third Reich* (London: MacDonald and Jane's Publishers Limited, Fourth Impression 1979)
Guhnfeldt, C., *Fornebu 9. April* (Oslo: Wings Forlag A/S, 1990)
Hoch, G., *Die Messerschmitt Me 109 in der Schweizer Flugwaffe – ein Stück Zeitgeschichte* (Waldenburg: Eigenverlag Autor, Second Edition, 2004)
Kay, A. L., & Smith, J. R., *German Aircraft of the Second World War* (London: Putnam Aeronautical Books, 2002)
Kosin, R., *The German Fighter since 1915* (London: Putnam, an imprint of Conway Maritime Press Ltd, 1988)
Lang, G., *Messerschmitt Bf 110 G / Me 110 H* (Stangelheim: Flugzeug Profil, UNITEC-Medienvertrieb, no year of publication listed)
Middlebrook, M., *The Nuremberg Raid 30–31 March 1944* (London: Penguin Group, 1986)
Petrović, O., & Nikolić, D., *Yugoslav Fighter Colours 1918–1941 Vol. 2* (Sandomierz: STRATUS s.j., 2021)
Price, A., *Battle over the Reich* (Shepperton: Ian Allan Ltd, Shepperton, Second impression, 1974); *Messerschmitt Bf 110 Night Fighters* (Windsor: Profile Publications Limited, 1971); *The Last Year of the Luftwaffe* (London: Greenhill Books, 2001)
Ramsey, W. G., *The Battle of Britain: Then and Now* (London, UK, ATB Books 1986)
Report No. 260-28, 'Analysis of the Messerschmitt Me-110 Airplane', Vultee Aircraft, Inc. Engineering and Development Dept., December 1941. (Glendale: Aero Publishers, Inc., no year listed)
Shores, C., & Cull, B., with Malizia, N., *Air War for Yugoslavia Greece and Crete 1940–41* (London: Grub Street, 1999)
Shores, C., & Massimello, G., with Guest, R., Olynyk, F., & Bock, W., *A History of the Mediterranean Air War 1940–1945 Volume Two: North African Desert February 1942–March 1943* (London: Grub Street, 2012); *A History of the Mediterranean Air War 1945–1945 Volume Three: Tunisia and the End in North Africa November 1942–May 1943* (London: Grub Street, 2016)
Shores, C., *Dust Clouds in the Middle East* (London: Grub Street, 2010); *Fledgling Eagles: the complete account of air operations during the phoney war and the Norwegian campaign 1940* (London: Grub Street, 1998 reprint)
Shores, C., Massimello, G., & Guest, R., *A History of the Mediterranean Air War 1940–1945 Volume One: North Africa June 1940–January 1942* (London: Grub Street, 2012)
Sobolew, D. A., *Deutsche Spuren in der Sowjetischen Luftfahrtgeschichte* (Berlin: Verlag E.S. Mittler & Sohn GmbH, 2000)
van Ishoven, A., *Messerschmitt Bf 110 at War* (Shepperton: Ian Allan Ltd, 1985); *Messerschmitt* (London, Gentry Books Limited, 1975)
Wetter, E., *Geheimer Nachtjäger in der Schweiz* (Frauenfeld: Allgemeine Schweizerische Militärzeitschrift, Huber & Co. AG, Frauenfeld 1989)
Widfeldt, B., *Tyska nödlandare 1939–1945* (Nässjö: Air Historic Research, Nässjö, 2007)
Williamson, G., *Luftwaffe Handbook 1935–1945* (Stroud: Sutton Publishing Limited, 2006)
Windrow, M. C., *The Messerschmitt Bf 110* (Windsor: Profile Publications Limited, 1965)

Internet

www.aircrewrememberancesociety3.com
www.airhistory.org.uk
www.flensted.eu.com
www.forcedlandingcollection.se
www.leteckabadatelna.cz
www.luftwaffe.cz
www.rafmuseum.org.uk
www.pressreader.com Swiss Shadowplay
www.warbird.ch
www.ww2.dk

Index

Aalborg 36-38, 40
Achterberg, Günther 141
Arkangelskiy, Alexandr A. 142
Armstrong Whitworth Whitley 77, 79-80
Augsburg-Haunstetten 29, 55
Avro Lancaster 98, 141

Baghdad 62-64
Bandi, Hans 134
Bansemir, *Dipl.-Ing.* Wilhelm 15
Becker, Martin 85, 92
Belgrade 58, 144
Bell YFM-1 Airacuda 22
BFW M.23 54
Bloch 152 19
Blomberg, Axel von 63-64
Breguet 690 18
Bristol Blenheim 42, 59, 63, 66, 98, 100
Brown, Eric 46, 120, 148

Cairo 66
Centre NC 600 18
Churchill, Winston 36, 49, 56
Copenhagen 37, 106
Curtiss Hawk 36, 143

Denmark 36-38, 50, 84, 93, 106, 115, 134, 137, 145-146, 148
Derna 66-68, 105
Dewoitine D.630/631 18
DH.82A Tiger Moth 136
DH.86 68
DH.98 Mosquito 92
Dornier Do 17Z-10 105, 129
Dornier Do 18 34
Dornier Do 215 69, 143
Dornier Do 217 140-141
Douhet, Giulio 13
Drewes, Martin 63-64
Dudgeon, A. G. 64, 136
Dübendorf 87-88, 141-142

EKW C-35 44-45
EKW C-3603 89

Fairey Fulmar 73
Fairey Albacore 73
Falck, Wolfgang 32-35, 37-38, 47
Farnborough 135, 137-138, 148
Finland 36, 73-74, 133, 150-151
Fliegerführer Irak 9, 63-64, 116
Focke-Wulf Fw 57 14-16, 23
Focke-Wulf Fw 58 *Weihe* 134, 138, 153
Fokker C.V 37, 42
Fokker D.XXI 37
Fokker G.I 15, 21
Fornebu 36, 38-40, 98
France 11, 18-19, 21, 29, 42-44, 46, 50, 76-77, 84-85, 100-101, 104, 107-108, 111, 113-116, 135, 140
Friedrichshafen 87, 147

Gänzler, Wilhelm 99
George, Ogwyn Francis 39
Gloster Gauntlet 37
Gloster Gladiator 36, 38-40, 62, 64, 98, 146
Gloster F.9/37 22
Gollob, Gordon 39-40
Göring, Hermann 44, 48, 50, 76, 138
Great Britain 11, 36, 46-49, 51-52, 54-56, 76, 86, 104, 114, 123, 131, 135, 137, 140, 147-149

Habbaniya 62-64, 136
Handley Page Halifax 99
Hanriot H.220 18
Hansen, Werner 38-39
Hawkinge 50, 149
Heinkel He 46 32
Heinkel He 59 41, 146
Heinkel He 111 12, 32, 37-38, 40-41, 44, 50, 58, 63-64, 69, 96
Heinkel He 219 12, 83-84, 92-93, 100
Heinkel He 280 96
Heligoland Bight 11, 34-35, 79
Henschel Hs 124
Henschel Hs 127
Hirschegg 35
Hitler, Adolf 23, 28, 36, 48-49, 54, 56-57, 88
Horn, Alfred 55-56
Hungary 57, 110, 113, 133, 138-139

Iraq 62-64, 135
Italy 57-58, 62, 70, 90, 110, 112, 133, 140, 145, 149

Japan 57, 129, 133
Johnen, Wilhelm 87-89
Junck, Werner 63
Junkers Ju 52/3m 36-37, 39-42, 48, 58, 61, 63-64, 67, 69-70
Junkers Ju 88 12, 14, 26, 50, 59, 70, 76, 92-93, 98, 105-106, 109-111, 131, 143
Junkers Ju 90 63

Kaden, Helmut 55
Kammhuber, Josef 76-77, 83-84, 100, 129, 140
Kamprath, Joachim 87
Kawasaki Ki-45 *Toryu* (Nick) 133
Khomyakov, Valentin I. 143
Kirkenes 73, 104, 150
Krakow 32
Kraljevo 144

Lake Upmasjaure 41, 146
Lambert-Müller, Fred 134
La Martinerie 135
Lange, Bruno 141
Lent, Helmut 38-39, 97-98
Lockheed Hudson 40
Lockheed P-38 Lightning 22, 69-71
Loire-Nieuport 20 18

Mahle, Paul 87, 129
McLean, David 55
Messerschmitt, Willy 14, 24, 46, 54
Messerschmitt Bf 108 134
Messerschmitt Bf 109 12, 24-25, 29, 32, 35, 46, 51, 58, 83-84, 93, 95, 117, 121
Messerschmitt Bf 161 26-27
Messerschmitt Bf 162 26-27, 49
Messerschmitt Me 163 138
Messerschmitt Me 210 12, 27, 48, 95, 103, 138
Messerschmitt Me 261 28
Messerschmitt Me 321 95, 96
Messerschmitt Me 410 101, 113-114, 116
Methfessel, Werner 33
Milch, Erhard 14, 83-84
Molotov, Vjatjeslav 142
Mosul 63, 116, 136
Mütschele, Helmut 38

Nakajima J1N1 *Gekko* (Irving) 128
Narvik 36, 40-41
Neale, Bob 133
Nicolaus, *Dipl.-Ing.* Friedrich 16
Nuremberg 25, 53, 56, 85, 103

Okorokov, Yevgeni 143
Opalev, Vyacheslav G. 143
Osiek Maly 32
Oslo 36, 38-39, 98
Öttil, Johann 29-30
Öttil, Franz-Xaver 29-30

Paris 135
Payen Pa 321 18
Peenemünde 27, 99, 129
Pelly-Fry, James 136
Petlyakov Pe-2 26
Petsamo 73
Plekhanov, Ivan Ye. 143
Potez 630/631 18-20, 29
PZL P.11c 32
PZL.23 *Karas* 33
PZL.38 *Wilk* 18, 20-21
PZL.48 *Lampart* 20-21
PZL.50 *Jastrzab* 20
PZL.54 *Ryś* 21

Raschid airfield 64
Rechlin 25, 27, 93
Reims 33
Restemeyer, Werner 34, 50
Rethel, Walter 23
Romania 58, 110, 114, 133, 141, 144
Romano R.110 18

Saab 74, 134
Saab L 24 134
Savoia-Marchetti S.82 68, 70
Schenk, Helmut 96
Schnaufer, Wolfgang 99-100, 137
Schmid, Joseph 'Beppo' 84
Schoenert, Rudolf 129
Schwarz, Heinz 142
Schye, Birger 38
Short Sunderland 39, 98
Slovakia 141
Sopwith Dolphin 128
Spain 133
Stalin, Josef 142
Stalingrad 74-75, 101
Stavanger-Sola 38, 40, 104, 115-116, 150
Stein, Wolfgang 15
Stör, Willi 29, 54
Stratton, Plt Off. 35
Supermarine Spitfire 33, 43, 46-47, 55, 69, 86, 143
Sweden 36, 41, 73-74, 93, 134, 143, 146
Switzerland 19, 44, 87-89, 141-142

Tobruk 66, 69
Tratt, Eduard 75, 101
Treynogga, Helmut 91, 142
Tupolev, Oleg 142
Turnu Severin 144

Udet, Ernst 14, 24

Værløse 37
Veliki Radinci 144
Vickers Wellington 11, 34-35, 77, 82, 90-91, 98
Vienna 113, 139, 144
Villiers-sous-Chalamont 30
Vuillemin, Joseph 29

Walker, Johnny 35
Walz, Feldwebel 37
Welikije Luki 142
Wessel, Horst 113
Westerland 36, 81, 106
Westland COW fighter 128
Wiener Neustadt 21, 135, 139
Wilhelmshaven 34-35
Wurster, Hermann 23-24, 27

Yugoslavia 19, 57-58, 62, 113-114, 134, 144